THE scumbag

IMAGE COMICS, INC. · **Todd McFarlane**: President · **Jim Valentino**: Vice President · **Marc Silvestri**: Chief Executive Officer · **Erik Larsen**: Chief Financial Officer · **Robert Kirkman**: Chief Operating Officer · **Eric Stephenson**: Publisher / Chief Creative Officer · **Nicole Lapalme**: Controller · **Leanna Caunter**: Accounting Analyst · **Sue Korpela**: Accounting & HR Manager · **Marla Eizik**: Talent Liaison · **Jeff Boison**: Director of Sales & Publishing Planning · **Dirk Wood**: Director of International Sales & Licensing · **Alex Cox**: Director of Direct Market Sales · **Chloe Ramos**: Book Market & Library Sales Manager · **Emilio Bautista**: Digital Sales Coordinator · **Jon Schlaffman**: Specialty Sales Coordinator · **Kat Salazar**: Director of PR & Marketing · **Drew Fitzgerald**: Marketing Content Associate · **Heather Doornink**: Production Director · **Drew Gill**: Art Director · **Hilary DiLoreto**: Print Manager · **Tricia Ramos**: Traffic Manager · **Melissa Gifford**: Content Manager · **Erika Schnatz**: Senior Production Artist · **Ryan Brewer**: Production Artist · **Deanna Phelps**: Production Artist · **IMAGECOMICS.COM**

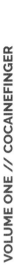

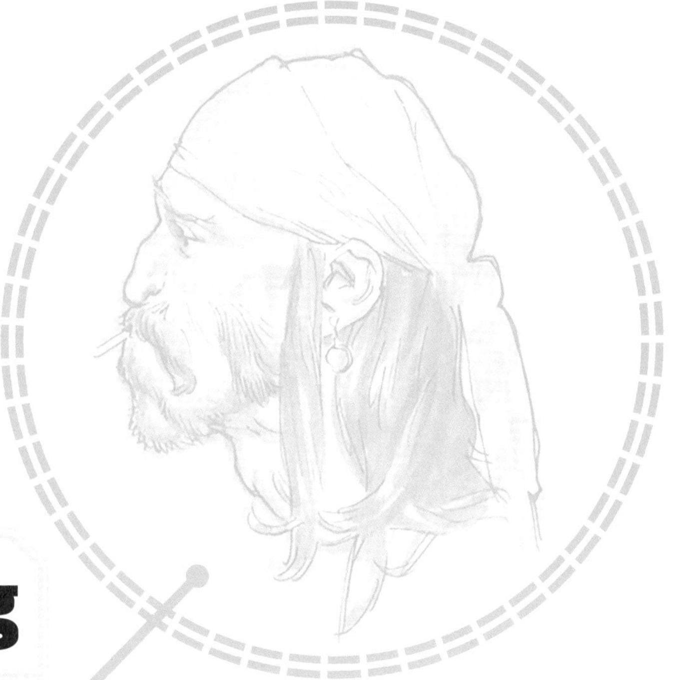

THE scumbag

VOLUME ONE // COCAINEFINGER

writer **RICK REMENDER**

artists **LEWIS LAROSA** [#1]

ANDREW ROBINSON [#2]

ERIC POWELL [#3]

ROLAND BOSCHI [#4]

WES CRAIG [#5]

colorist **MORENO DINISIO**

letterer **RUS WOOTON**

cover art **NIC KLEIN**

editor **WILL DENNIS**

designer **ERIKA SCHNATZ**

asst. editor **TYLER JENNES**

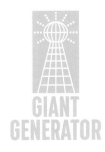

GIANT GENERATOR

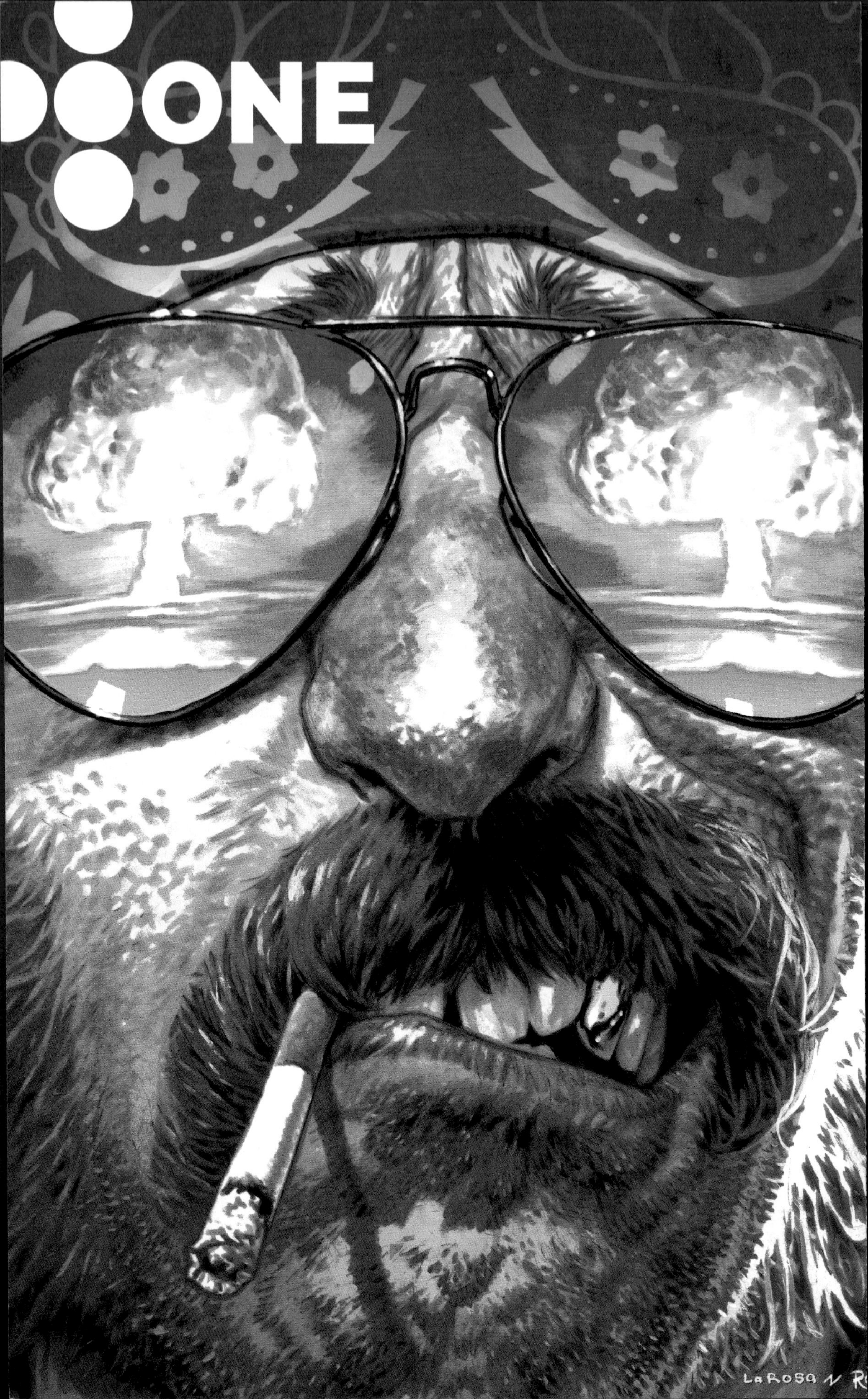
ONE
LaRosa

CHARLES BUKOWSKI SAID THE PROBLEM
WITH THE WORLD IS THAT THE INTELLIGENT
PEOPLE ARE FULL OF DOUBTS, WHILE THE
STUPID ONES ARE FULL OF CONFIDENCE.

NO MAN BETTER PROVES THAT POINT THAN
THE ONE I'M ABOUT TO INTRODUCE YOU TO.

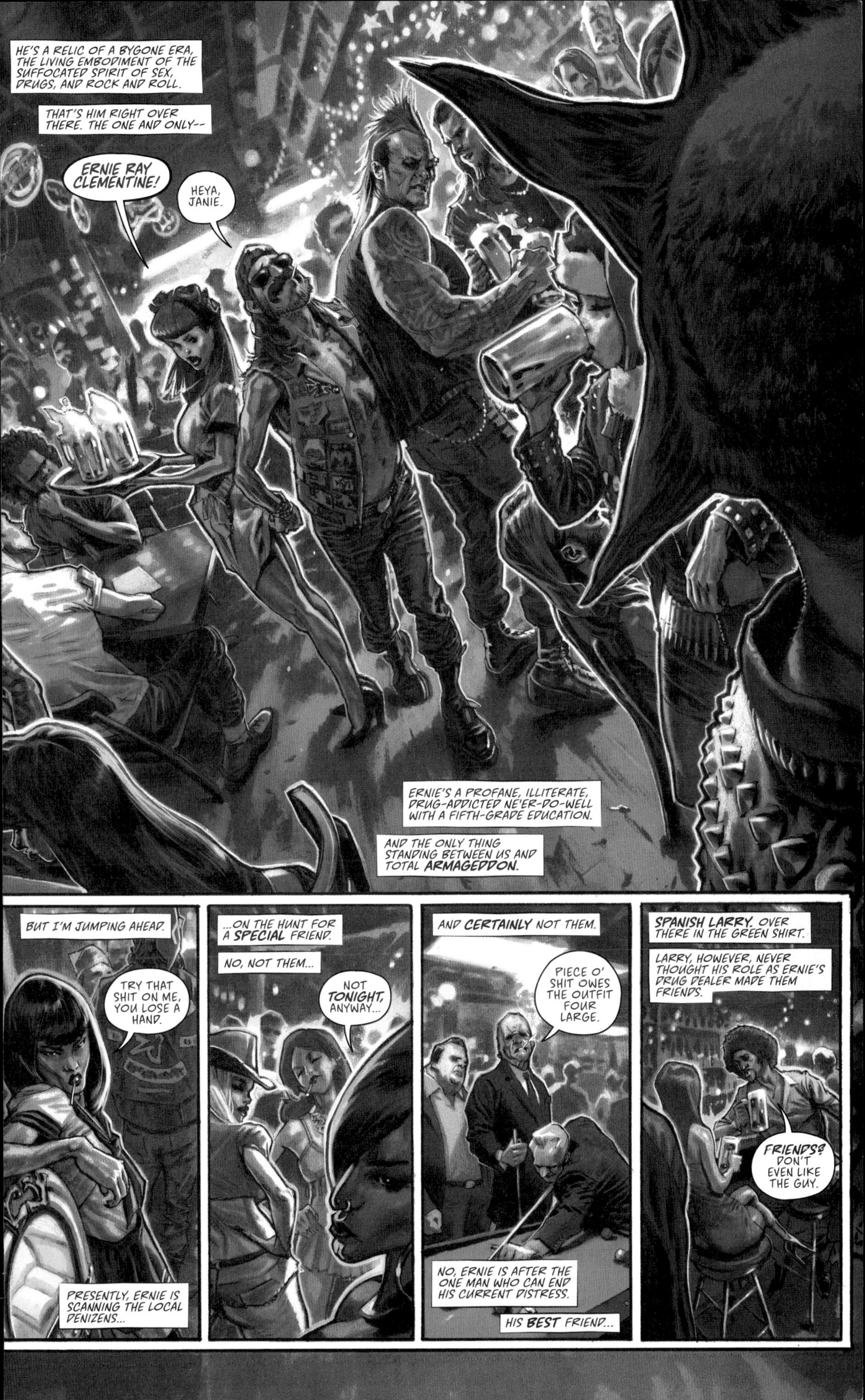
HE'S A RELIC OF A BYGONE ERA, THE LIVING EMBODIMENT OF THE SUFFOCATED SPIRIT OF SEX, DRUGS, AND ROCK AND ROLL.
THAT'S HIM RIGHT OVER THERE. THE ONE AND ONLY--
ERNIE RAY CLEMENTINE!
HEYA, JANIE.
ERNIE'S A PROFANE, ILLITERATE, DRUG-ADDICTED NE'ER-DO-WELL WITH A FIFTH-GRADE EDUCATION.
AND THE ONLY THING STANDING BETWEEN US AND TOTAL ARMAGEDDON.
BUT I'M JUMPING AHEAD.
TRY THAT SHIT ON ME, YOU LOSE A HAND.
PRESENTLY, ERNIE IS SCANNING THE LOCAL DENIZENS...
...ON THE HUNT FOR A SPECIAL FRIEND.
NO, NOT THEM...
NOT TONIGHT, ANYWAY...
AND CERTAINLY NOT THEM.
PIECE O' SHIT OWES THE OUTFIT FOUR LARGE.
NO, ERNIE IS AFTER THE ONE MAN WHO CAN END HIS CURRENT DISTRESS.
HIS BEST FRIEND...
SPANISH LARRY. OVER THERE IN THE GREEN SHIRT.
LARRY, HOWEVER, NEVER THOUGHT HIS ROLE AS ERNIE'S DRUG DEALER MADE THEM FRIENDS.
FRIENDS? DON'T EVEN LIKE THE GUY.

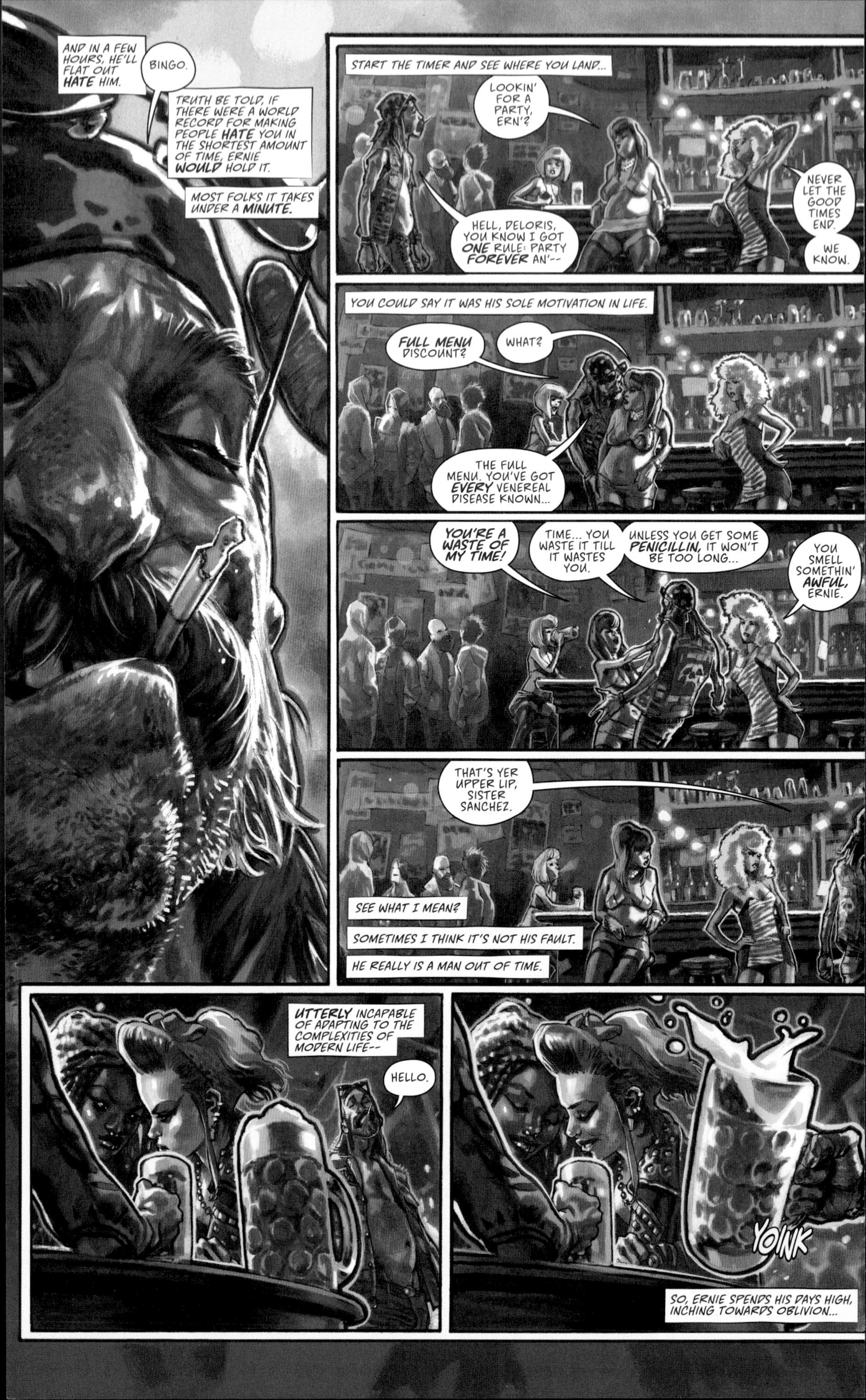
AND IN A FEW HOURS, HE'LL FLAT OUT HATE HIM.
BINGO.
TRUTH BE TOLD, IF THERE WERE A WORLD RECORD FOR MAKING PEOPLE HATE YOU IN THE SHORTEST AMOUNT OF TIME, ERNIE WOULD HOLD IT.
MOST FOLKS IT TAKES UNDER A MINUTE.
START THE TIMER AND SEE WHERE YOU LAND...
LOOKIN' FOR A PARTY, ERN'?
HELL, DELORIS, YOU KNOW I GOT ONE RULE: PARTY FOREVER AN'--
NEVER LET THE GOOD TIMES END.
WE KNOW.
YOU COULD SAY IT WAS HIS SOLE MOTIVATION IN LIFE.
FULL MENU DISCOUNT?
WHAT?
THE FULL MENU. YOU'VE GOT EVERY VENEREAL DISEASE KNOWN...
YOU'RE A WASTE OF MY TIME!
TIME... YOU WASTE IT TILL IT WASTES YOU.
UNLESS YOU GET SOME PENICILLIN, IT WON'T BE TOO LONG...
YOU SMELL SOMETHIN' AWFUL, ERNIE.
THAT'S YER UPPER LIP, SISTER SANCHEZ.
SEE WHAT I MEAN?
SOMETIMES I THINK IT'S NOT HIS FAULT.
HE REALLY IS A MAN OUT OF TIME.
UTTERLY INCAPABLE OF ADAPTING TO THE COMPLEXITIES OF MODERN LIFE--
HELLO.
YOINK
SO, ERNIE SPENDS HIS DAYS HIGH, INCHING TOWARDS OBLIVION...

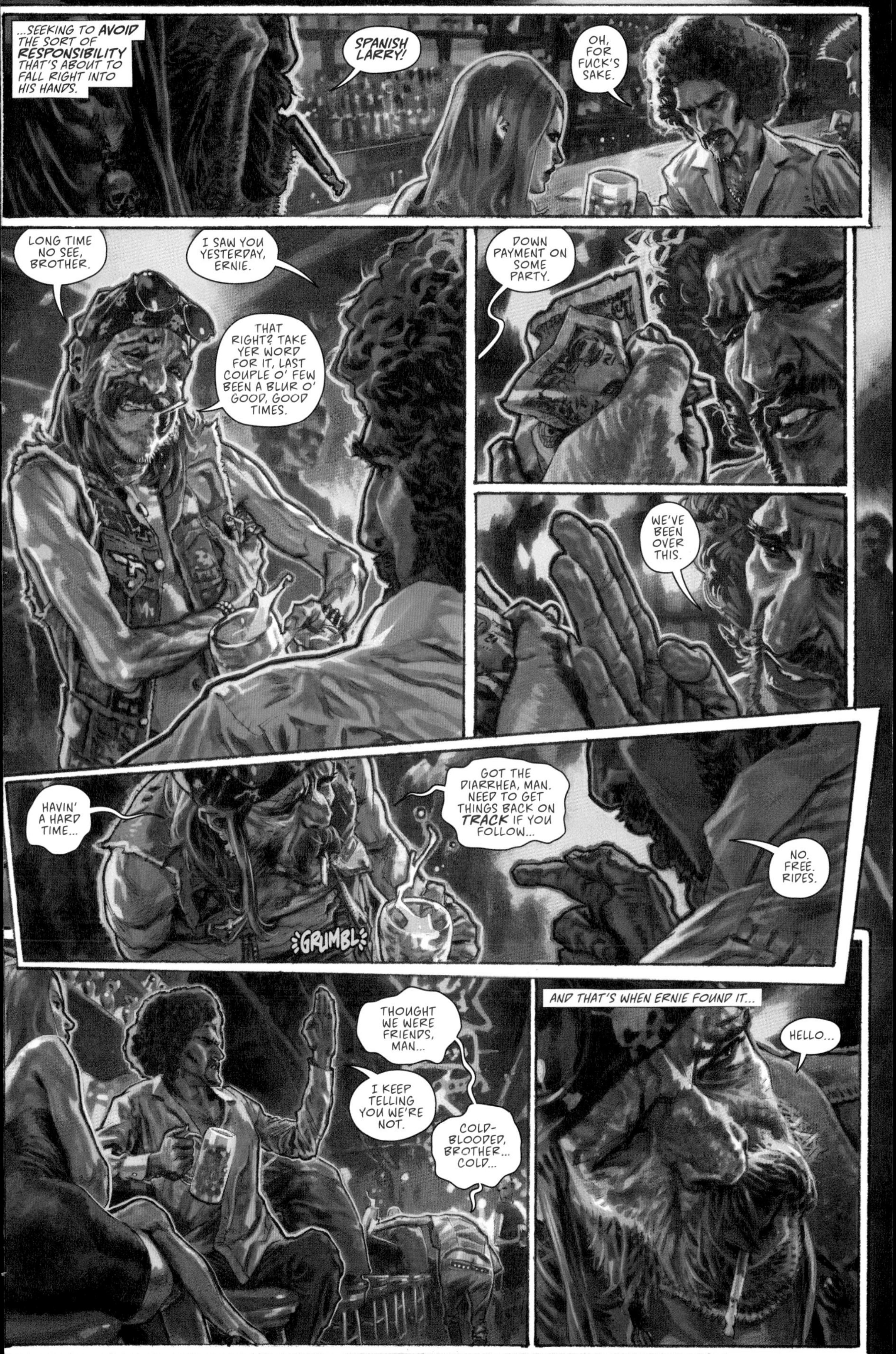

...SEEKING TO AVOID THE SORT OF RESPONSIBILITY THAT'S ABOUT TO FALL RIGHT INTO HIS HANDS.
SPANISH LARRY!
OH, FOR FUCK'S SAKE.
LONG TIME NO SEE, BROTHER.
I SAW YOU YESTERDAY, ERNIE.
THAT RIGHT? TAKE YER WORD FOR IT, LAST COUPLE O' FEW BEEN A BLUR O' GOOD, GOOD TIMES.
DOWN PAYMENT ON SOME PARTY.
WE'VE BEEN OVER THIS.
HAVIN' A HARD TIME...
GOT THE DIARRHEA, MAN. NEED TO GET THINGS BACK ON TRACK IF YOU FOLLOW...
NO. FREE. RIDES.
GRUMBL
THOUGHT WE WERE FRIENDS, MAN...
I KEEP TELLING YOU WE'RE NOT.
COLD-BLOODED, BROTHER... COLD...
AND THAT'S WHEN ERNIE FOUND IT...
HELLO...

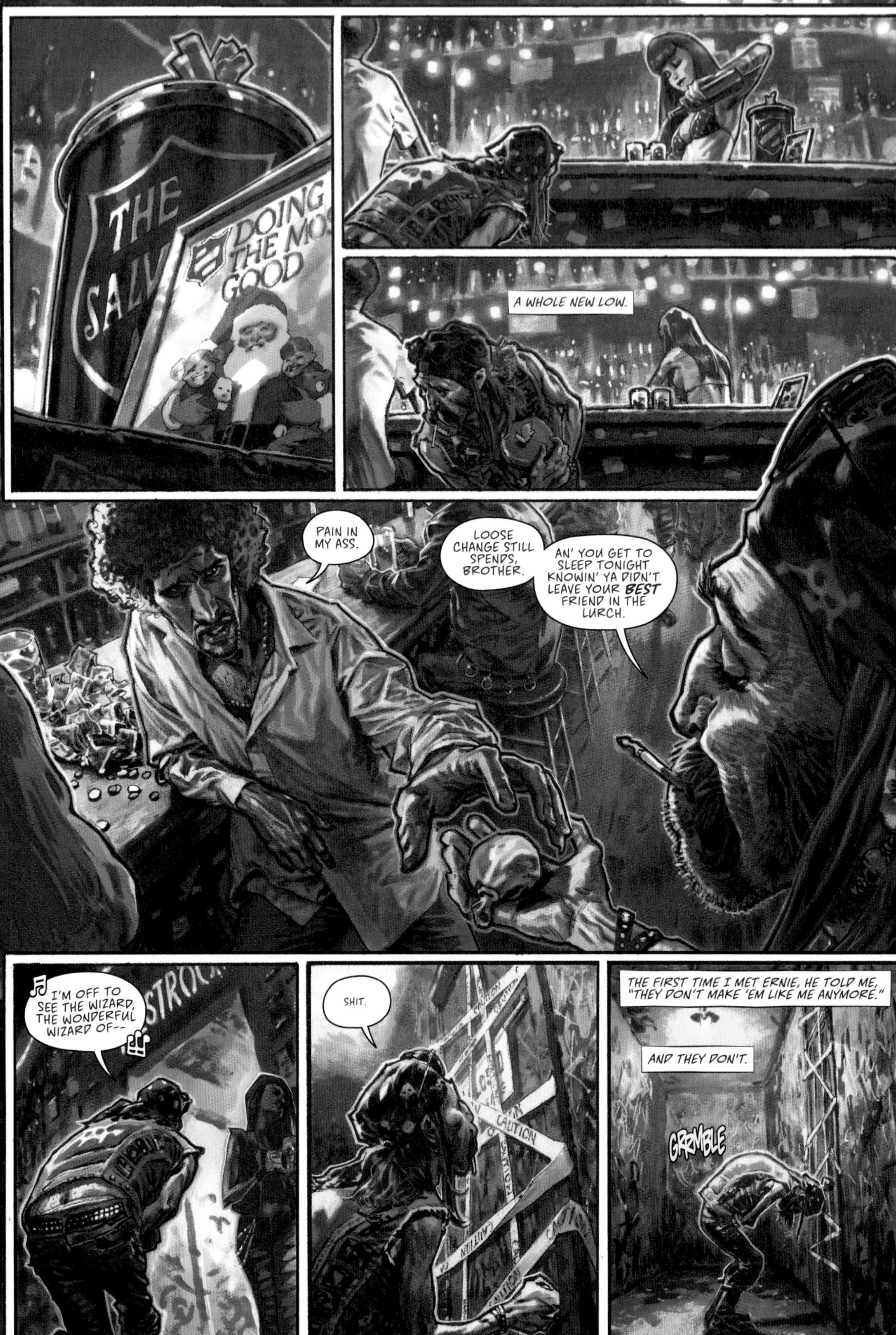
THE SALV
DOING THE MOS GOOD
A WHOLE NEW LOW.
PAIN IN MY ASS.
LOOSE CHANGE STILL SPENDS, BROTHER.
AN' YOU GET TO SLEEP TONIGHT KNOWIN' YA DIDN'T LEAVE YOUR BEST FRIEND IN THE LURCH.
I'M OFF TO SEE THE WIZARD, THE WONDERFUL WIZARD OF--
SHIT.
CAUTION
THE FIRST TIME I MET ERNIE, HE TOLD ME, "THEY DON'T MAKE 'EM LIKE ME ANYMORE."
AND THEY DON'T.
GRMBLE
AND FOR GOOD REASON.

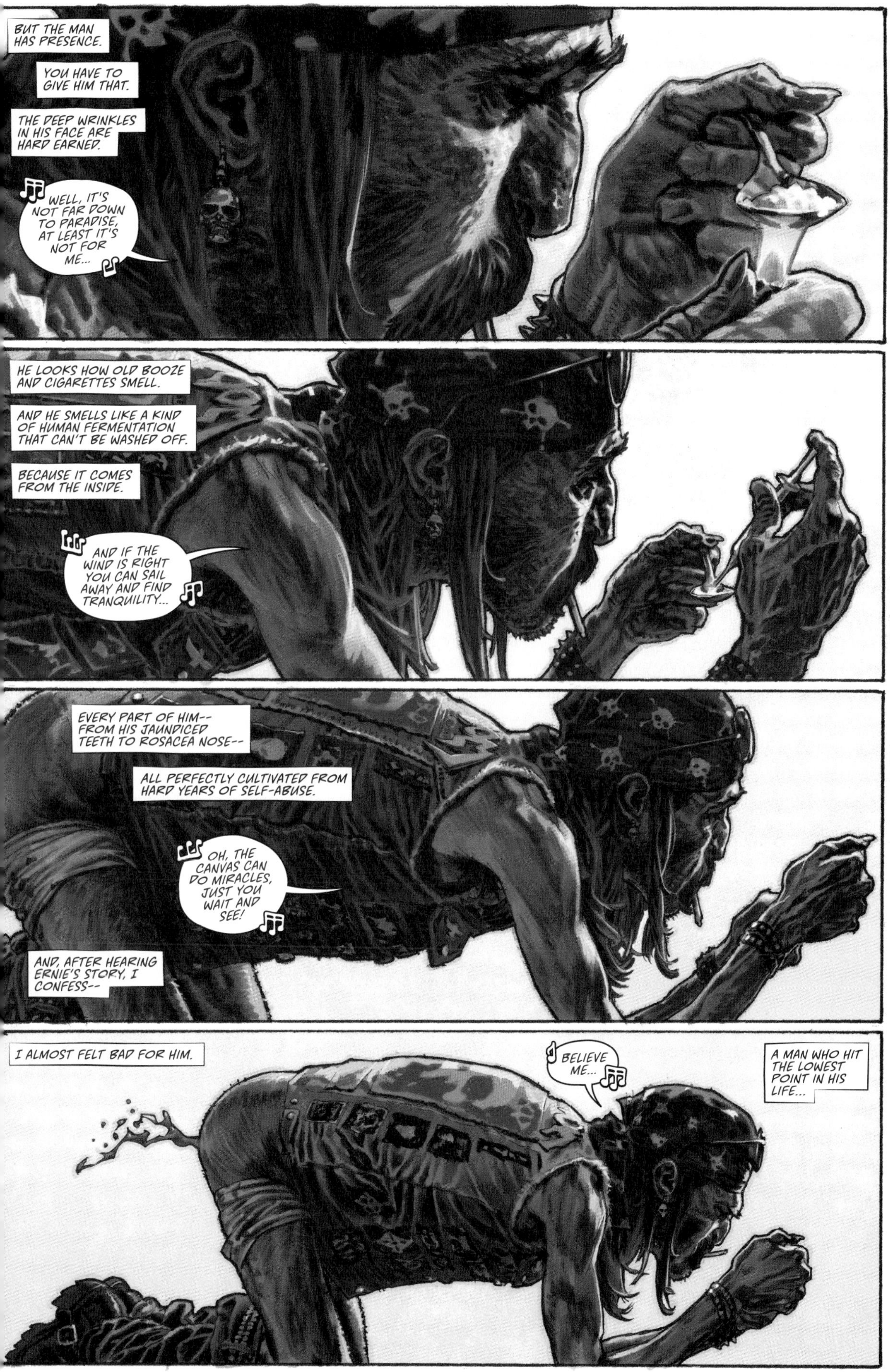
BUT THE MAN HAS PRESENCE.
YOU HAVE TO GIVE HIM THAT.
THE DEEP WRINKLES IN HIS FACE ARE HARD EARNED.
WELL, IT'S NOT FAR DOWN TO PARADISE, AT LEAST IT'S NOT FOR ME...
HE LOOKS HOW OLD BOOZE AND CIGARETTES SMELL.
AND HE SMELLS LIKE A KIND OF HUMAN FERMENTATION THAT CAN'T BE WASHED OFF.
BECAUSE IT COMES FROM THE INSIDE.
AND IF THE WIND IS RIGHT YOU CAN SAIL AWAY AND FIND TRANQUILITY...
EVERY PART OF HIM-- FROM HIS JAUNDICED TEETH TO ROSACEA NOSE--
ALL PERFECTLY CULTIVATED FROM HARD YEARS OF SELF-ABUSE.
OH, THE CANVAS CAN DO MIRACLES, JUST YOU WAIT AND SEE!
AND, AFTER HEARING ERNIE'S STORY, I CONFESS--
I ALMOST FELT BAD FOR HIM.
BELIEVE ME...
A MAN WHO HIT THE LOWEST POINT IN HIS LIFE...

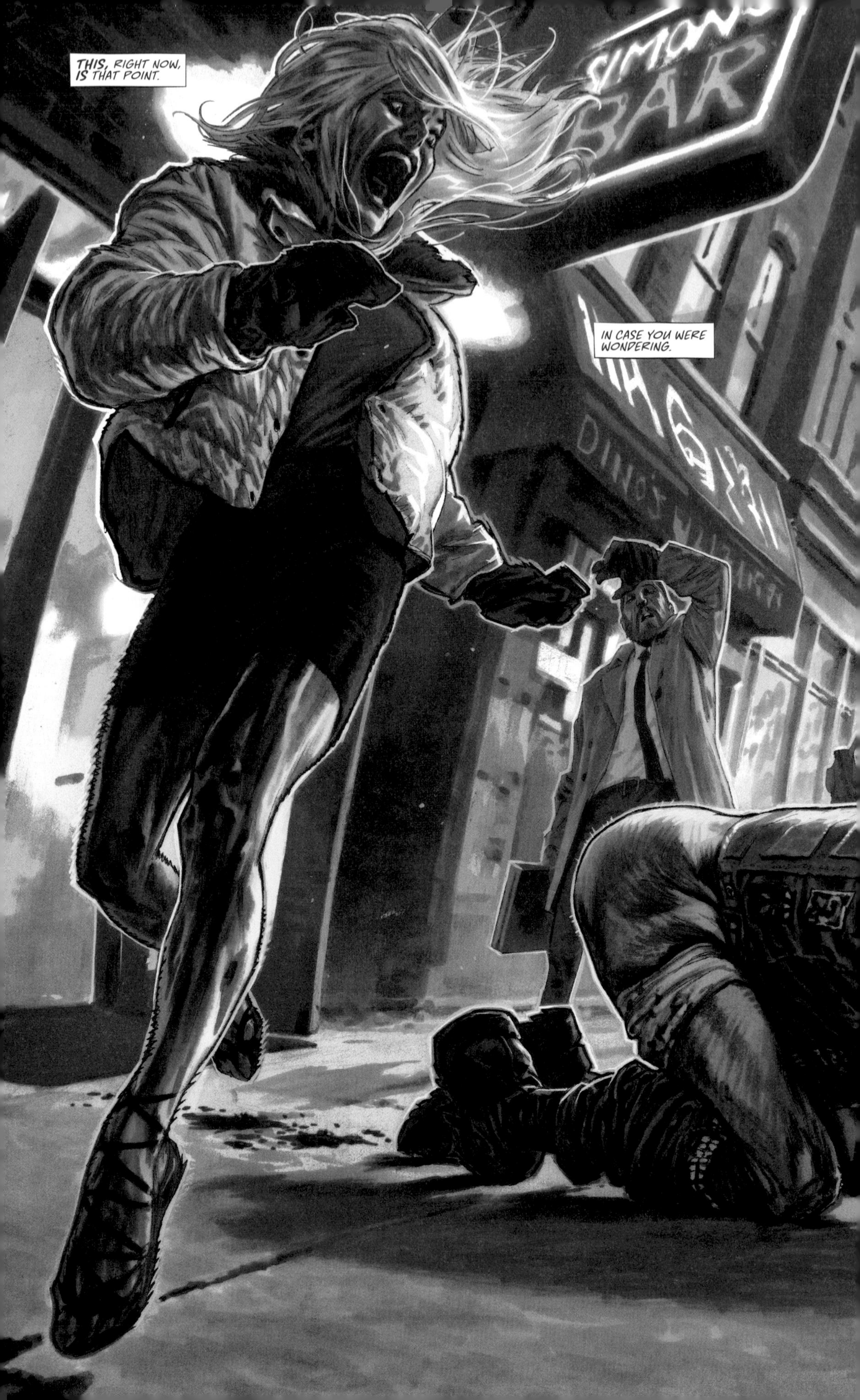
THIS, RIGHT NOW, IS THAT POINT.
BAR
IN CASE YOU WERE WONDERING.

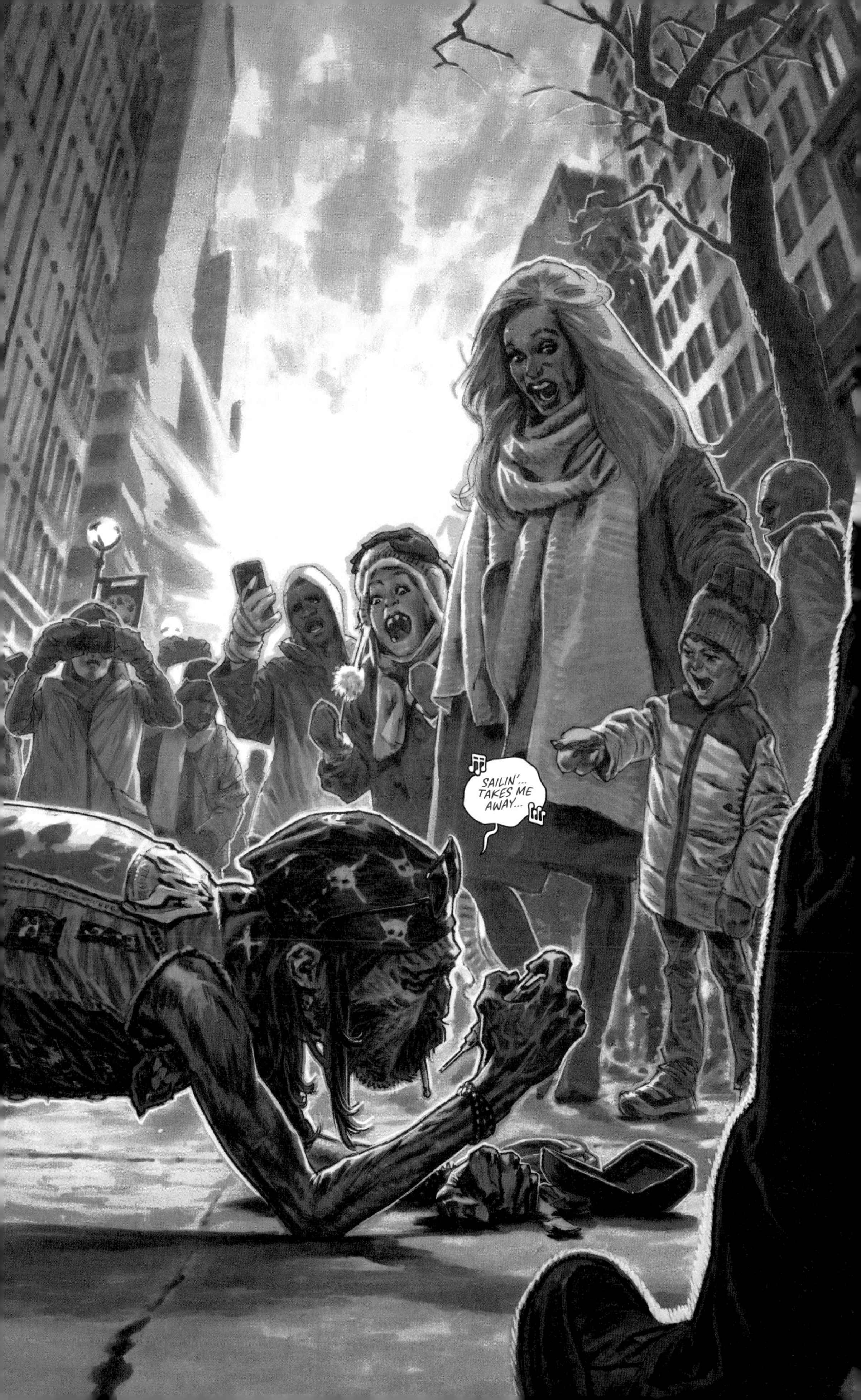
SAILIN'... TAKES ME AWAY...

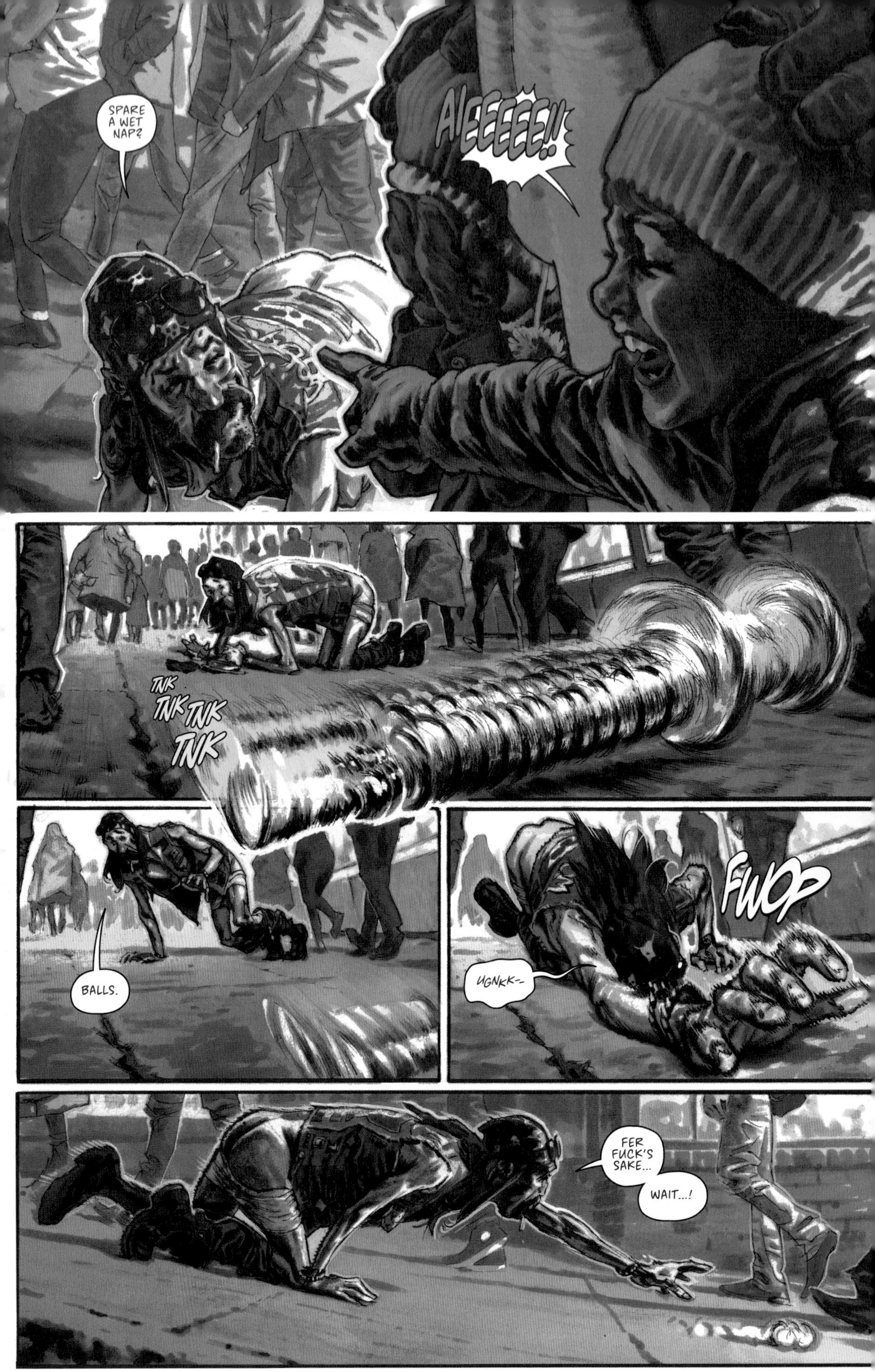
SPARE A WET NAP?
AIEEEEEE!!
TNK TNK TNK TNK
BALLS.
FWOP
UGNKK--
FER FUCK'S SAKE...
WAIT...!

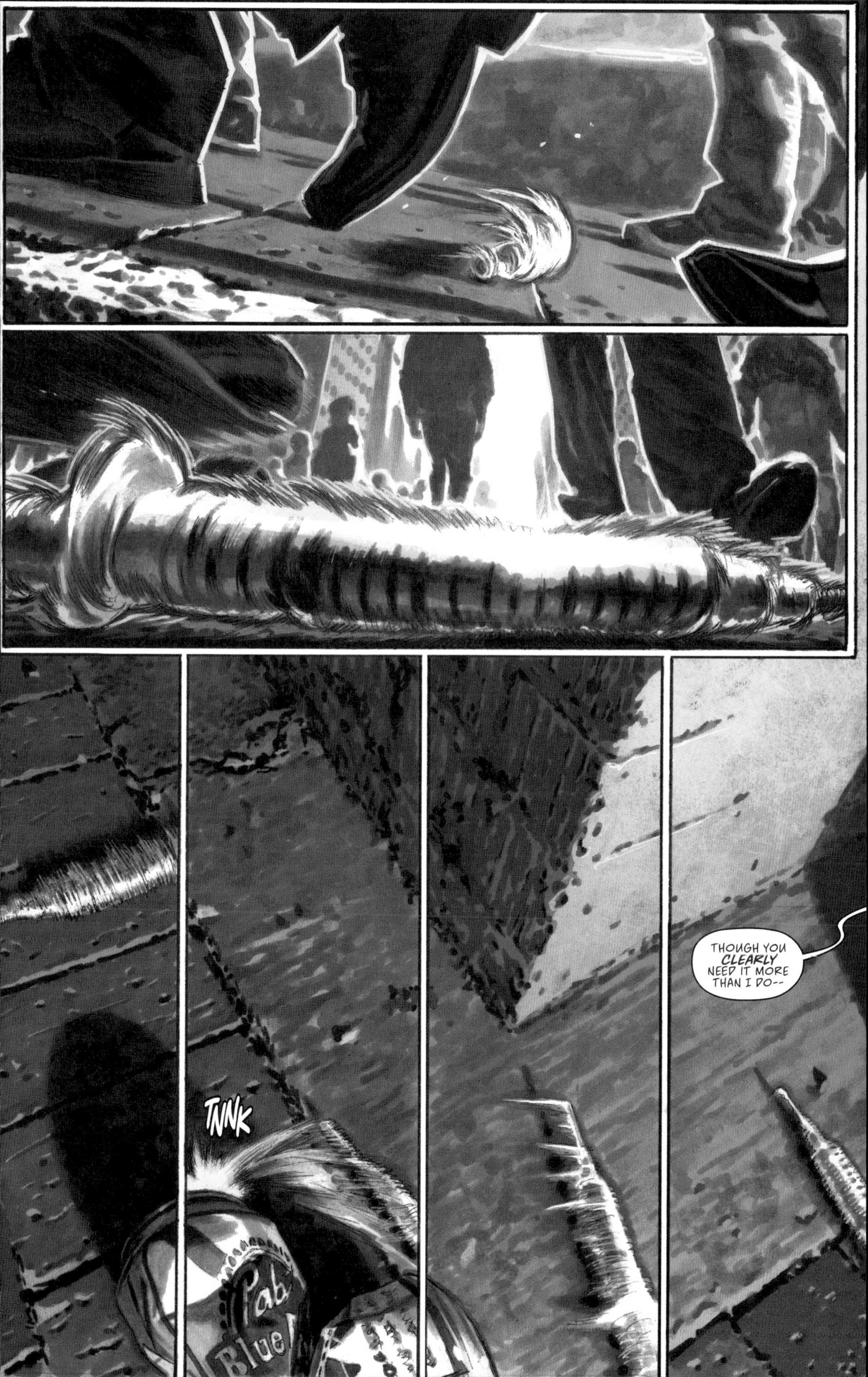
TNNK
THOUGH YOU CLEARLY NEED IT MORE THAN I DO--

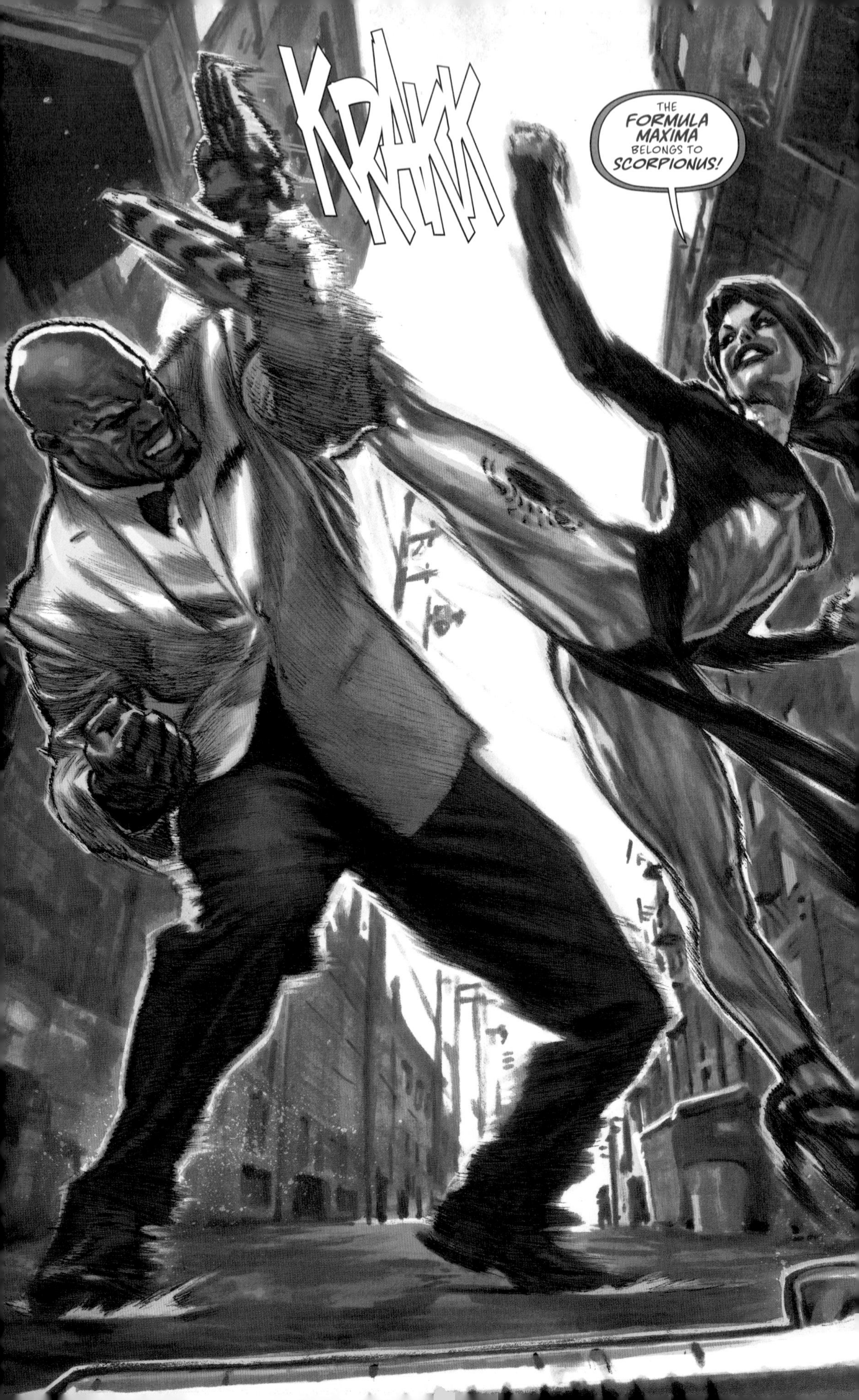
KRAKK
THE FORMULA MAXIMA BELONGS TO SCORPIONUS!

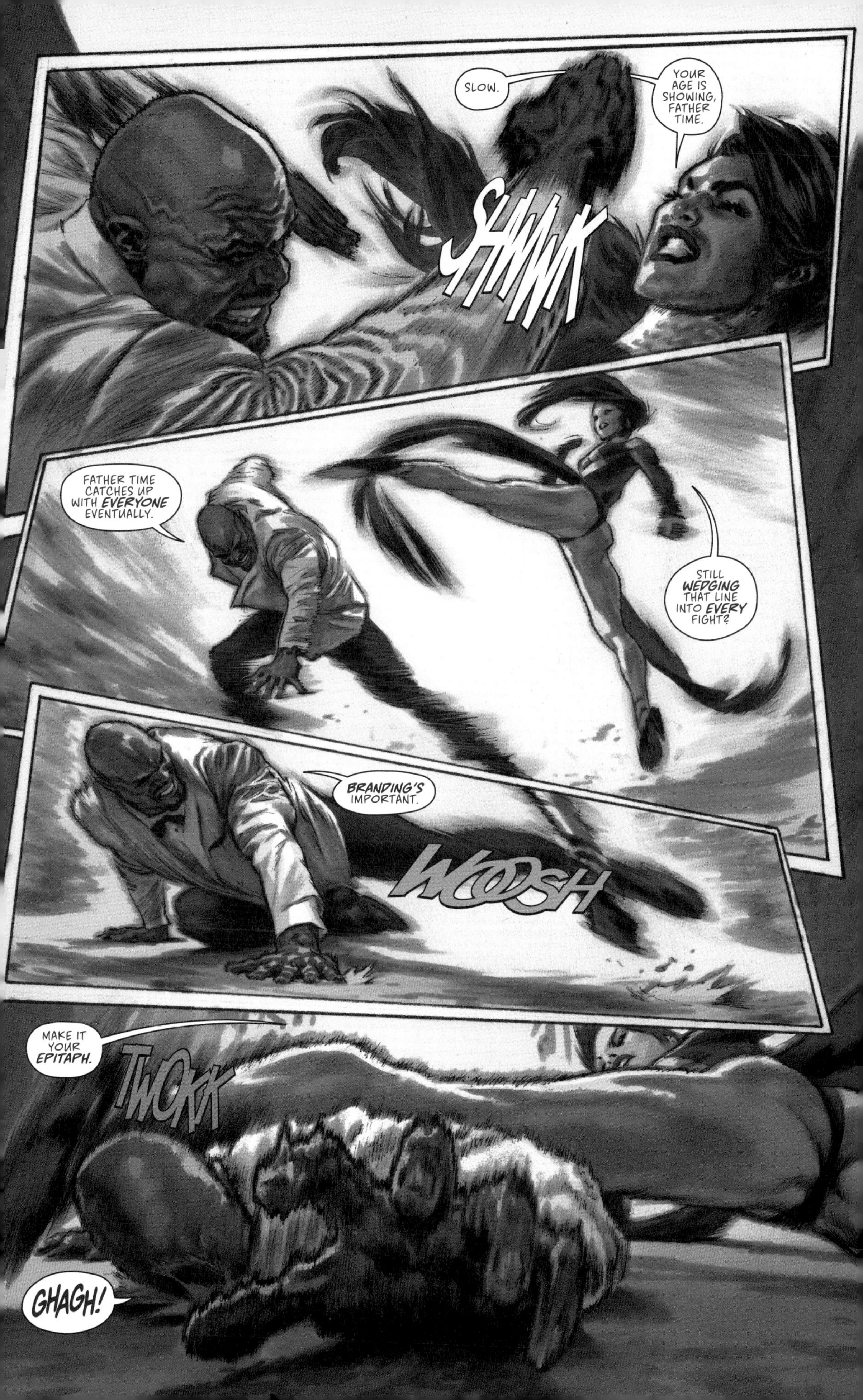
SLOW.
YOUR AGE IS SHOWING, FATHER TIME.
SHNNK
FATHER TIME CATCHES UP WITH EVERYONE EVENTUALLY.
STILL WEDGING THAT LINE INTO EVERY FIGHT?
BRANDING'S IMPORTANT.
WOOSH
MAKE IT YOUR EPITAPH.
TWOKK
GHAGH!

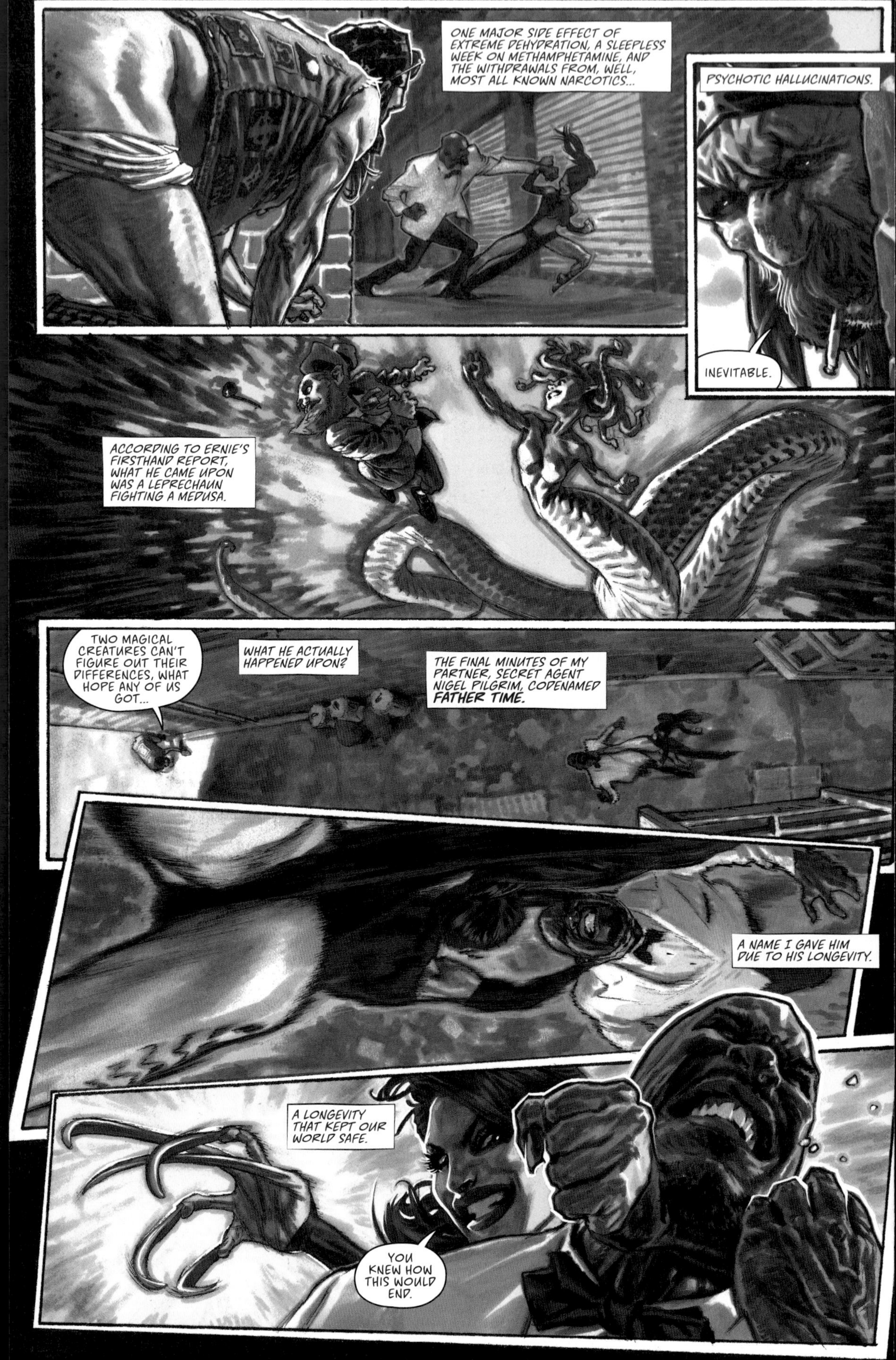

ONE MAJOR SIDE EFFECT OF EXTREME DEHYDRATION, A SLEEPLESS WEEK ON METHAMPHETAMINE, AND THE WITHDRAWALS FROM, WELL, MOST ALL KNOWN NARCOTICS...
PSYCHOTIC HALLUCINATIONS.
INEVITABLE.
ACCORDING TO ERNIE'S FIRSTHAND REPORT, WHAT HE CAME UPON WAS A LEPRECHAUN FIGHTING A MEDUSA.
TWO MAGICAL CREATURES CAN'T FIGURE OUT THEIR DIFFERENCES, WHAT HOPE ANY OF US GOT...
WHAT HE ACTUALLY HAPPENED UPON?
THE FINAL MINUTES OF MY PARTNER, SECRET AGENT NIGEL PILGRIM, CODENAMED **FATHER TIME.**
A NAME I GAVE HIM DUE TO HIS LONGEVITY.
A LONGEVITY THAT KEPT OUR WORLD SAFE.
YOU KNEW HOW THIS WOULD END.

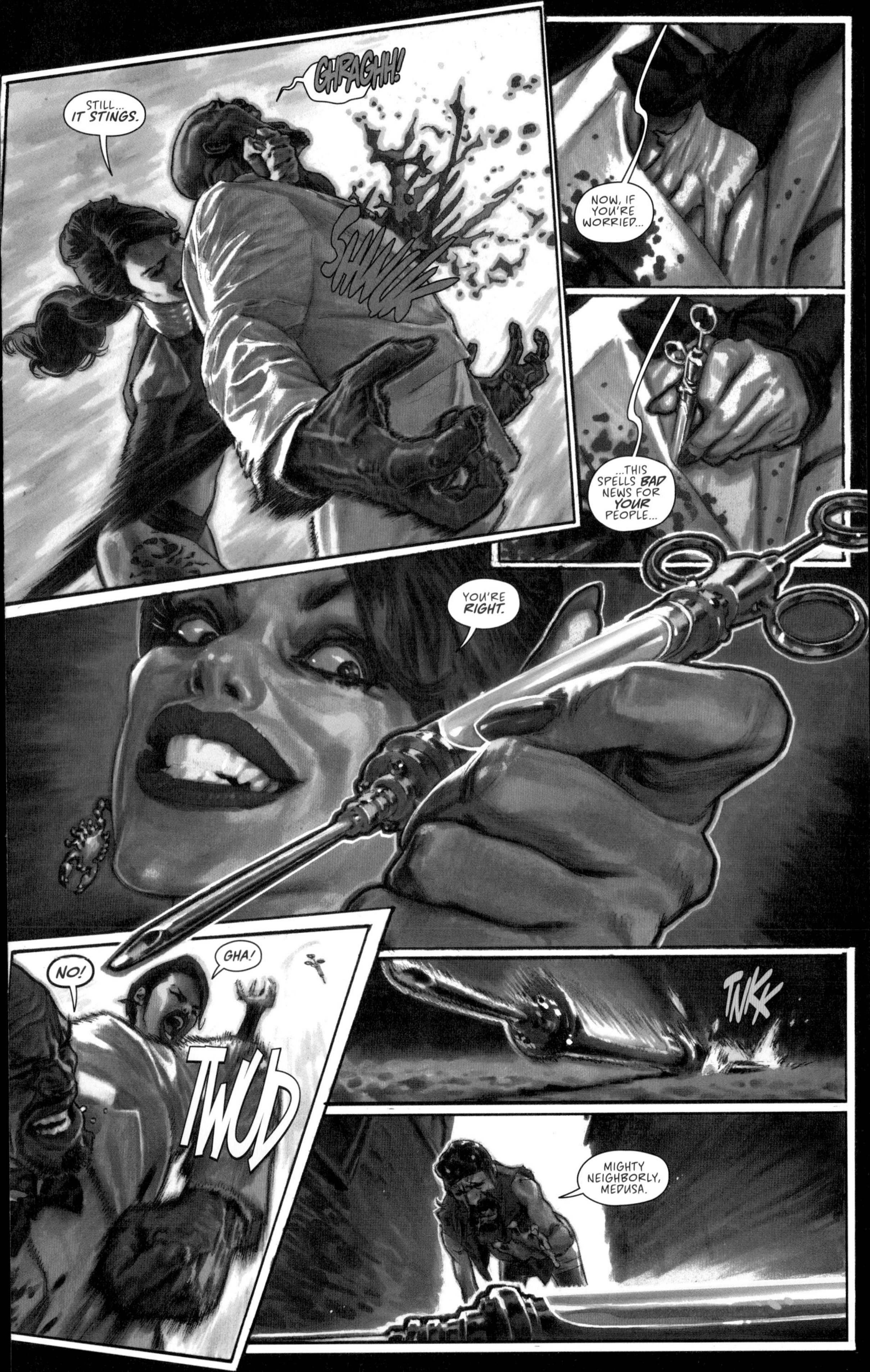
STILL... IT STINGS.
GHRAGHH!
SHUNK
NOW, IF YOU'RE WORRIED...
...THIS SPELLS BAD NEWS FOR YOUR PEOPLE...
YOU'RE RIGHT.
NO!
GHA!
TWUD
TNKK
MIGHTY NEIGHBORLY, MEDUSA.

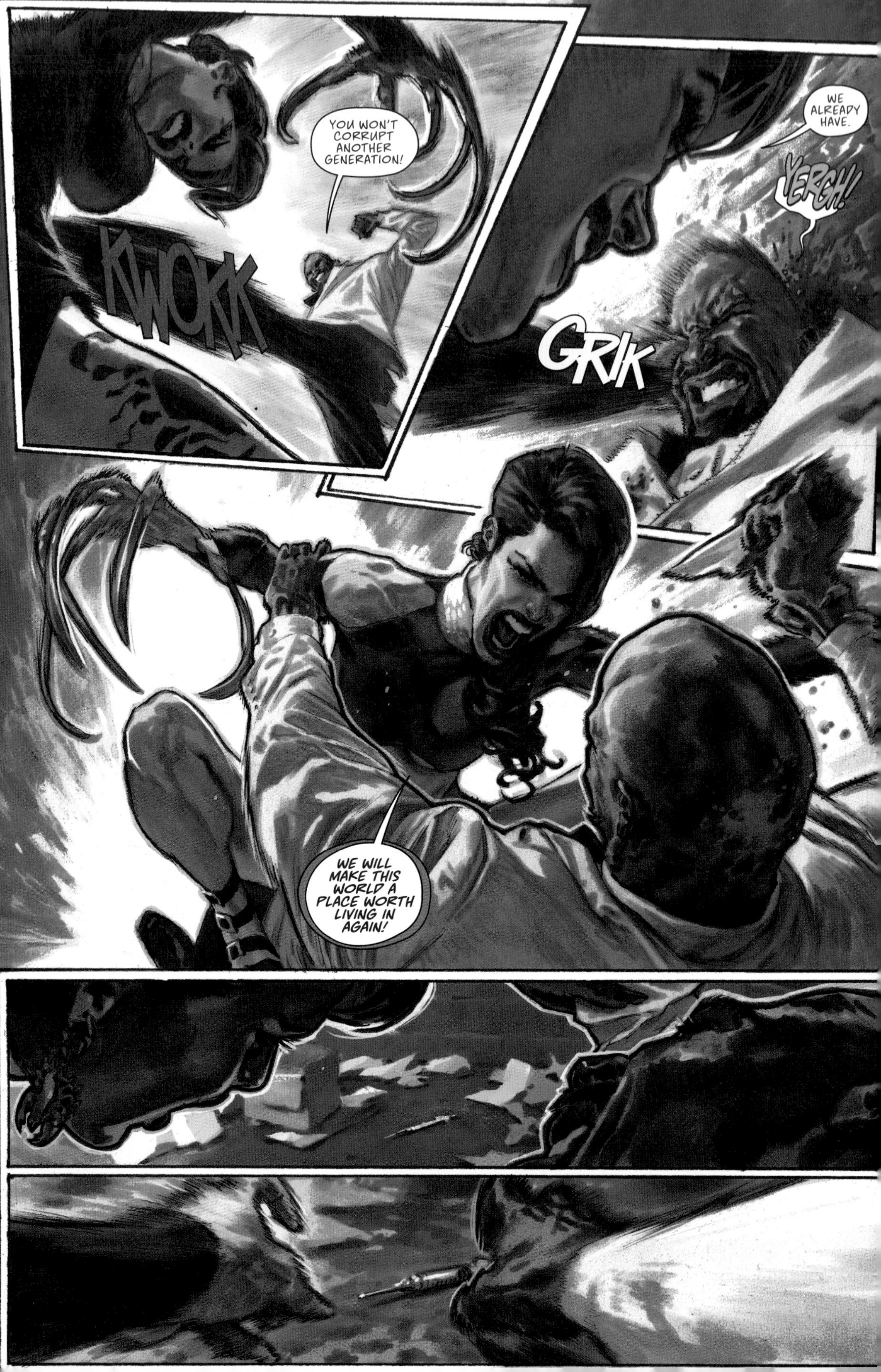
YOU WON'T CORRUPT ANOTHER GENERATION!
KWOKK
WE ALREADY HAVE.
YERGH!
GRIK
WE WILL MAKE THIS WORLD A PLACE WORTH LIVING IN AGAIN!

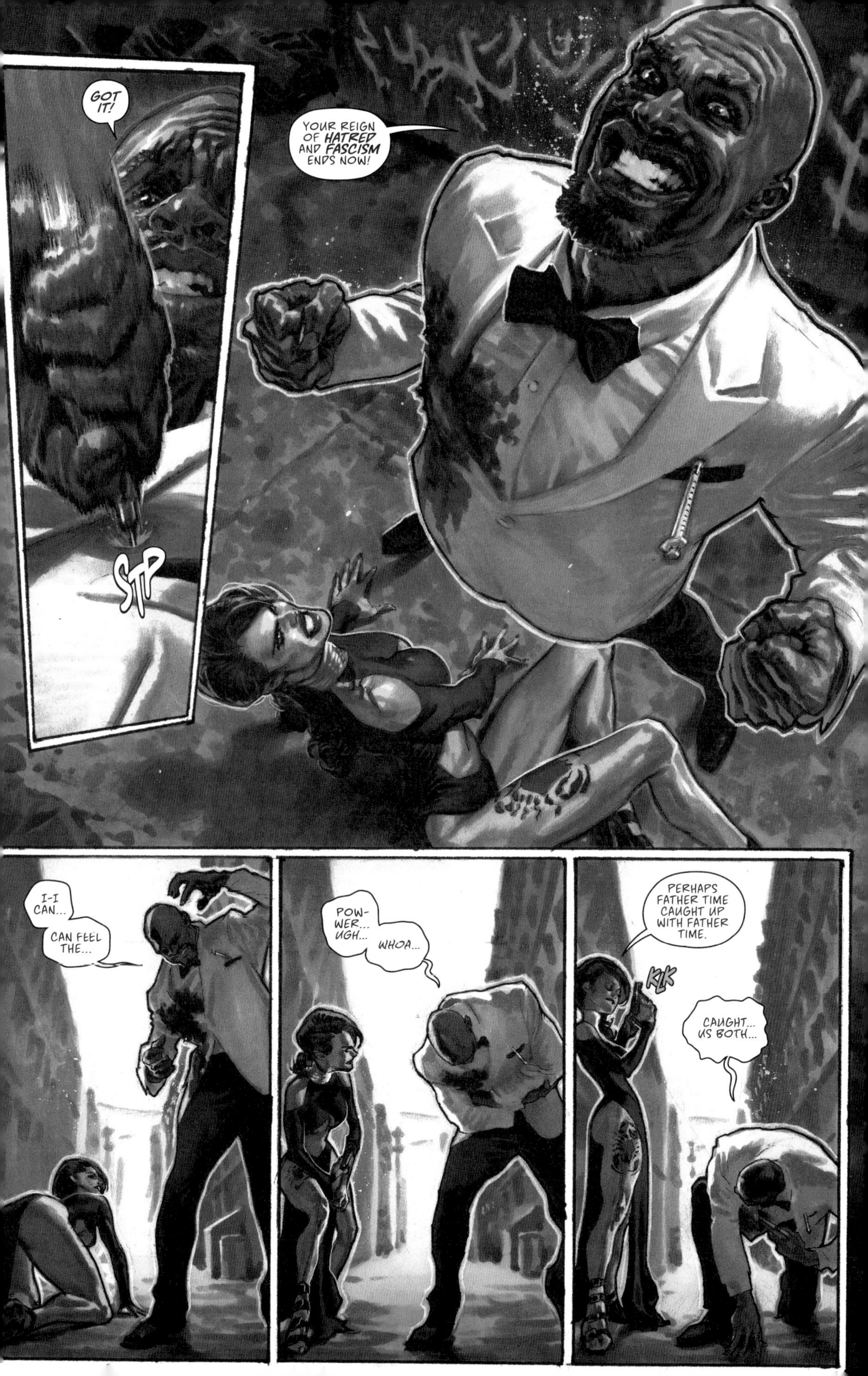
GOT IT!
STP
YOUR REIGN OF HATRED AND FASCISM ENDS NOW!
I-I CAN...
CAN FEEL THE...
POW-WER... UGH...
WHOA...
PERHAPS FATHER TIME CAUGHT UP WITH FATHER TIME.
KLK
CAUGHT... US BOTH...

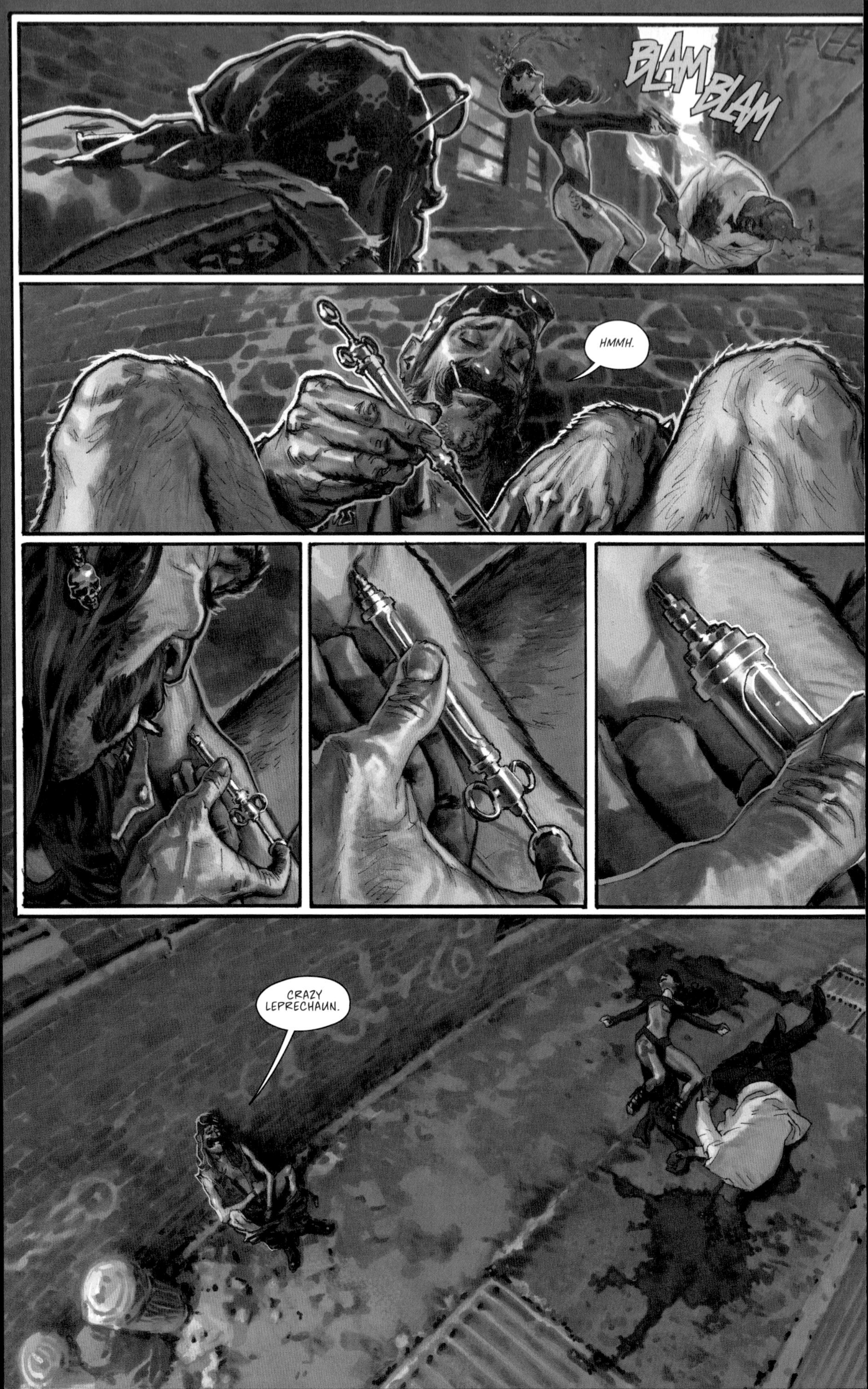
BLAM BLAM
HMMH.
CRAZY LEPRECHAUN.

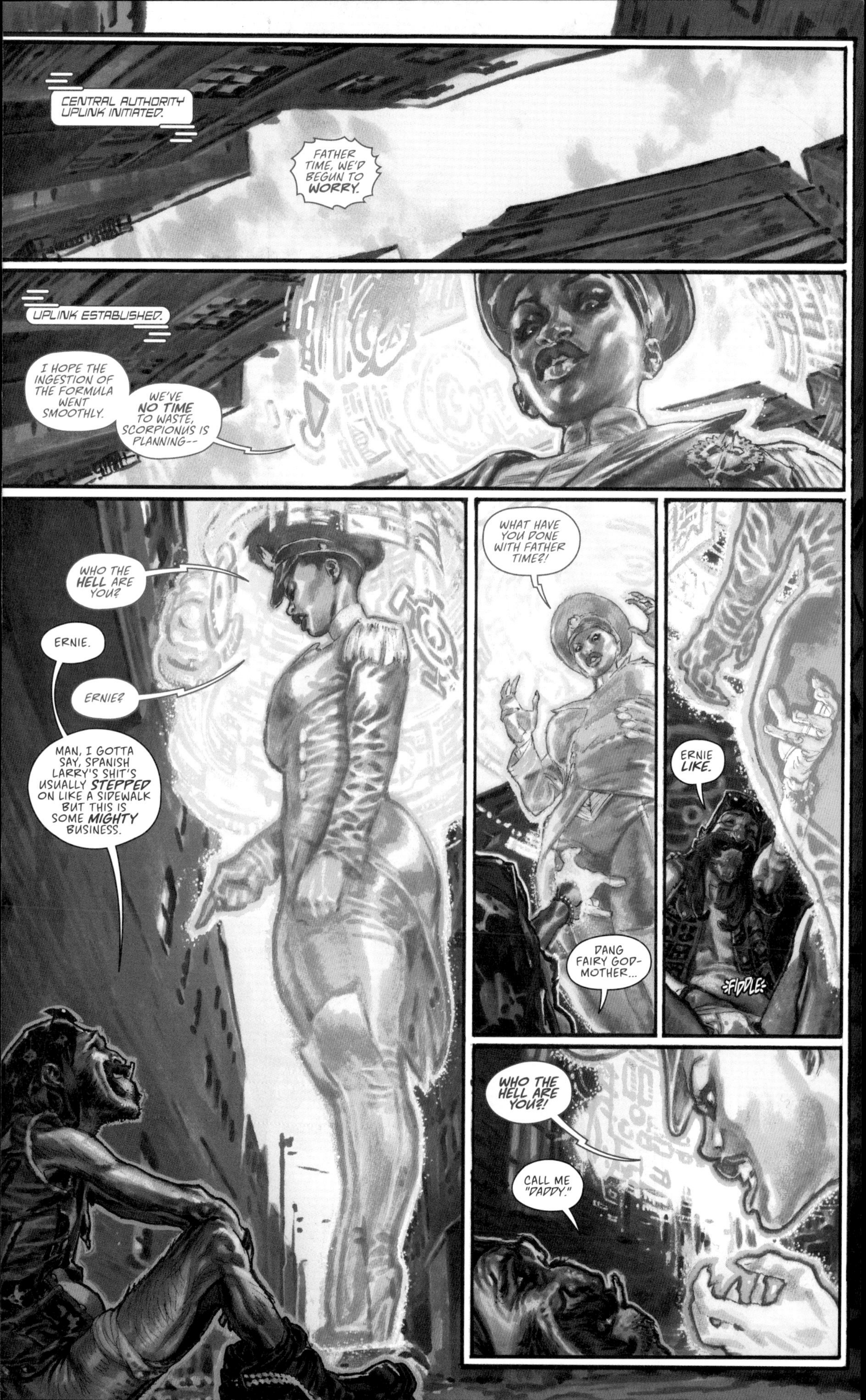
CENTRAL AUTHORITY UPLINK INITIATED.
FATHER TIME, WE'D BEGUN TO WORRY.
UPLINK ESTABLISHED.
I HOPE THE INGESTION OF THE FORMULA WENT SMOOTHLY.
WE'VE NO TIME TO WASTE, SCORPIONUS IS PLANNING--
WHO THE HELL ARE YOU?
ERNIE.
ERNIE?
MAN, I GOTTA SAY, SPANISH LARRY'S SHIT'S USUALLY STEPPED ON LIKE A SIDEWALK BUT THIS IS SOME MIGHTY BUSINESS.
WHAT HAVE YOU DONE WITH FATHER TIME?!
DANG FAIRY GOD-MOTHER...
ERNIE LIKE.
FIDDLE
WHO THE HELL ARE YOU?!
CALL ME "DADDY."

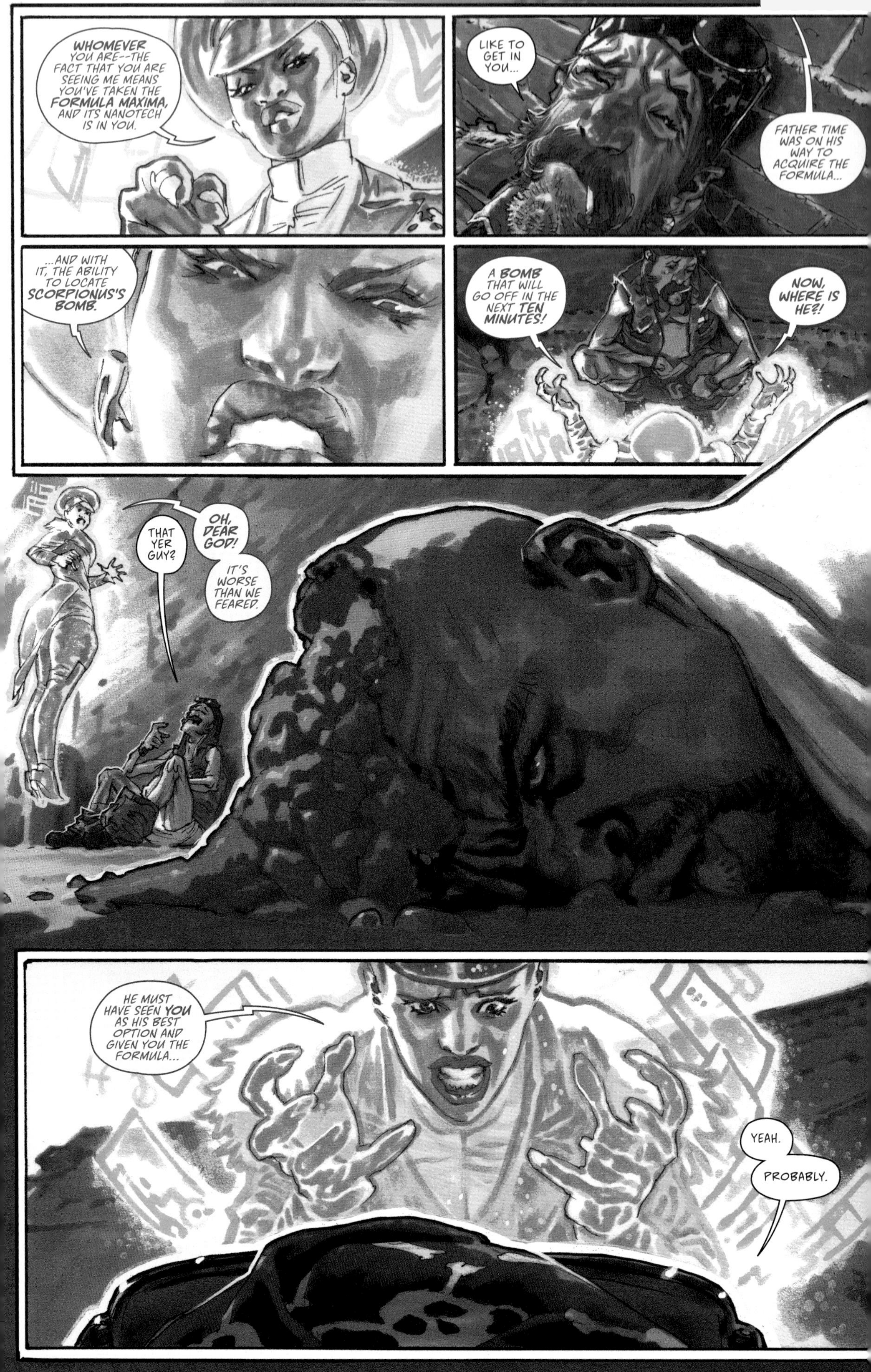
WHOMEVER YOU ARE--THE FACT THAT YOU ARE SEEING ME MEANS YOU'VE TAKEN THE FORMULA MAXIMA, AND ITS NANOTECH IS IN YOU.
LIKE TO GET IN YOU...
FATHER TIME WAS ON HIS WAY TO ACQUIRE THE FORMULA...
...AND WITH IT, THE ABILITY TO LOCATE SCORPIONUS'S BOMB.
A BOMB THAT WILL GO OFF IN THE NEXT TEN MINUTES!
NOW, WHERE IS HE?!
THAT YER GUY?
OH, DEAR GOD!
IT'S WORSE THAN WE FEARED.
HE MUST HAVE SEEN YOU AS HIS BEST OPTION AND GIVEN YOU THE FORMULA...
YEAH.
PROBABLY.

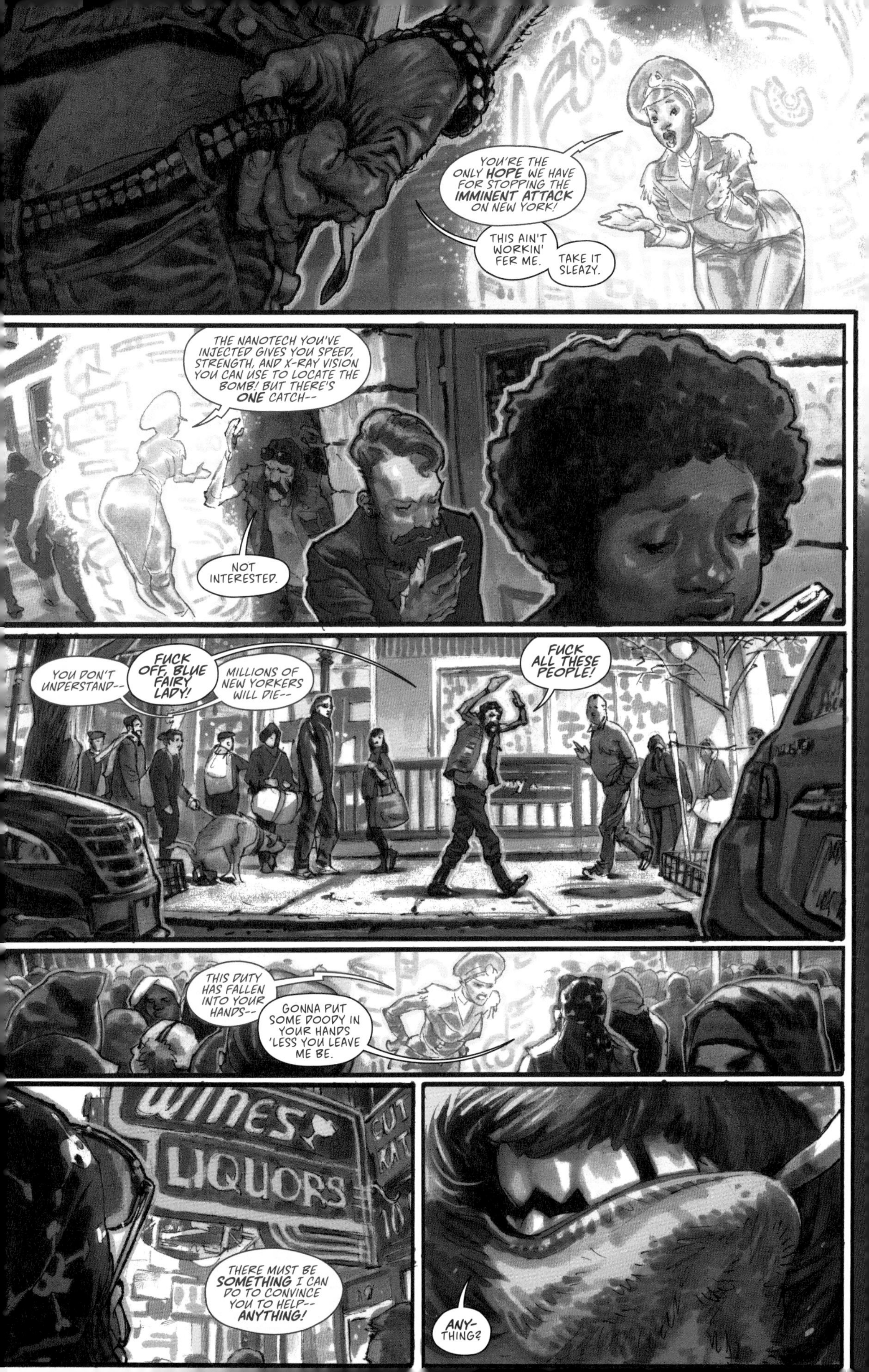
YOU'RE THE ONLY HOPE WE HAVE FOR STOPPING THE IMMINENT ATTACK ON NEW YORK!
THIS AIN'T WORKIN' FER ME.
TAKE IT SLEAZY.
THE NANOTECH YOU'VE INJECTED GIVES YOU SPEED, STRENGTH, AND X-RAY VISION YOU CAN USE TO LOCATE THE BOMB! BUT THERE'S ONE CATCH--
NOT INTERESTED.
YOU DON'T UNDERSTAND--
FUCK OFF, BLUE FAIRY LADY!
MILLIONS OF NEW YORKERS WILL DIE--
FUCK ALL THESE PEOPLE!
THIS DUTY HAS FALLEN INTO YOUR HANDS--
GONNA PUT SOME DOODY IN YOUR HANDS 'LESS YOU LEAVE ME BE.
WINES
LIQUORS
THERE MUST BE SOMETHING I CAN DO TO CONVINCE YOU TO HELP-- ANYTHING!
ANY-THING?

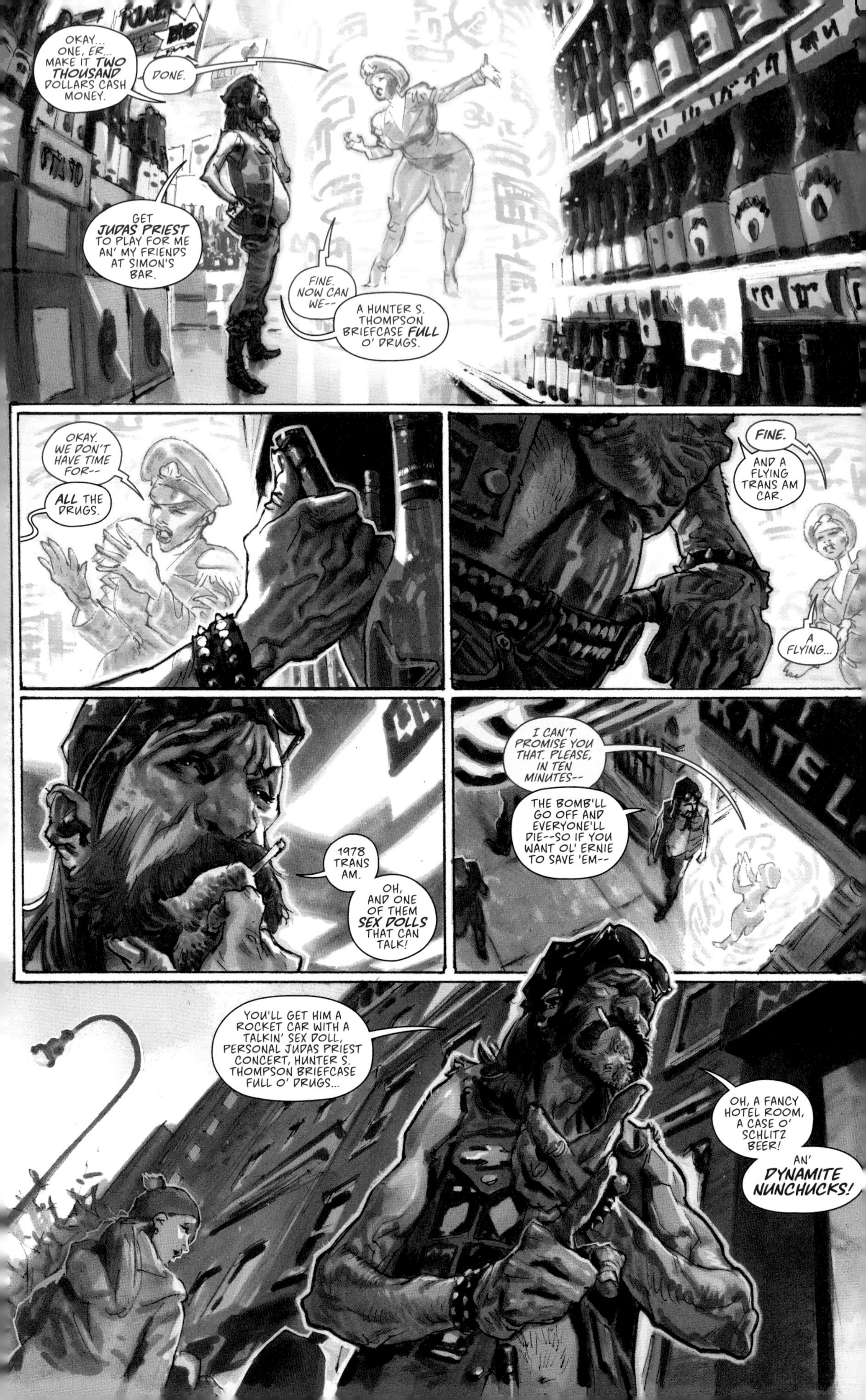
OKAY... ONE, ER... MAKE IT TWO THOUSAND DOLLARS CASH MONEY.
DONE.
GET JUDAS PRIEST TO PLAY FOR ME AN' MY FRIENDS AT SIMON'S BAR.
FINE. NOW CAN WE--
A HUNTER S. THOMPSON BRIEFCASE FULL O' DRUGS.
OKAY. WE DON'T HAVE TIME FOR--
ALL THE DRUGS.
FINE.
AND A FLYING TRANS AM CAR.
A FLYING...
1978 TRANS AM.
OH, AND ONE OF THEM SEX DOLLS THAT CAN TALK!
I CAN'T PROMISE YOU THAT. PLEASE, IN TEN MINUTES--
THE BOMB'LL GO OFF AND EVERYONE'LL DIE--SO IF YOU WANT OL' ERNIE TO SAVE 'EM--
YOU'LL GET HIM A ROCKET CAR WITH A TALKIN' SEX DOLL, PERSONAL JUDAS PRIEST CONCERT, HUNTER S. THOMPSON BRIEFCASE FULL O' DRUGS...
OH, A FANCY HOTEL ROOM, A CASE O' SCHLITZ BEER!
AN' DYNAMITE NUNCHUCKS!

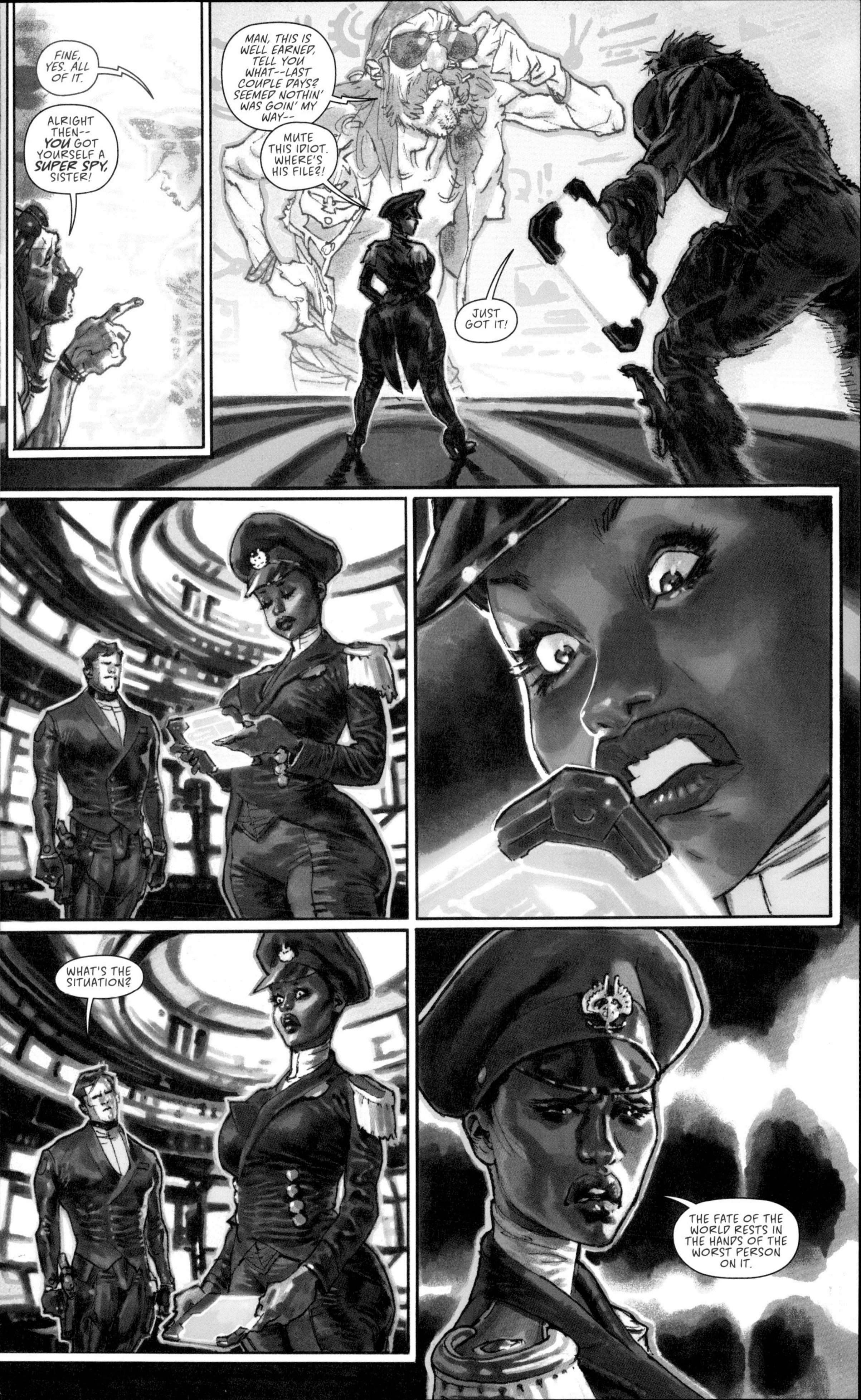
FINE, YES. ALL OF IT.
ALRIGHT THEN--YOU GOT YOURSELF A SUPER SPY, SISTER!
MAN, THIS IS WELL EARNED, TELL YOU WHAT--LAST COUPLE DAYS? SEEMED NOTHIN' WAS GOIN' MY WAY--
MUTE THIS IDIOT. WHERE'S HIS FILE?!
JUST GOT IT!
WHAT'S THE SITUATION?
THE FATE OF THE WORLD RESTS IN THE HANDS OF THE WORST PERSON ON IT.

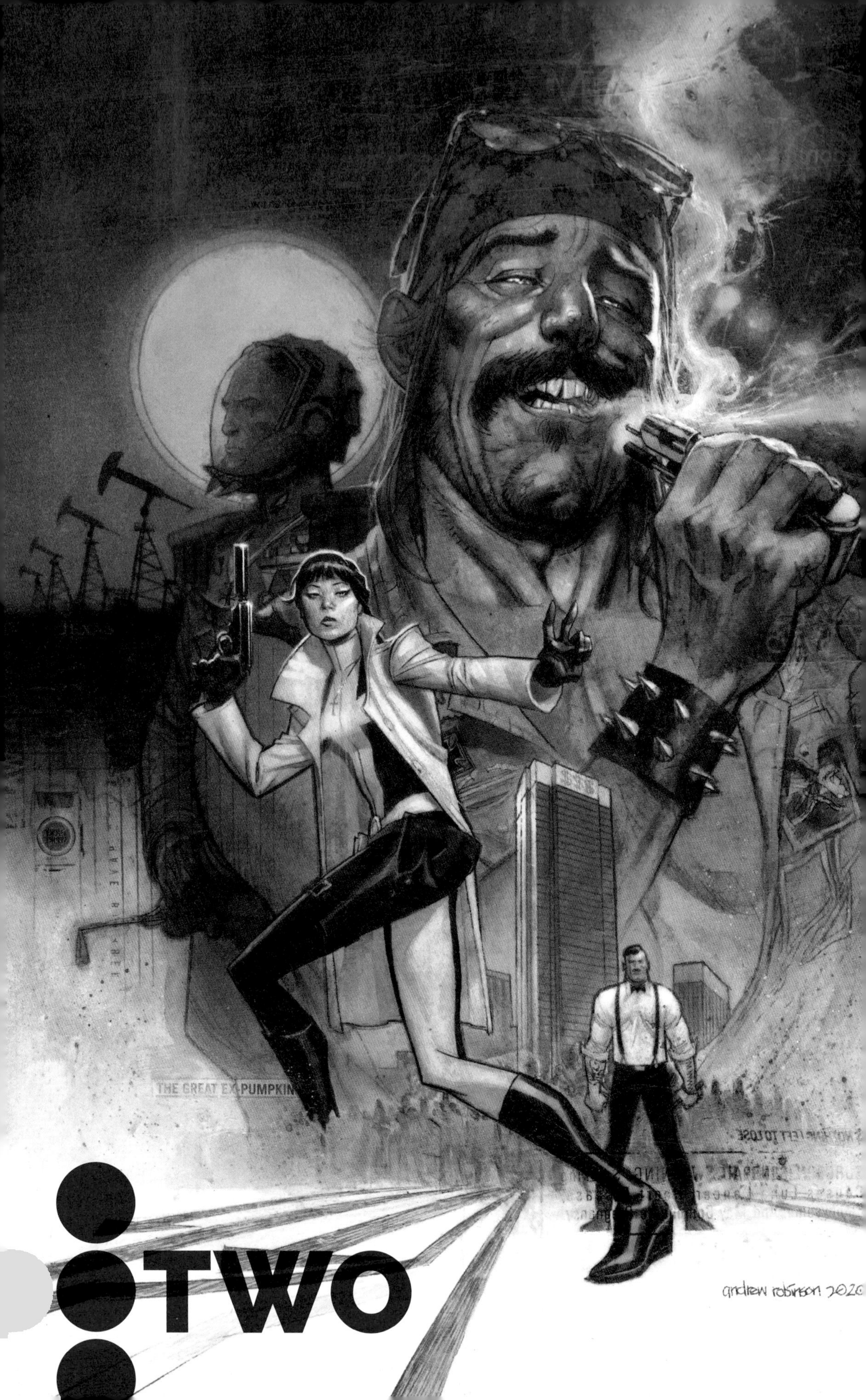
THE GREAT EX-PUMPKIN
andrew robinson 2020

TWO

MY THERAPIST ONCE TOLD ME I NEED
TO LEARN TO **"LOVE MYSELF."**

IT MADE ME WONDER... HOW **MANY** PEOPLE
HAS SHE SAID THAT BANAL BULLSHIT TO?

DOES IT APPLY TO **EVERYONE?**

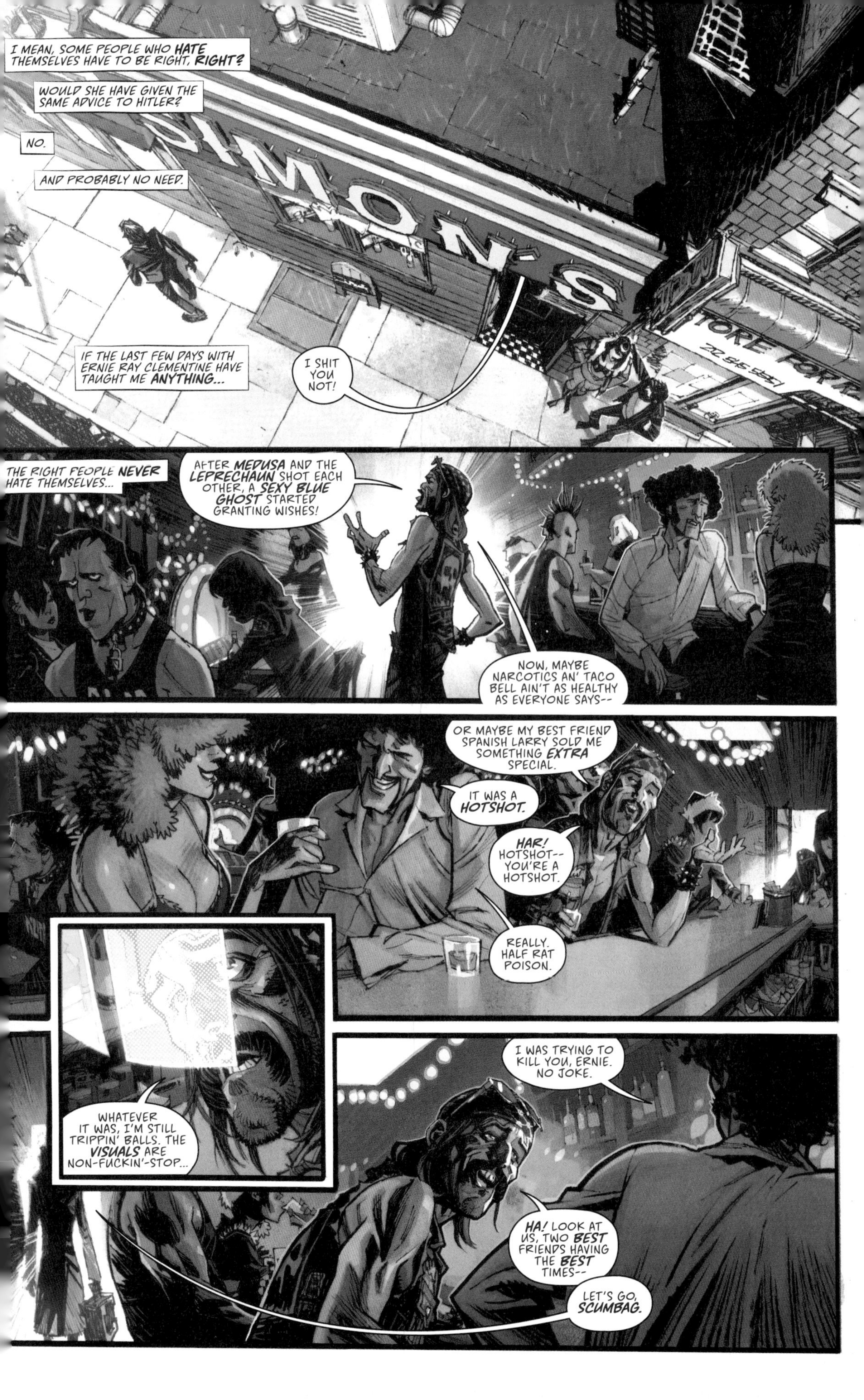
I MEAN, SOME PEOPLE WHO HATE THEMSELVES HAVE TO BE RIGHT, RIGHT?
WOULD SHE HAVE GIVEN THE SAME ADVICE TO HITLER?
NO.
AND PROBABLY NO NEED.
IF THE LAST FEW DAYS WITH ERNIE RAY CLEMENTINE HAVE TAUGHT ME ANYTHING...
I SHIT YOU NOT!
THE RIGHT PEOPLE NEVER HATE THEMSELVES...
AFTER MEDUSA AND THE LEPRECHAUN SHOT EACH OTHER, A SEXY BLUE GHOST STARTED GRANTING WISHES!
NOW, MAYBE NARCOTICS AN' TACO BELL AIN'T AS HEALTHY AS EVERYONE SAYS--
OR MAYBE MY BEST FRIEND SPANISH LARRY SOLD ME SOMETHING EXTRA SPECIAL.
IT WAS A HOTSHOT.
HAR! HOTSHOT-- YOU'RE A HOTSHOT.
REALLY. HALF RAT POISON.
WHATEVER IT WAS, I'M STILL TRIPPIN' BALLS. THE VISUALS ARE NON-FUCKIN'-STOP...
I WAS TRYING TO KILL YOU, ERNIE. NO JOKE.
HA! LOOK AT US, TWO BEST FRIENDS HAVING THE BEST TIMES--
LET'S GO, SCUMBAG.

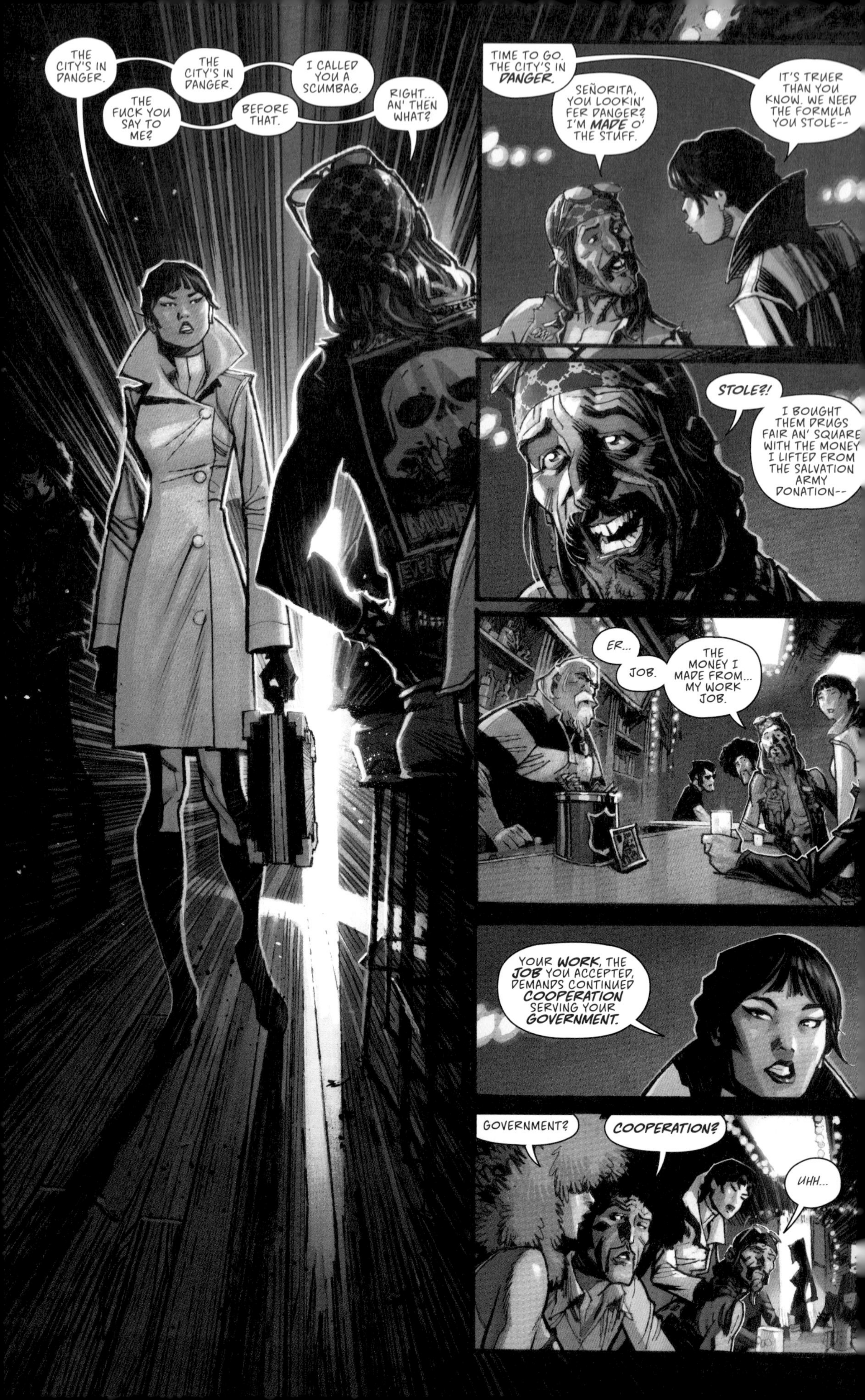

THE CITY'S IN DANGER.
THE FUCK YOU SAY TO ME?
THE CITY'S IN DANGER.
BEFORE THAT.
I CALLED YOU A SCUMBAG.
RIGHT... AN' THEN WHAT?
TIME TO GO. THE CITY'S IN DANGER.
SEÑORITA, YOU LOOKIN' FER DANGER? I'M MADE O' THE STUFF.
IT'S TRUER THAN YOU KNOW. WE NEED THE FORMULA YOU STOLE--
STOLE?!
I BOUGHT THEM DRUGS FAIR AN' SQUARE WITH THE MONEY I LIFTED FROM THE SALVATION ARMY DONATION--
ER...
JOB.
THE MONEY I MADE FROM... MY WORK JOB.
YOUR WORK, THE JOB YOU ACCEPTED, DEMANDS CONTINUED COOPERATION SERVING YOUR GOVERNMENT.
GOVERNMENT?
COOPERATION?
UHH...

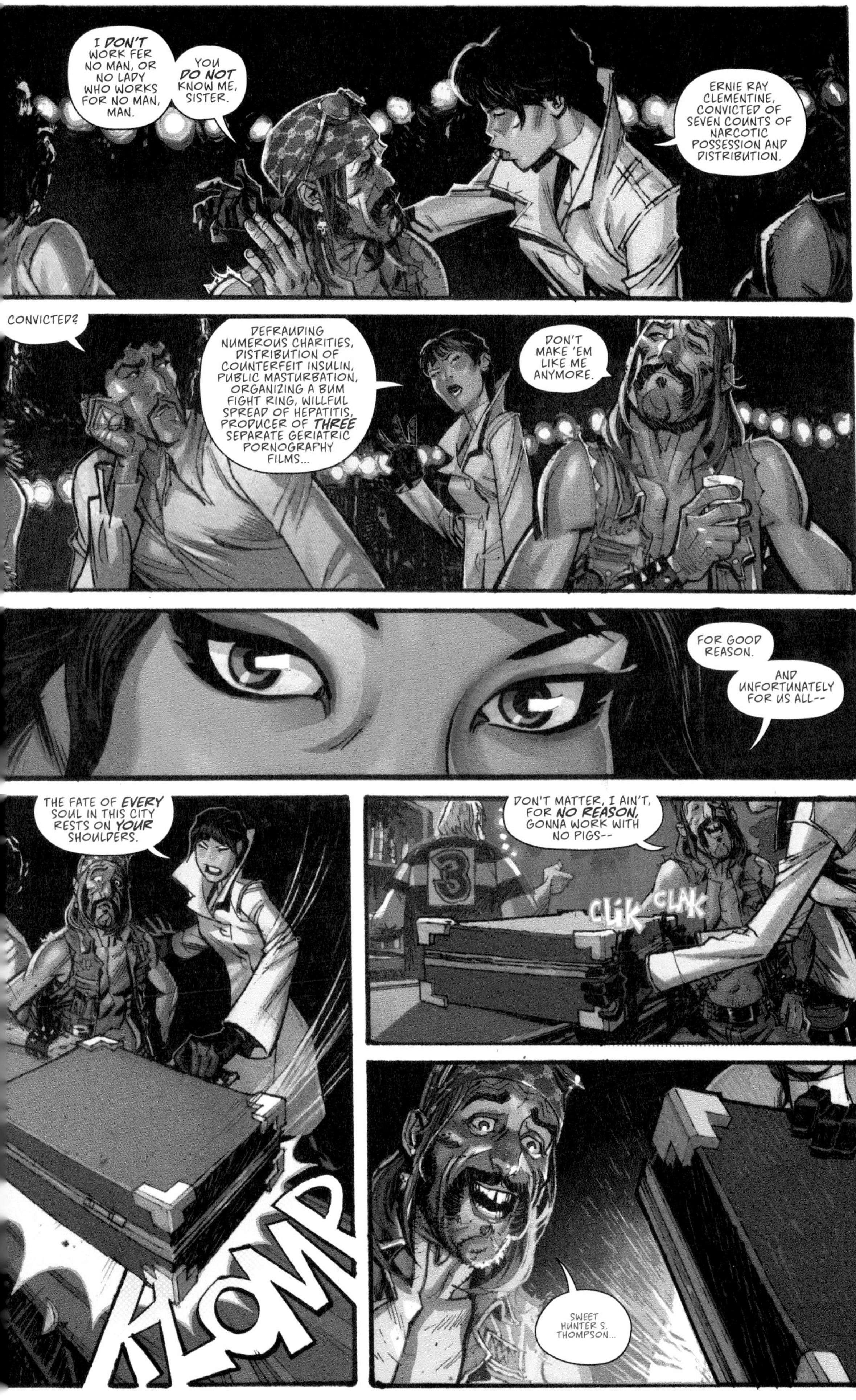
I **DON'T** WORK FER NO MAN, OR NO LADY WHO WORKS FOR NO MAN, MAN.
YOU **DO NOT** KNOW ME, SISTER.
ERNIE RAY CLEMENTINE, CONVICTED OF SEVEN COUNTS OF NARCOTIC POSSESSION AND DISTRIBUTION.
CONVICTED?
DEFRAUDING NUMEROUS CHARITIES, DISTRIBUTION OF COUNTERFEIT INSULIN, PUBLIC MASTURBATION, ORGANIZING A BUM FIGHT RING, WILLFUL SPREAD OF HEPATITIS, PRODUCER OF **THREE** SEPARATE GERIATRIC PORNOGRAPHY FILMS...
DON'T MAKE 'EM LIKE ME ANYMORE.
FOR GOOD REASON.
AND UNFORTUNATELY FOR US ALL--
THE FATE OF **EVERY** SOUL IN THIS CITY RESTS ON **YOUR** SHOULDERS.
KLOMP
DON'T MATTER, I AIN'T, FOR **NO REASON,** GONNA WORK WITH NO PIGS--
CLIK
CLAK
SWEET HUNTER S. THOMPSON...

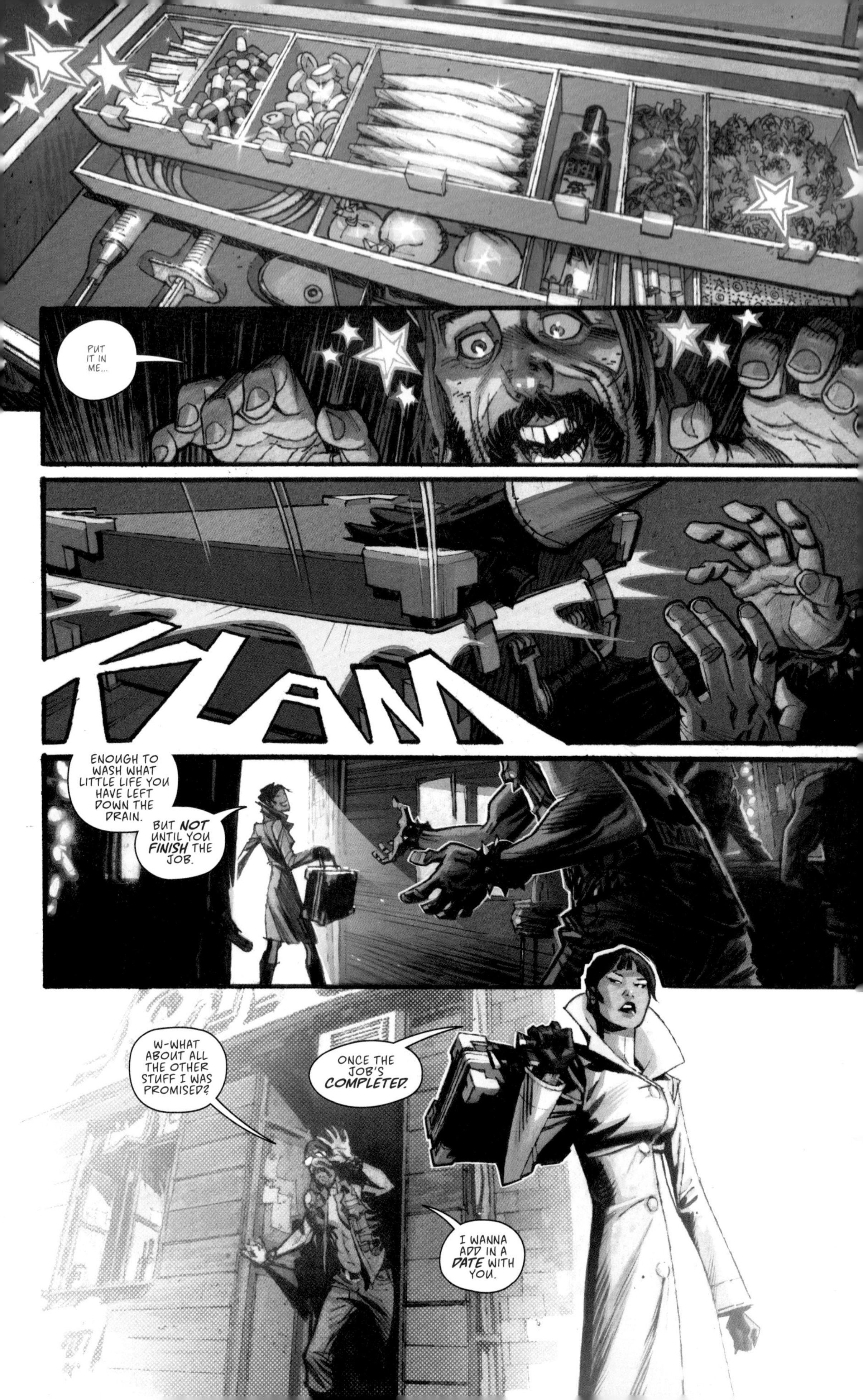
PUT IT IN ME...
KLAM
ENOUGH TO WASH WHAT LITTLE LIFE YOU HAVE LEFT DOWN THE DRAIN.
BUT NOT UNTIL YOU FINISH THE JOB.
W-WHAT ABOUT ALL THE OTHER STUFF I WAS PROMISED?
ONCE THE JOB'S COMPLETED.
I WANNA ADD IN A DATE WITH YOU.

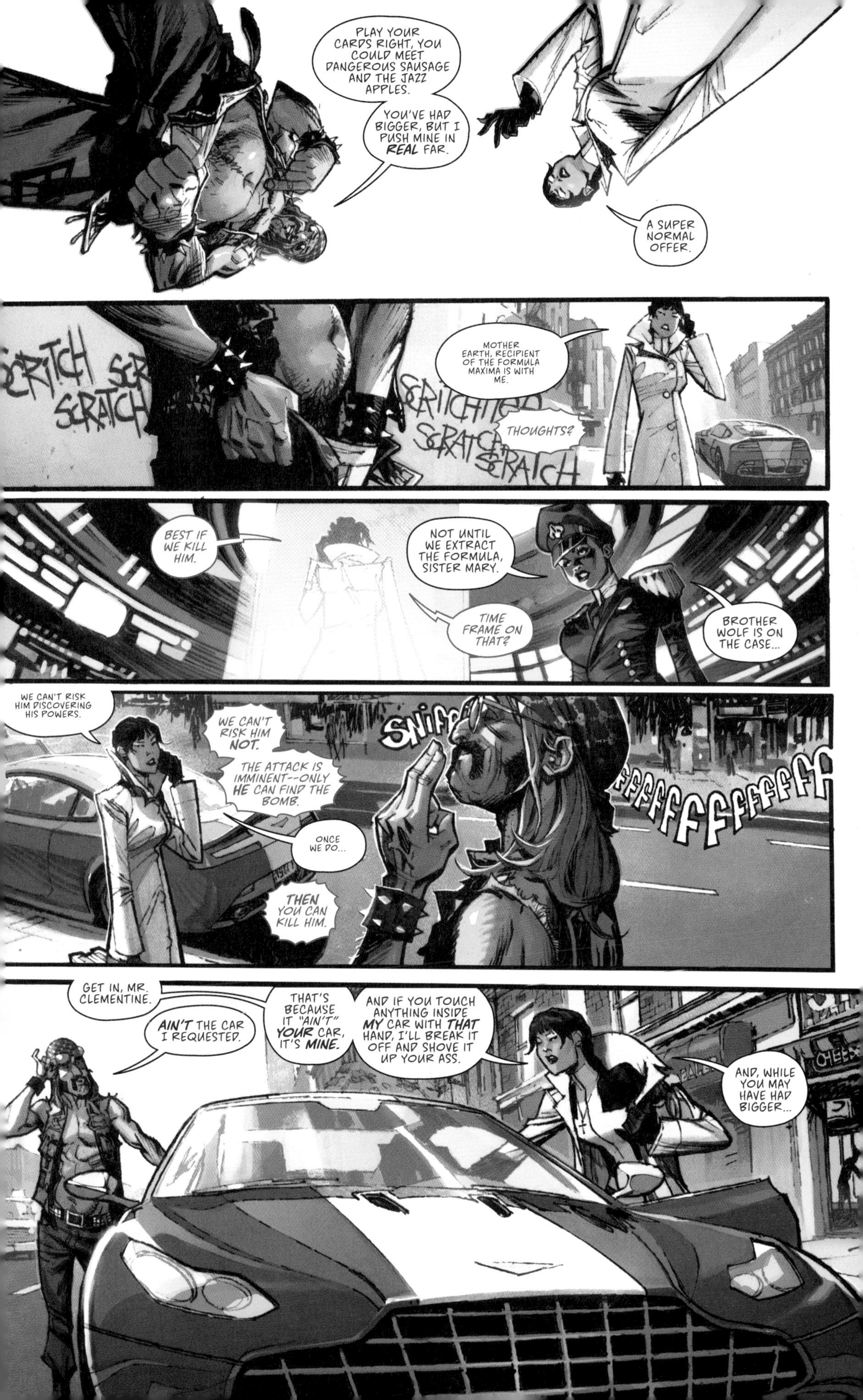

PLAY YOUR CARDS RIGHT, YOU COULD MEET DANGEROUS SAUSAGE AND THE JAZZ APPLES.
YOU'VE HAD BIGGER, BUT I PUSH MINE IN REAL FAR.
A SUPER NORMAL OFFER.
SCRITCH SCR SCRATCH
MOTHER EARTH, RECIPIENT OF THE FORMULA MAXIMA IS WITH ME.
THOUGHTS?
SCRITCH SCRATCH SCRATCH
BEST IF WE KILL HIM.
NOT UNTIL WE EXTRACT THE FORMULA, SISTER MARY.
TIME FRAME ON THAT?
BROTHER WOLF IS ON THE CASE...
WE CAN'T RISK HIM DISCOVERING HIS POWERS.
WE CAN'T RISK HIM NOT.
THE ATTACK IS IMMINENT--ONLY HE CAN FIND THE BOMB.
SNIFFFFFFFFFFFFFFF
ONCE WE DO...
THEN YOU CAN KILL HIM.
GET IN, MR. CLEMENTINE.
AIN'T THE CAR I REQUESTED.
THAT'S BECAUSE IT "AIN'T" YOUR CAR, IT'S MINE.
AND IF YOU TOUCH ANYTHING INSIDE MY CAR WITH THAT HAND, I'LL BREAK IT OFF AND SHOVE IT UP YOUR ASS.
AND, WHILE YOU MAY HAVE HAD BIGGER...

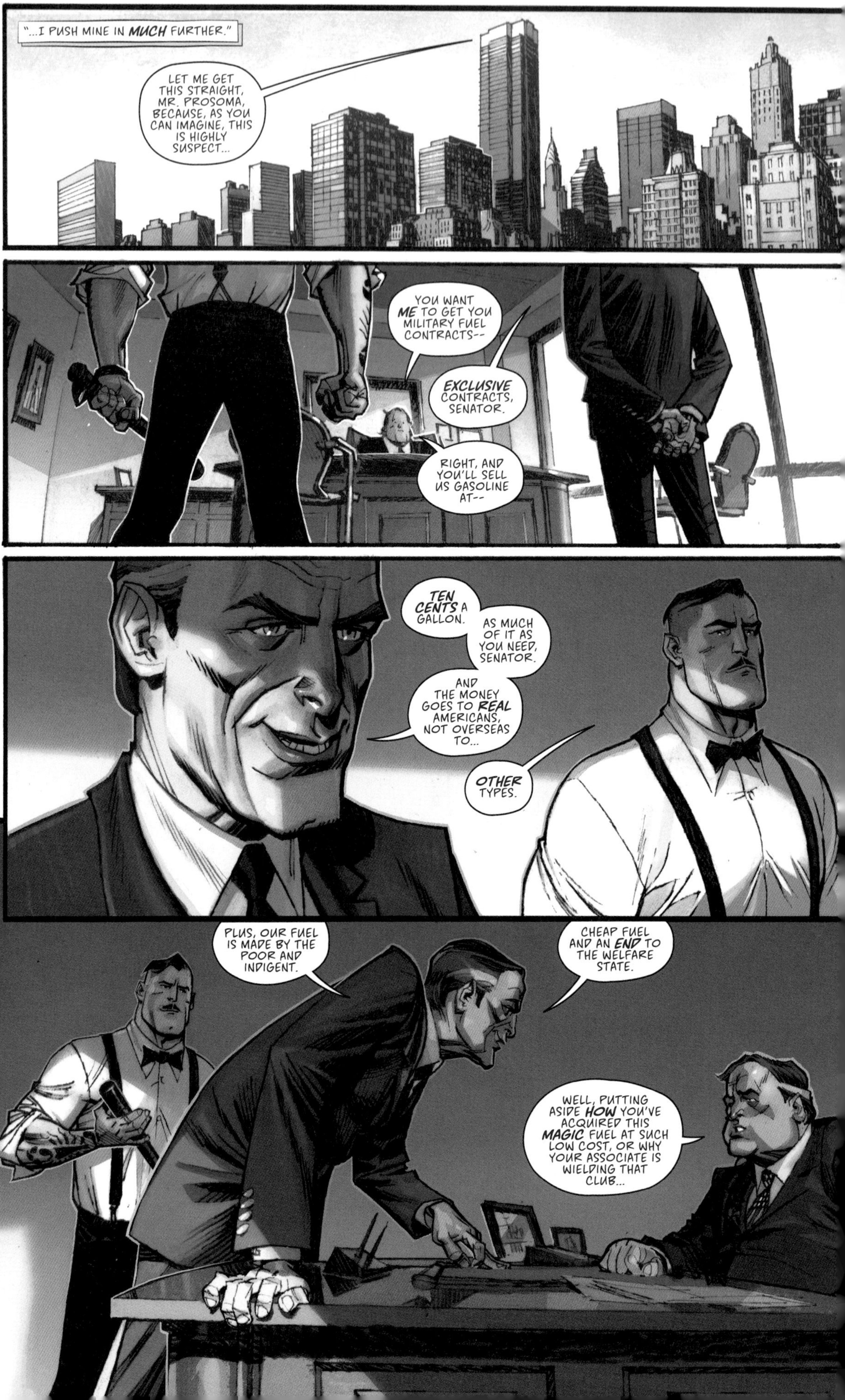
"...I PUSH MINE IN MUCH FURTHER."
LET ME GET THIS STRAIGHT, MR. PROSOMA, BECAUSE, AS YOU CAN IMAGINE, THIS IS HIGHLY SUSPECT...
YOU WANT ME TO GET YOU MILITARY FUEL CONTRACTS--
EXCLUSIVE CONTRACTS, SENATOR.
RIGHT, AND YOU'LL SELL US GASOLINE AT--
TEN CENTS A GALLON.
AS MUCH OF IT AS YOU NEED, SENATOR.
AND THE MONEY GOES TO REAL AMERICANS, NOT OVERSEAS TO...
OTHER TYPES.
PLUS, OUR FUEL IS MADE BY THE POOR AND INDIGENT.
CHEAP FUEL AND AN END TO THE WELFARE STATE.
WELL, PUTTING ASIDE HOW YOU'VE ACQUIRED THIS MAGIC FUEL AT SUCH LOW COST, OR WHY YOUR ASSOCIATE IS WIELDING THAT CLUB...

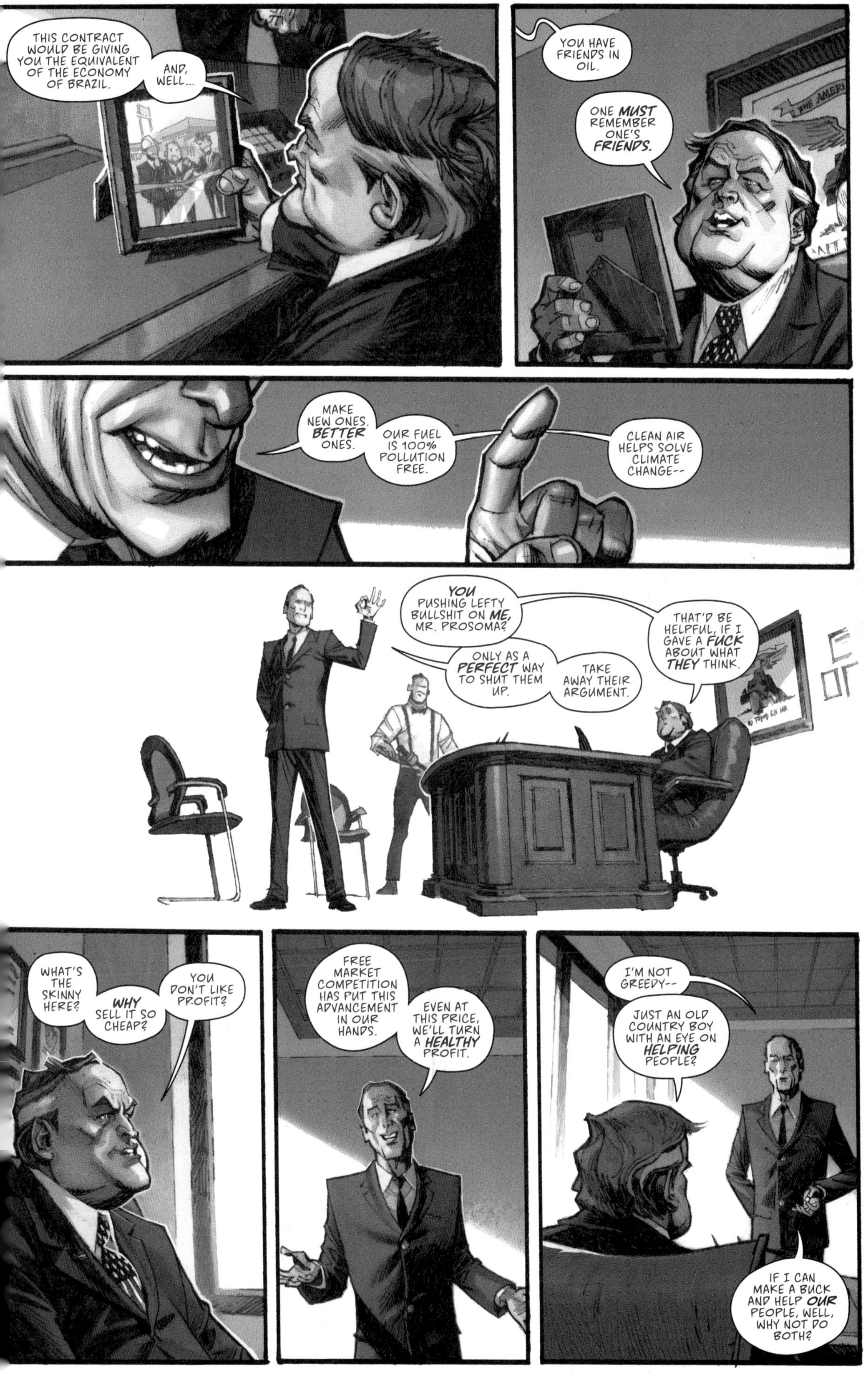

THIS CONTRACT WOULD BE GIVING YOU THE EQUIVALENT OF THE ECONOMY OF BRAZIL.
AND, WELL...
YOU HAVE FRIENDS IN OIL.
ONE MUST REMEMBER ONE'S FRIENDS.
MAKE NEW ONES. BETTER ONES.
OUR FUEL IS 100% POLLUTION FREE.
CLEAN AIR HELPS SOLVE CLIMATE CHANGE--
YOU PUSHING LEFTY BULLSHIT ON ME, MR. PROSOMA?
THAT'D BE HELPFUL, IF I GAVE A FUCK ABOUT WHAT THEY THINK.
ONLY AS A PERFECT WAY TO SHUT THEM UP.
TAKE AWAY THEIR ARGUMENT.
WHAT'S THE SKINNY HERE?
WHY SELL IT SO CHEAP?
YOU DON'T LIKE PROFIT?
FREE MARKET COMPETITION HAS PUT THIS ADVANCEMENT IN OUR HANDS.
EVEN AT THIS PRICE, WE'LL TURN A HEALTHY PROFIT.
I'M NOT GREEDY--
JUST AN OLD COUNTRY BOY WITH AN EYE ON HELPING PEOPLE?
IF I CAN MAKE A BUCK AND HELP OUR PEOPLE, WELL, WHY NOT DO BOTH?

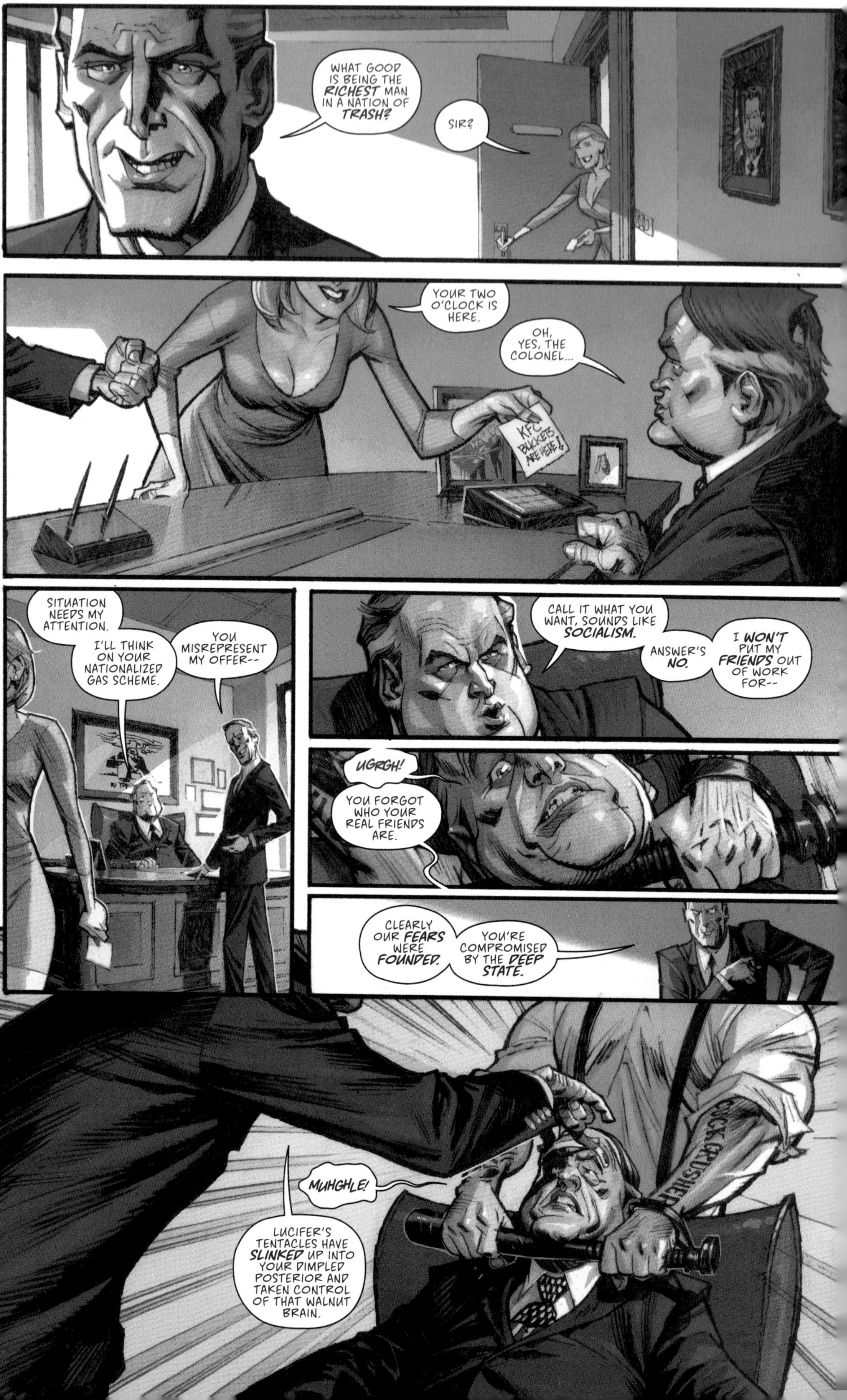
WHAT GOOD IS BEING THE RICHEST MAN IN A NATION OF TRASH?
SIR?
YOUR TWO O'CLOCK IS HERE.
OH, YES, THE COLONEL...
KFC BUCKETS ARE HERE!
SITUATION NEEDS MY ATTENTION.
I'LL THINK ON YOUR NATIONALIZED GAS SCHEME.
YOU MISREPRESENT MY OFFER--
CALL IT WHAT YOU WANT, SOUNDS LIKE SOCIALISM.
ANSWER'S NO.
I WON'T PUT MY FRIENDS OUT OF WORK FOR--
UGRGH!
YOU FORGOT WHO YOUR REAL FRIENDS ARE.
CLEARLY OUR FEARS WERE FOUNDED.
YOU'RE COMPROMISED BY THE DEEP STATE.
MUHGHLE!
LUCIFER'S TENTACLES HAVE SLINKED UP INTO YOUR DIMPLED POSTERIOR AND TAKEN CONTROL OF THAT WALNUT BRAIN.

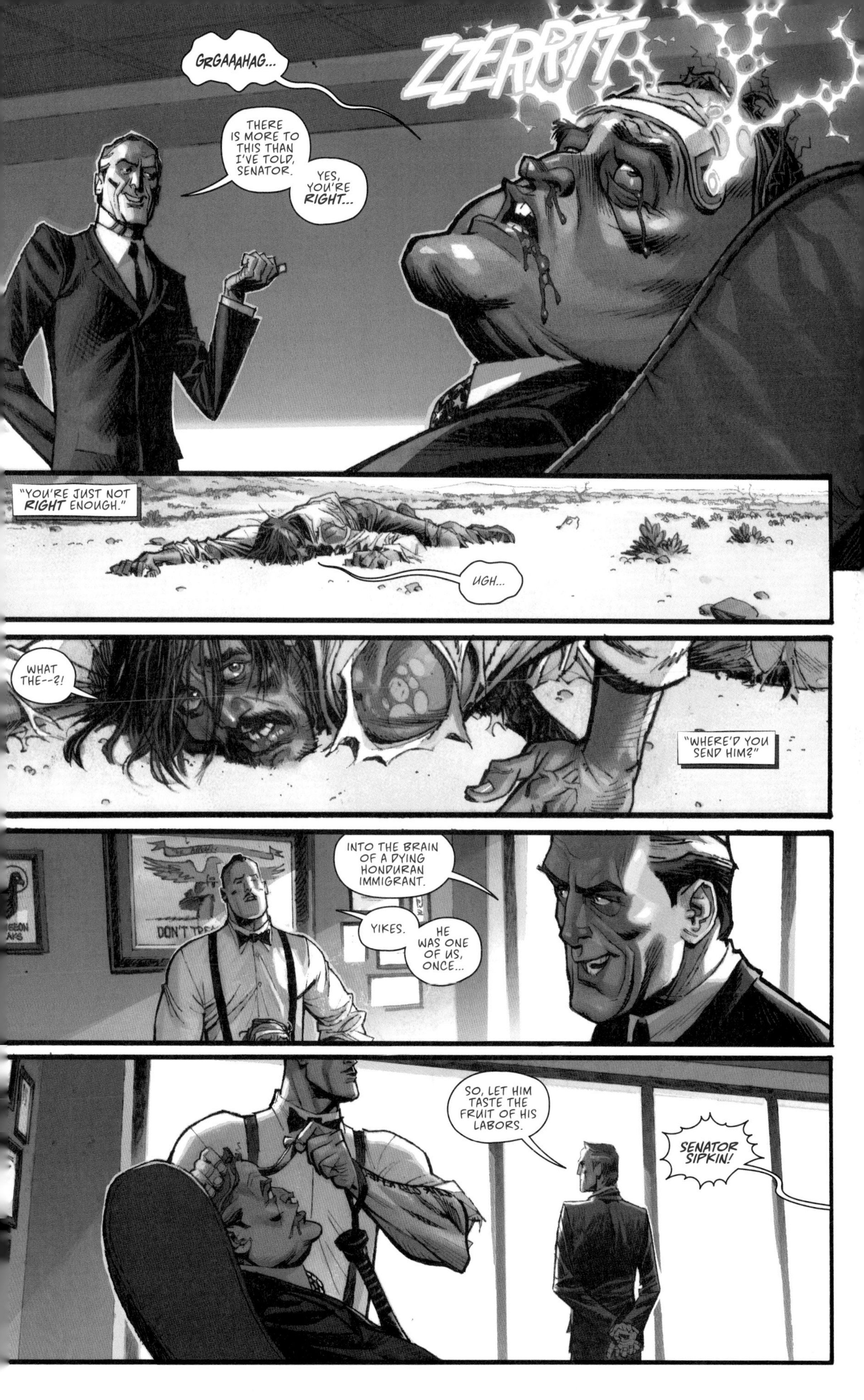
GRGAAAHAG...
ZZERRTT
THERE IS MORE TO THIS THAN I'VE TOLD, SENATOR.
YES, YOU'RE RIGHT...
"YOU'RE JUST NOT RIGHT ENOUGH."
UGH...
WHAT THE--?!
"WHERE'D YOU SEND HIM?"
INTO THE BRAIN OF A DYING HONDURAN IMMIGRANT.
YIKES.
HE WAS ONE OF US, ONCE...
SO, LET HIM TASTE THE FRUIT OF HIS LABORS.
SENATOR SIPKIN!

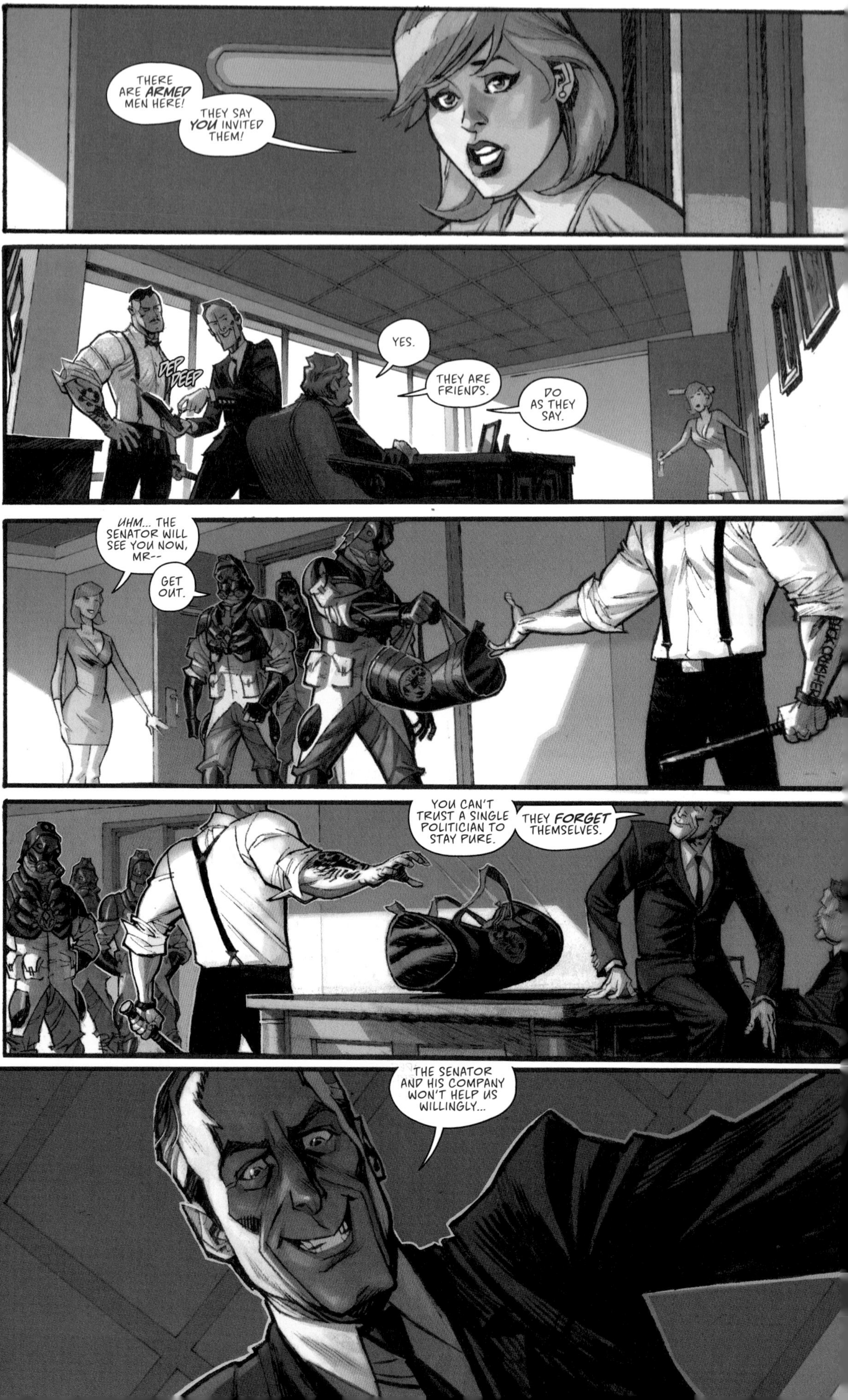
THERE ARE ARMED MEN HERE!
THEY SAY YOU INVITED THEM!
DEP DEEP
YES.
THEY ARE FRIENDS.
DO AS THEY SAY.
UHM... THE SENATOR WILL SEE YOU NOW, MR--
GET OUT.
YOU CAN'T TRUST A SINGLE POLITICIAN TO STAY PURE.
THEY FORGET THEMSELVES.
THE SENATOR AND HIS COMPANY WON'T HELP US WILLINGLY...

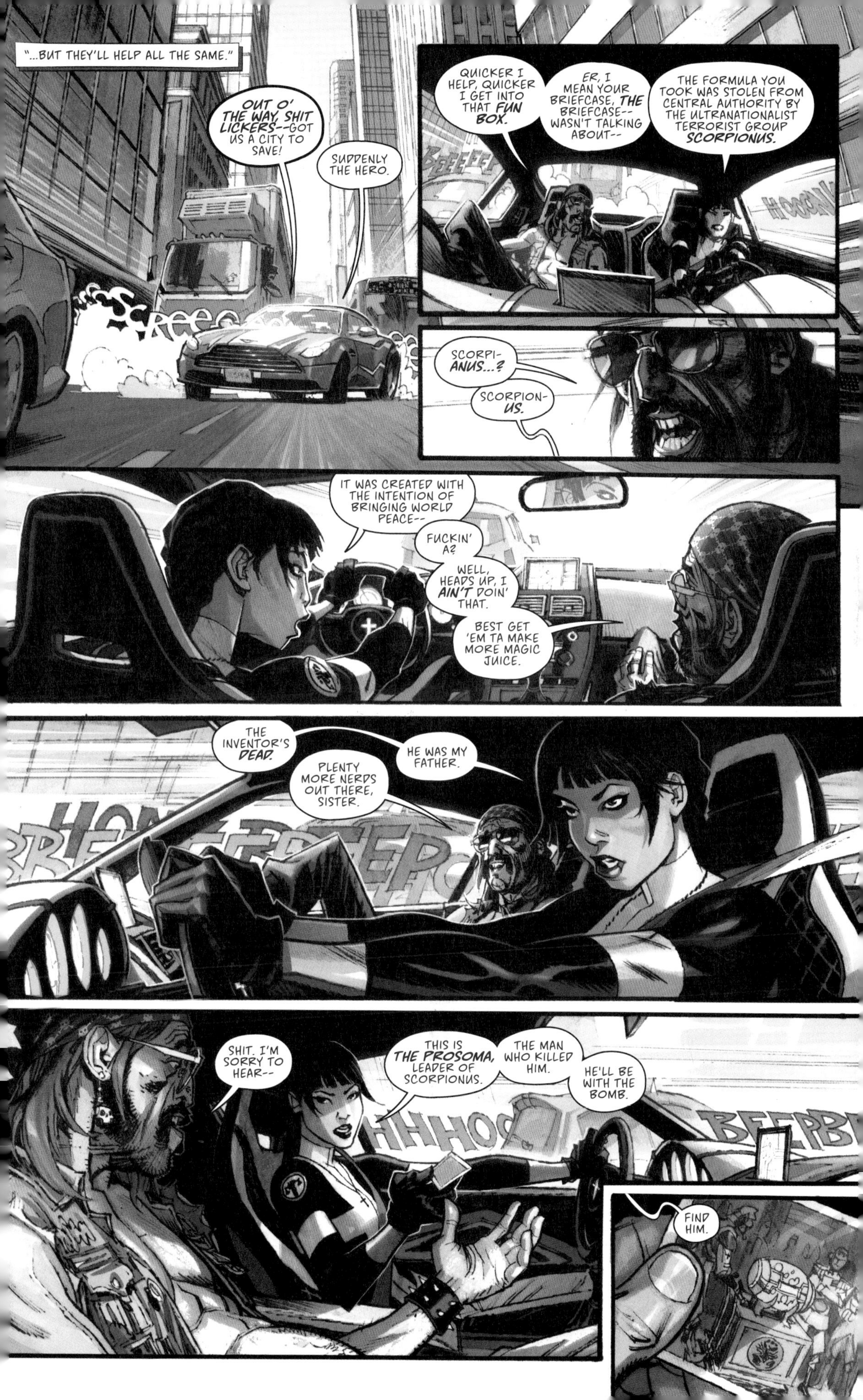
"...BUT THEY'LL HELP ALL THE SAME."
OUT O' THE WAY, SHIT LICKERS--GOT US A CITY TO SAVE!
SUDDENLY THE HERO.
QUICKER I HELP, QUICKER I GET INTO THAT FUN BOX.
ER, I MEAN YOUR BRIEFCASE, THE BRIEFCASE--WASN'T TALKING ABOUT--
THE FORMULA YOU TOOK WAS STOLEN FROM CENTRAL AUTHORITY BY THE ULTRANATIONALIST TERRORIST GROUP SCORPIONUS.
SCORPI-ANUS...?
SCORPION-US.
IT WAS CREATED WITH THE INTENTION OF BRINGING WORLD PEACE--
FUCKIN' A?
WELL, HEADS UP, I AIN'T DOIN' THAT.
BEST GET 'EM TA MAKE MORE MAGIC JUICE.
THE INVENTOR'S DEAD.
HE WAS MY FATHER.
PLENTY MORE NERDS OUT THERE, SISTER.
SHIT. I'M SORRY TO HEAR--
THIS IS THE PROSOMA, LEADER OF SCORPIONUS.
THE MAN WHO KILLED HIM.
HE'LL BE WITH THE BOMB.
FIND HIM.

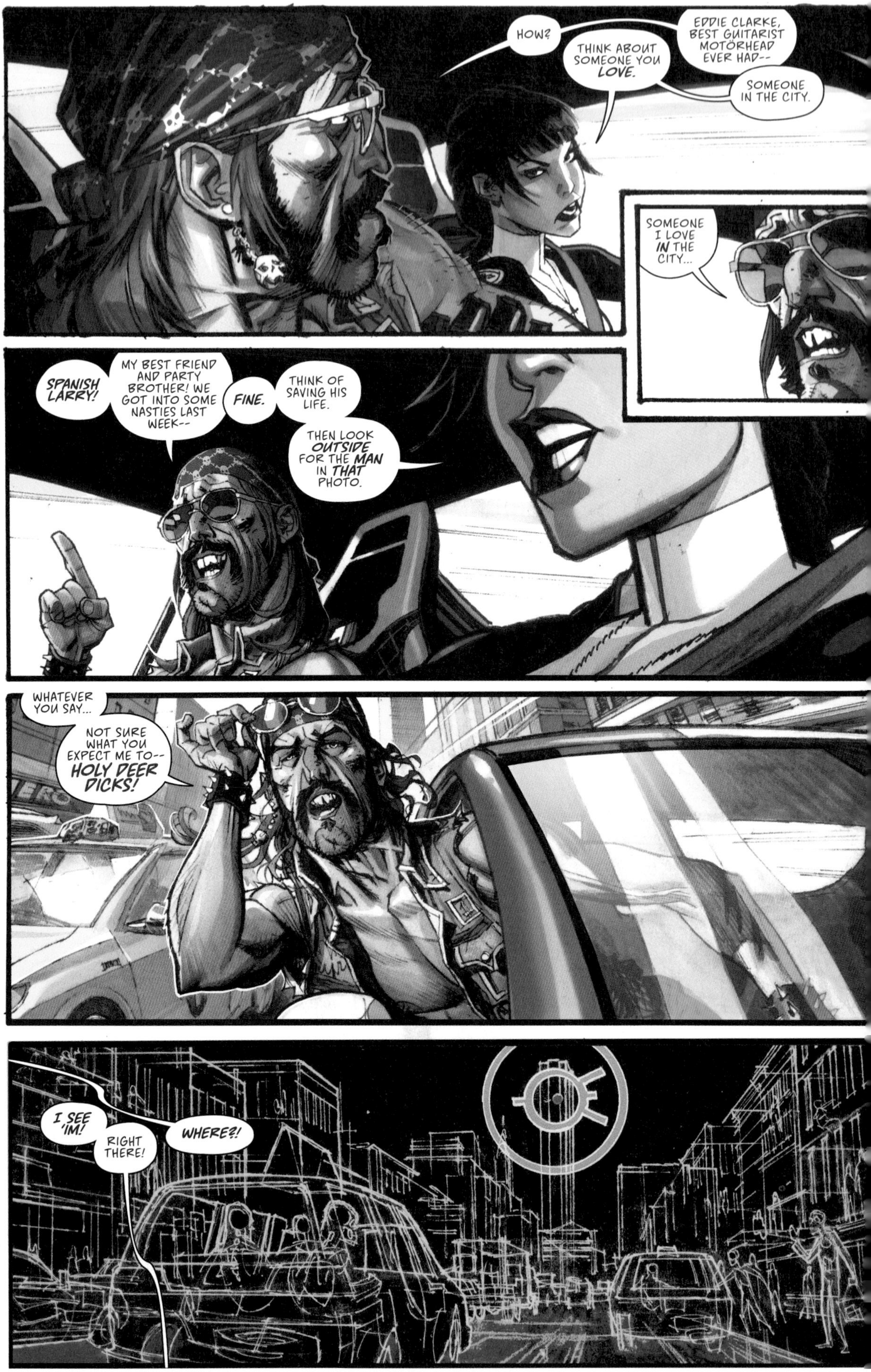
HOW?
THINK ABOUT SOMEONE YOU **LOVE.**
EDDIE CLARKE, BEST GUITARIST MOTÖRHEAD EVER HAD--
SOMEONE IN THE CITY.
SOMEONE I LOVE **IN** THE CITY...
SPANISH LARRY!
MY BEST FRIEND AND PARTY BROTHER! WE GOT INTO SOME NASTIES LAST WEEK--
FINE.
THINK OF SAVING HIS LIFE.
THEN LOOK **OUTSIDE** FOR THE **MAN** IN **THAT** PHOTO.
WHATEVER YOU SAY...
NOT SURE WHAT YOU EXPECT ME TO-- **HOLY DEER DICKS!**
I SEE 'IM!
RIGHT THERE!
WHERE?!

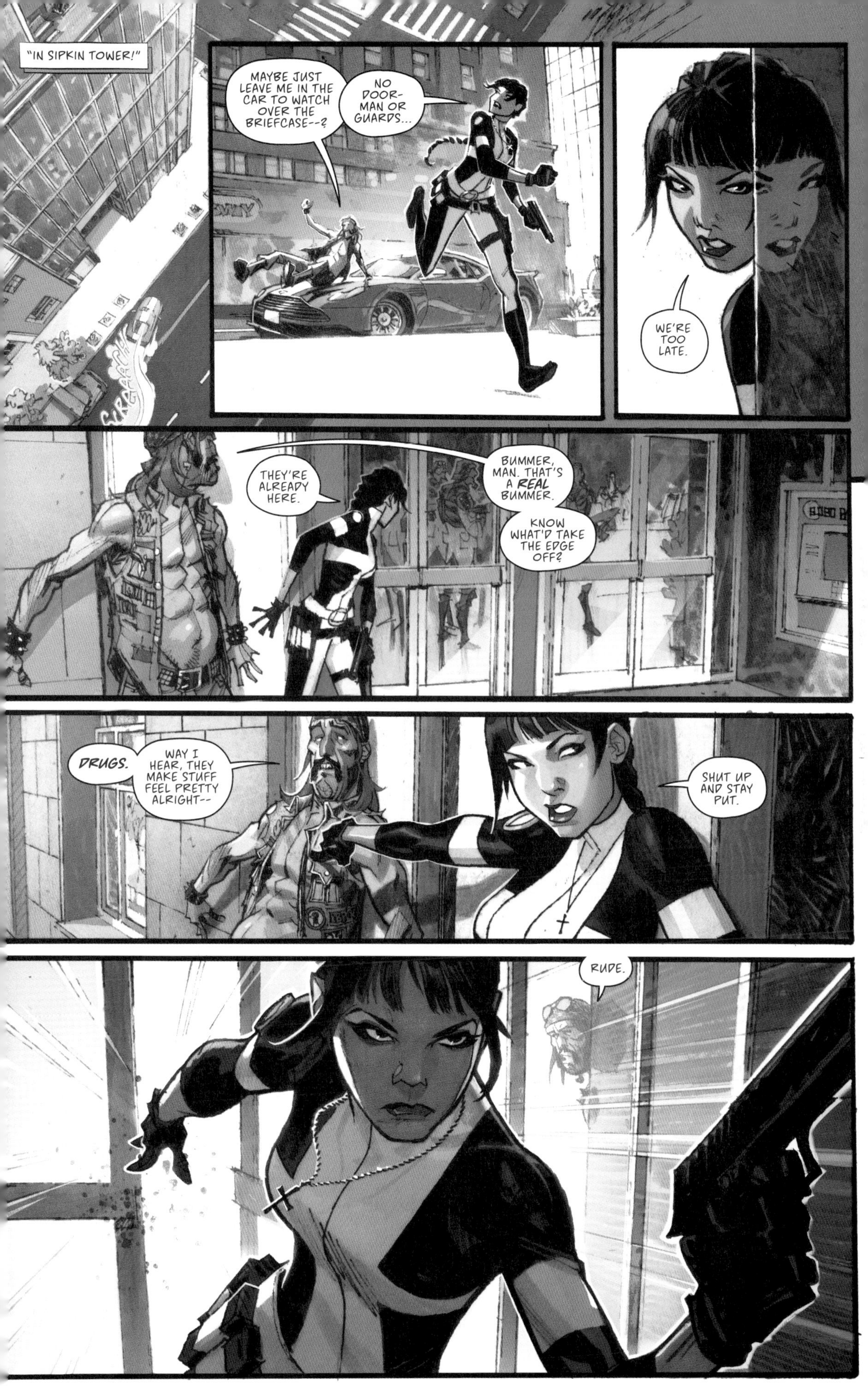
"IN SIPKIN TOWER!"
MAYBE JUST LEAVE ME IN THE CAR TO WATCH OVER THE BRIEFCASE--?
NO DOOR-MAN OR GUARDS...
WE'RE TOO LATE.
THEY'RE ALREADY HERE.
BUMMER, MAN. THAT'S A REAL BUMMER.
KNOW WHAT'D TAKE THE EDGE OFF?
DRUGS.
WAY I HEAR, THEY MAKE STUFF FEEL PRETTY ALRIGHT--
SHUT UP AND STAY PUT.
RUDE.

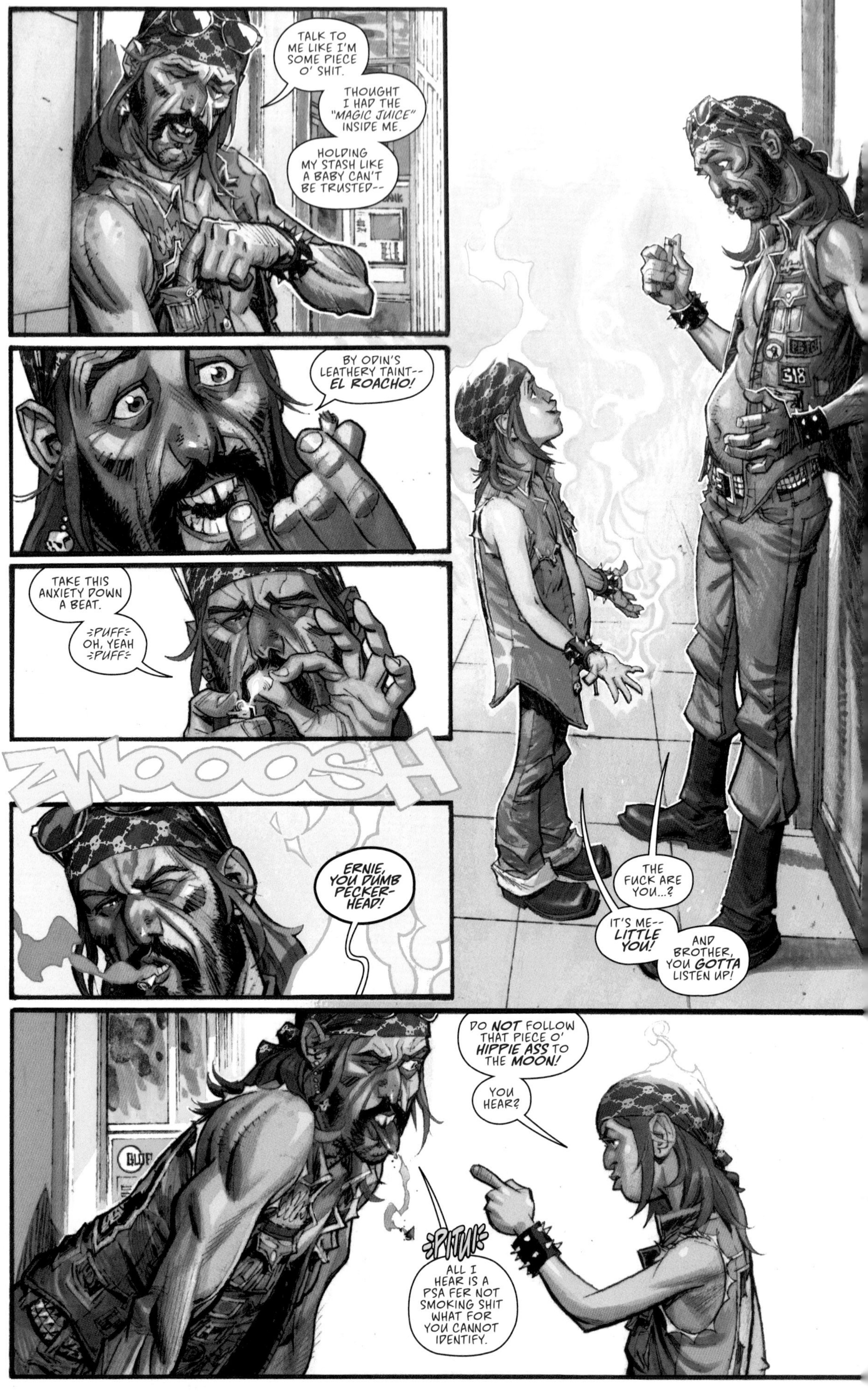

TALK TO ME LIKE I'M SOME PIECE O' SHIT.
THOUGHT I HAD THE "MAGIC JUICE" INSIDE ME.
HOLDING MY STASH LIKE A BABY CAN'T BE TRUSTED--
BY ODIN'S LEATHERY TAINT-- EL ROACHO!
TAKE THIS ANXIETY DOWN A BEAT.
PUFF OH, YEAH PUFF
ZWOOOSH
ERNIE, YOU DUMB PECKER-HEAD!
THE FUCK ARE YOU...?
IT'S ME-- LITTLE YOU!
AND BROTHER, YOU GOTTA LISTEN UP!
DO NOT FOLLOW THAT PIECE O' HIPPIE ASS TO THE MOON!
YOU HEAR?
PTUI
ALL I HEAR IS A PSA FER NOT SMOKING SHIT WHAT FOR YOU CANNOT IDENTIFY.

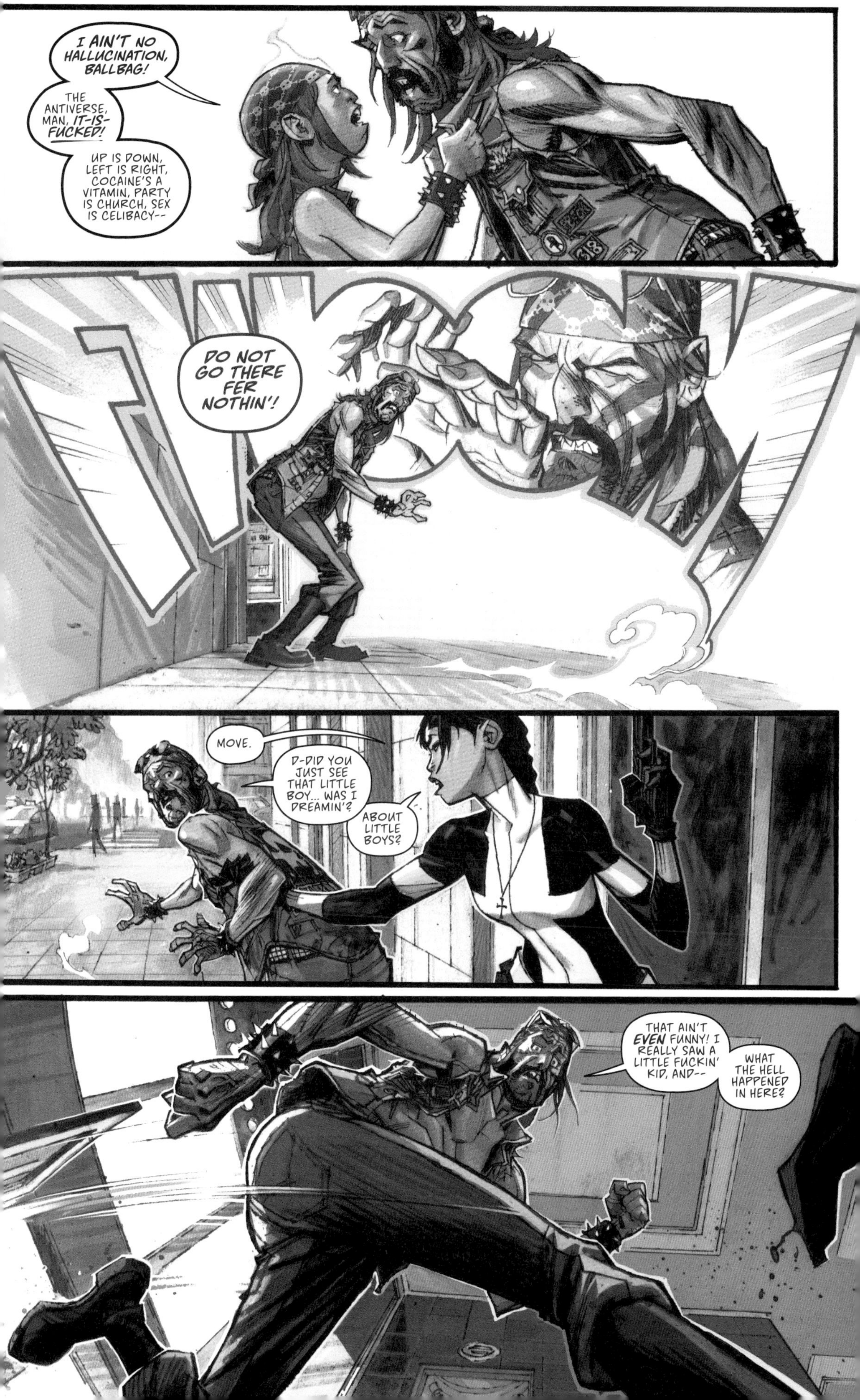
I AIN'T NO HALLUCINATION, BALLBAG!
THE ANTIVERSE, MAN, IT-IS-FUCKED!
UP IS DOWN, LEFT IS RIGHT, COCAINE'S A VITAMIN, PARTY IS CHURCH, SEX IS CELIBACY--
DO NOT GO THERE FER NOTHIN'!
MOVE.
D-DID YOU JUST SEE THAT LITTLE BOY... WAS I DREAMIN'?
ABOUT LITTLE BOYS?
THAT AIN'T EVEN FUNNY! I REALLY SAW A LITTLE FUCKIN' KID, AND--
WHAT THE HELL HAPPENED IN HERE?

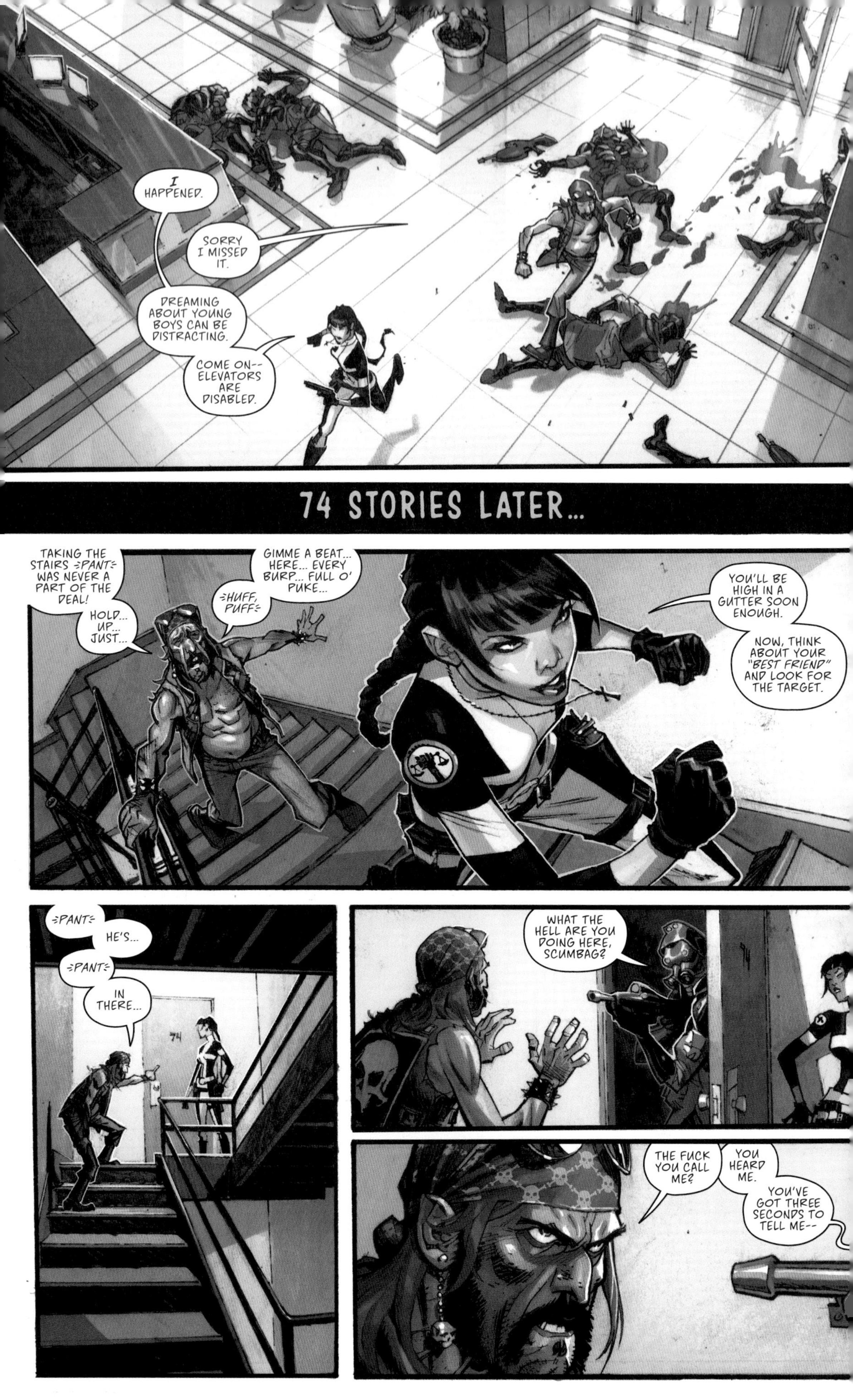
I HAPPENED.
SORRY I MISSED IT.
DREAMING ABOUT YOUNG BOYS CAN BE DISTRACTING.
COME ON-- ELEVATORS ARE DISABLED.
74 STORIES LATER...
TAKING THE STAIRS =PANT= WAS NEVER A PART OF THE DEAL!
HOLD... UP... JUST...
=HUFF, PUFF=
GIMME A BEAT... HERE... EVERY BURP... FULL O' PUKE...
YOU'LL BE HIGH IN A GUTTER SOON ENOUGH.
NOW, THINK ABOUT YOUR "BEST FRIEND" AND LOOK FOR THE TARGET.
=PANT=
HE'S...
=PANT=
IN THERE...
WHAT THE HELL ARE YOU DOING HERE, SCUMBAG?
THE FUCK YOU CALL ME?
YOU HEARD ME.
YOU'VE GOT THREE SECONDS TO TELL ME--

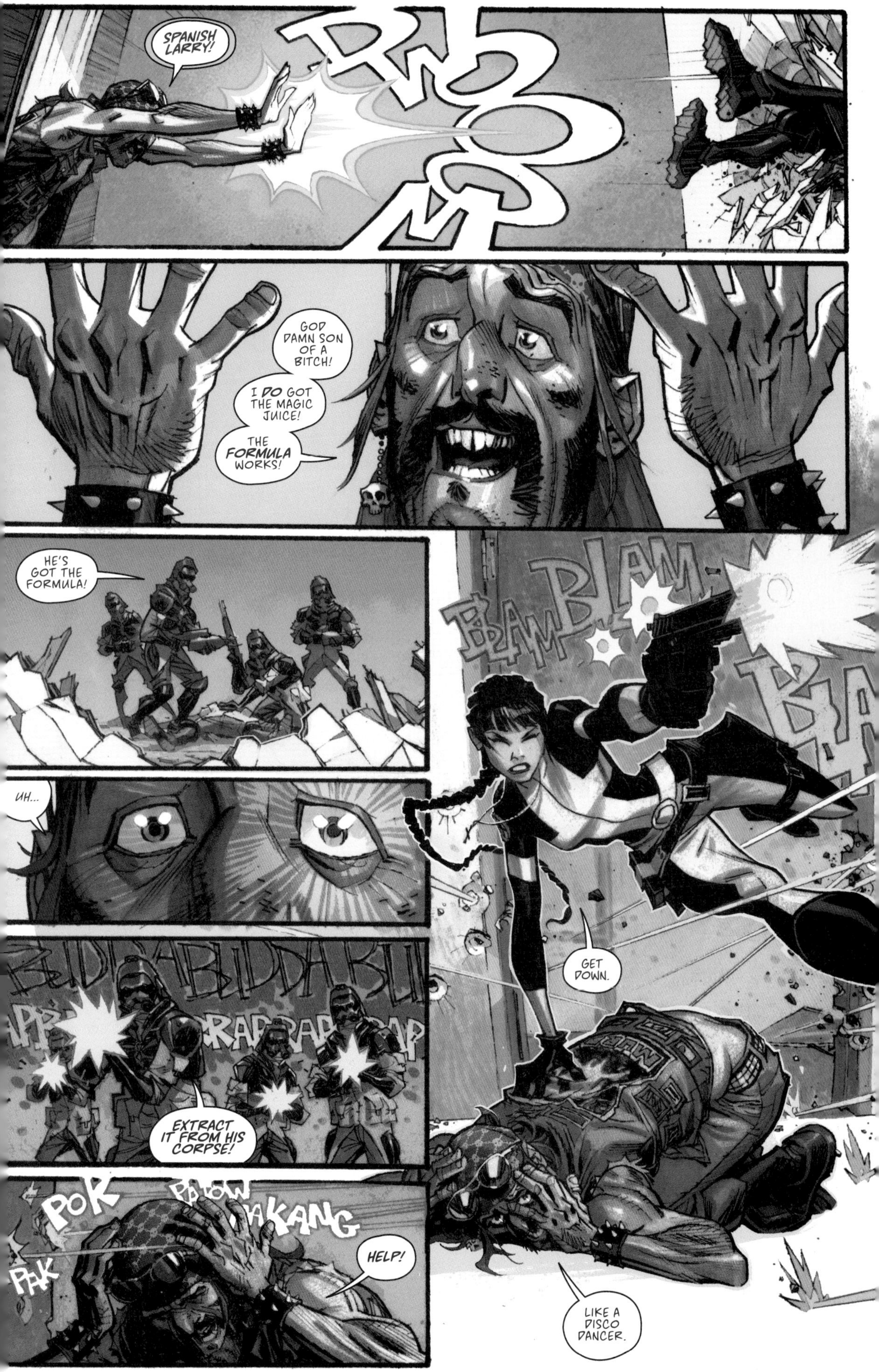

SPANISH LARRY!
BWOOOM
GOD DAMN SON OF A BITCH!
I DO GOT THE MAGIC JUICE!
THE FORMULA WORKS!
HE'S GOT THE FORMULA!
BLAM BLAM
UH...
GET DOWN.
BIDDABIDDABIDDA
RAP RAP RAP RAP
EXTRACT IT FROM HIS CORPSE!
POK
KAKANG
PAK
HELP!
LIKE A DISCO DANCER.

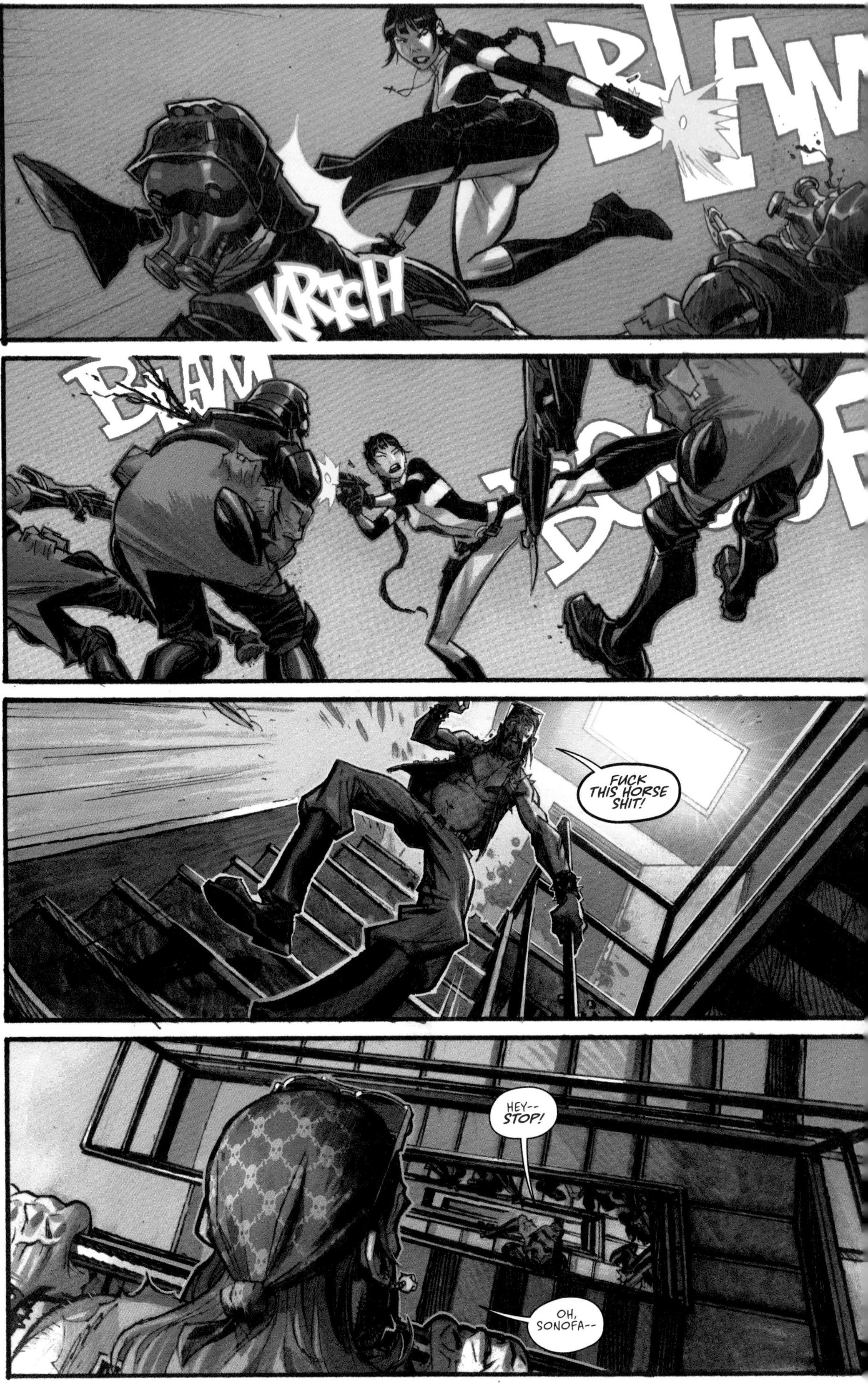
BLAM
KRTCH
BLAM
FUCK THIS HORSE SHIT!
HEY-- STOP!
OH, SONOFA--

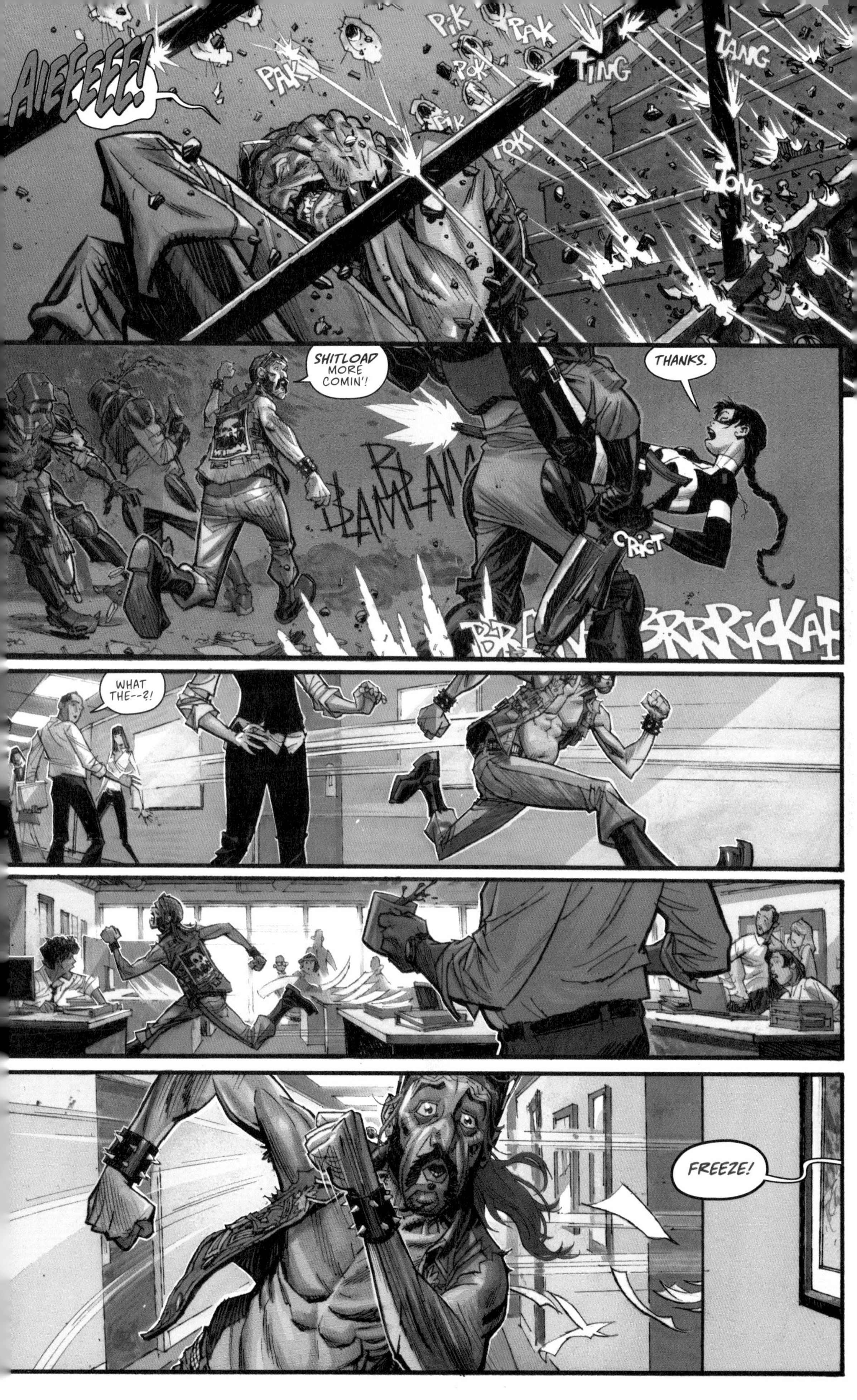
AIEEEEE!
PIK
PAK
PAK
POK
PIK
POK
TING
TANG
TONG
SHITLOAD MORE COMIN'!
THANKS.
BLAMBLAM
CRICT
BRRRICKAP
WHAT THE--?!
FREEZE!

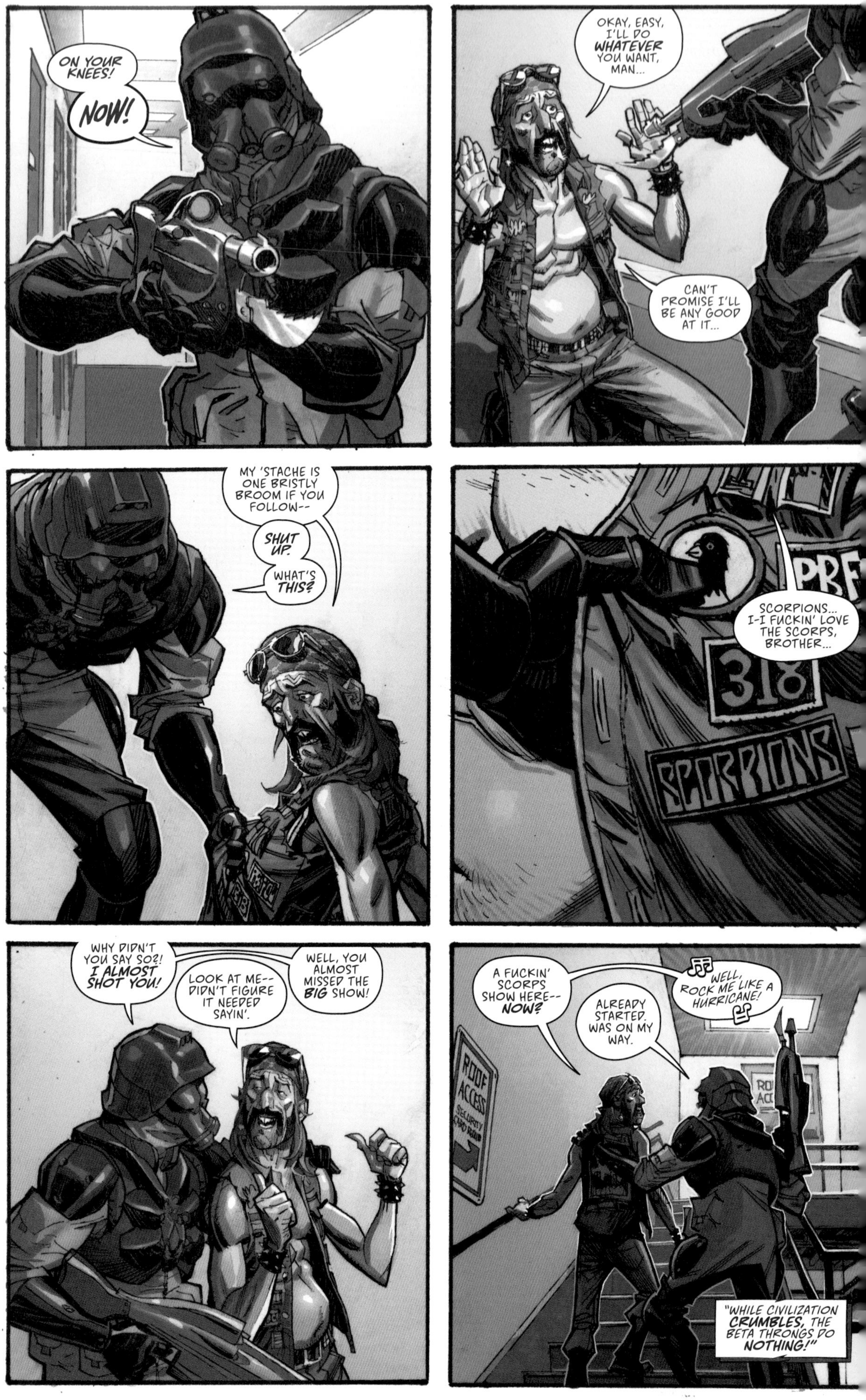
ON YOUR KNEES!
NOW!
OKAY, EASY, I'LL DO WHATEVER YOU WANT, MAN...
CAN'T PROMISE I'LL BE ANY GOOD AT IT...
MY 'STACHE IS ONE BRISTLY BROOM IF YOU FOLLOW--
SHUT UP.
WHAT'S THIS?
PBF
318
SCORPIONS
SCORPIONS... I-I FUCKIN' LOVE THE SCORPS, BROTHER...
WHY DIDN'T YOU SAY SO?! I ALMOST SHOT YOU!
LOOK AT ME-- DIDN'T FIGURE IT NEEDED SAYIN'.
WELL, YOU ALMOST MISSED THE BIG SHOW!
A FUCKIN' SCORPS SHOW HERE-- NOW?
ALREADY STARTED. WAS ON MY WAY.
WELL, ROCK ME LIKE A HURRICANE!
ROOF ACCESS
"WHILE CIVILIZATION CRUMBLES, THE BETA THRONGS DO NOTHING!"

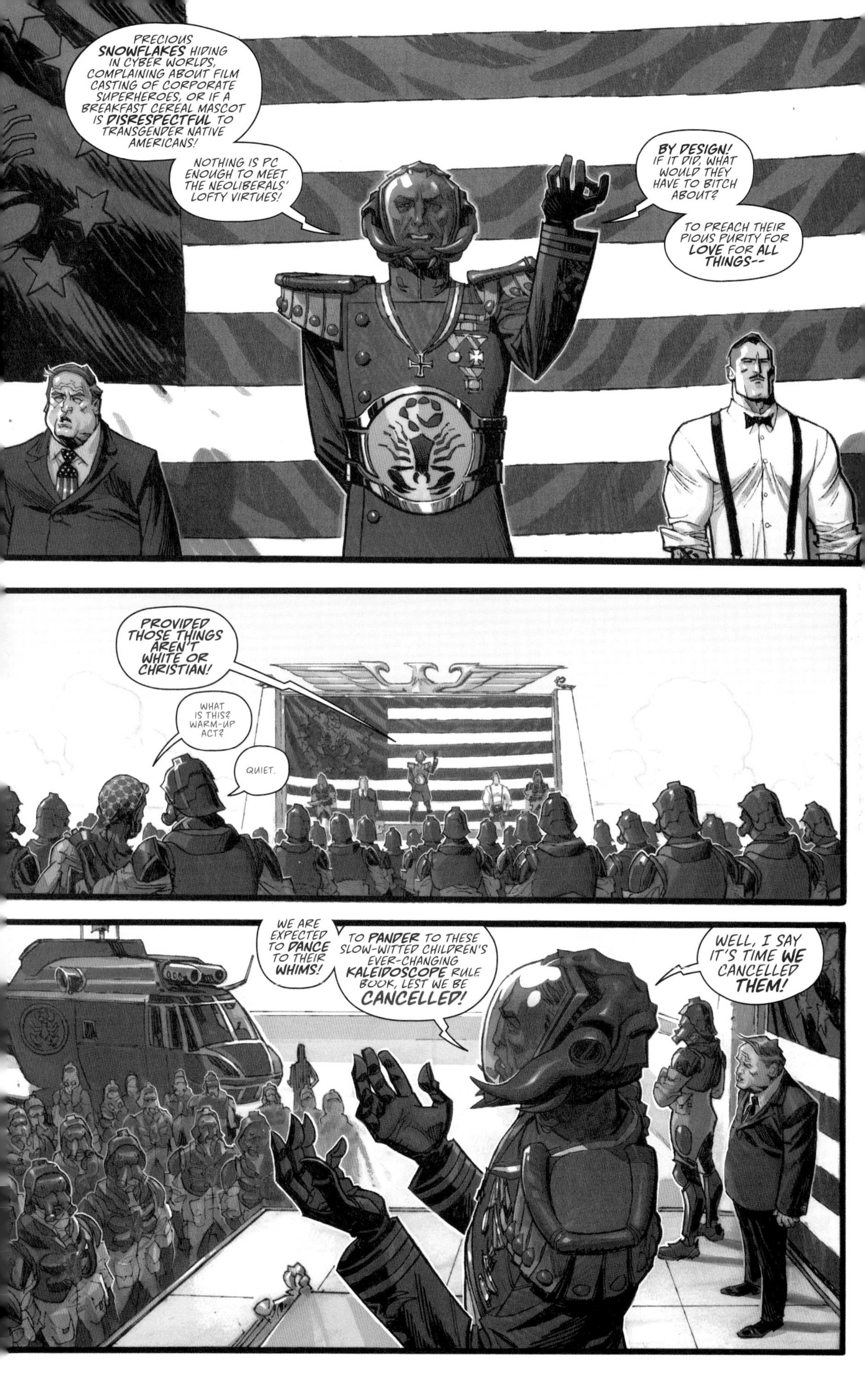
PRECIOUS SNOWFLAKES HIDING IN CYBER WORLDS, COMPLAINING ABOUT FILM CASTING OF CORPORATE SUPERHEROES, OR IF A BREAKFAST CEREAL MASCOT IS DISRESPECTFUL TO TRANSGENDER NATIVE AMERICANS!
NOTHING IS PC ENOUGH TO MEET THE NEOLIBERALS' LOFTY VIRTUES!
BY DESIGN! IF IT DID, WHAT WOULD THEY HAVE TO BITCH ABOUT?
TO PREACH THEIR PIOUS PURITY FOR LOVE FOR ALL THINGS--
PROVIDED THOSE THINGS AREN'T WHITE OR CHRISTIAN!
WHAT IS THIS? WARM-UP ACT?
QUIET.
WE ARE EXPECTED TO DANCE TO THEIR WHIMS!
TO PANDER TO THESE SLOW-WITTED CHILDREN'S EVER-CHANGING KALEIDOSCOPE RULE BOOK, LEST WE BE CANCELLED!
WELL, I SAY IT'S TIME WE CANCELLED THEM!

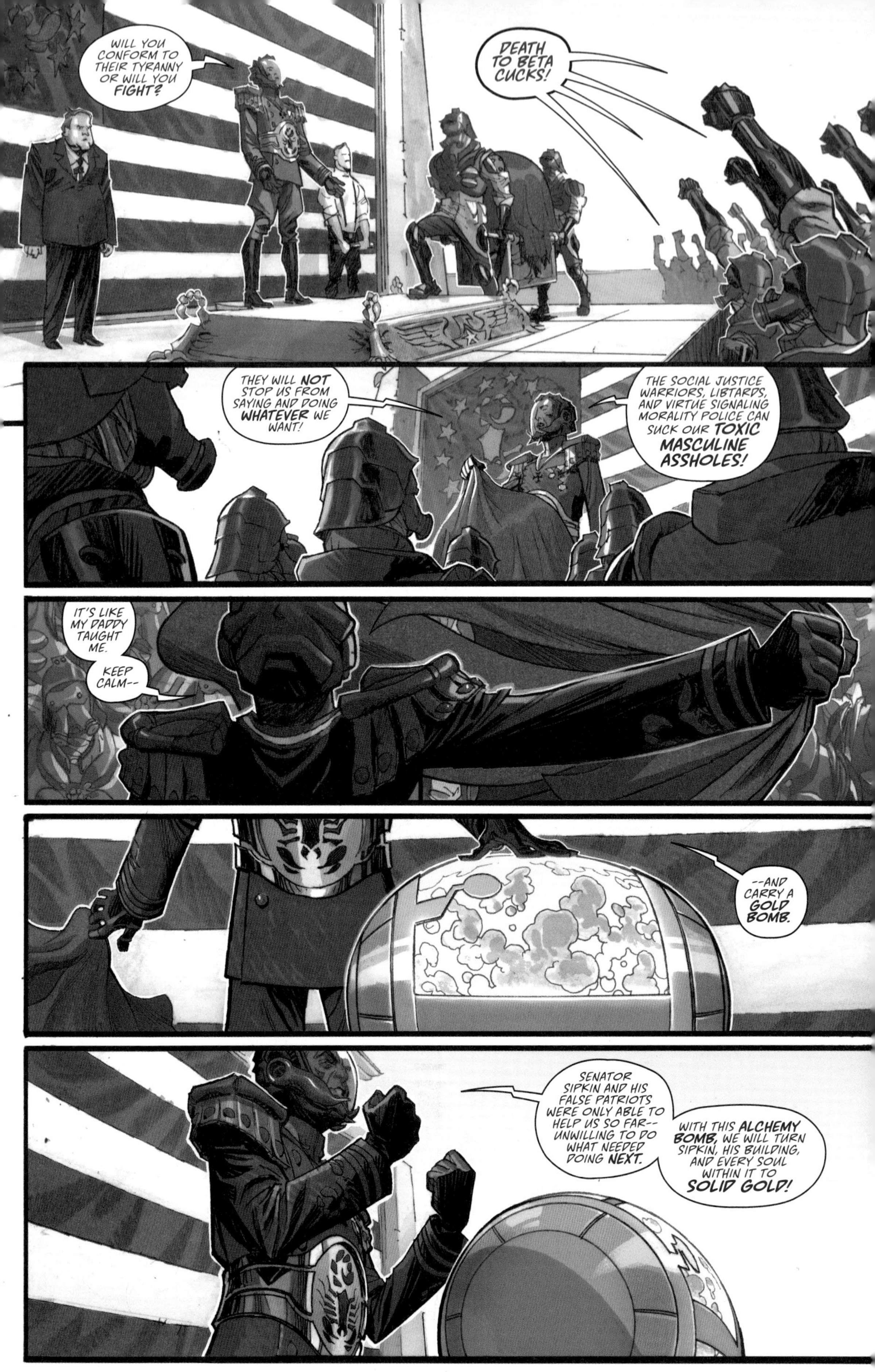

WILL YOU CONFORM TO THEIR TYRANNY OR WILL YOU FIGHT?
DEATH TO BETA CUCKS!
THEY WILL NOT STOP US FROM SAYING AND DOING WHATEVER WE WANT!
THE SOCIAL JUSTICE WARRIORS, LIBTARDS, AND VIRTUE SIGNALING MORALITY POLICE CAN SUCK OUR TOXIC MASCULINE ASSHOLES!
IT'S LIKE MY DADDY TAUGHT ME.
KEEP CALM--
--AND CARRY A GOLD BOMB.
SENATOR SIPKIN AND HIS FALSE PATRIOTS WERE ONLY ABLE TO HELP US SO FAR-- UNWILLING TO DO WHAT NEEDED DOING NEXT.
WITH THIS ALCHEMY BOMB, WE WILL TURN SIPKIN, HIS BUILDING, AND EVERY SOUL WITHIN IT TO SOLID GOLD!

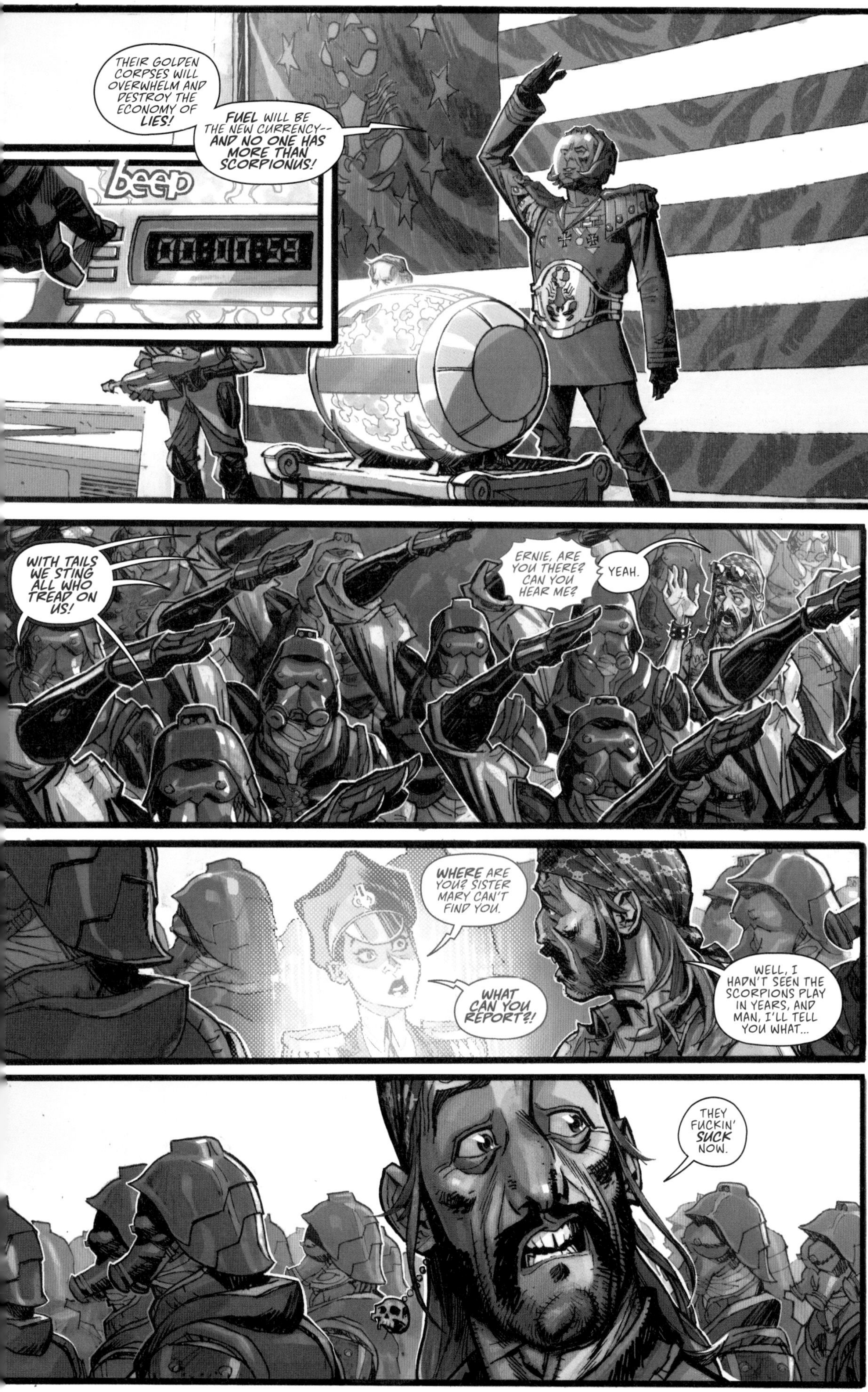
THEIR GOLDEN CORPSES WILL OVERWHELM AND DESTROY THE ECONOMY OF LIES!
FUEL WILL BE THE NEW CURRENCY-- AND NO ONE HAS MORE THAN SCORPIONUS!
beep
WITH TAILS WE STING ALL WHO TREAD ON US!
ERNIE, ARE YOU THERE? CAN YOU HEAR ME?
YEAH.
WHERE ARE YOU? SISTER MARY CAN'T FIND YOU.
WHAT CAN YOU REPORT?!
WELL, I HADN'T SEEN THE SCORPIONS PLAY IN YEARS, AND MAN, I'LL TELL YOU WHAT...
THEY FUCKIN' SUCK NOW.

THREE

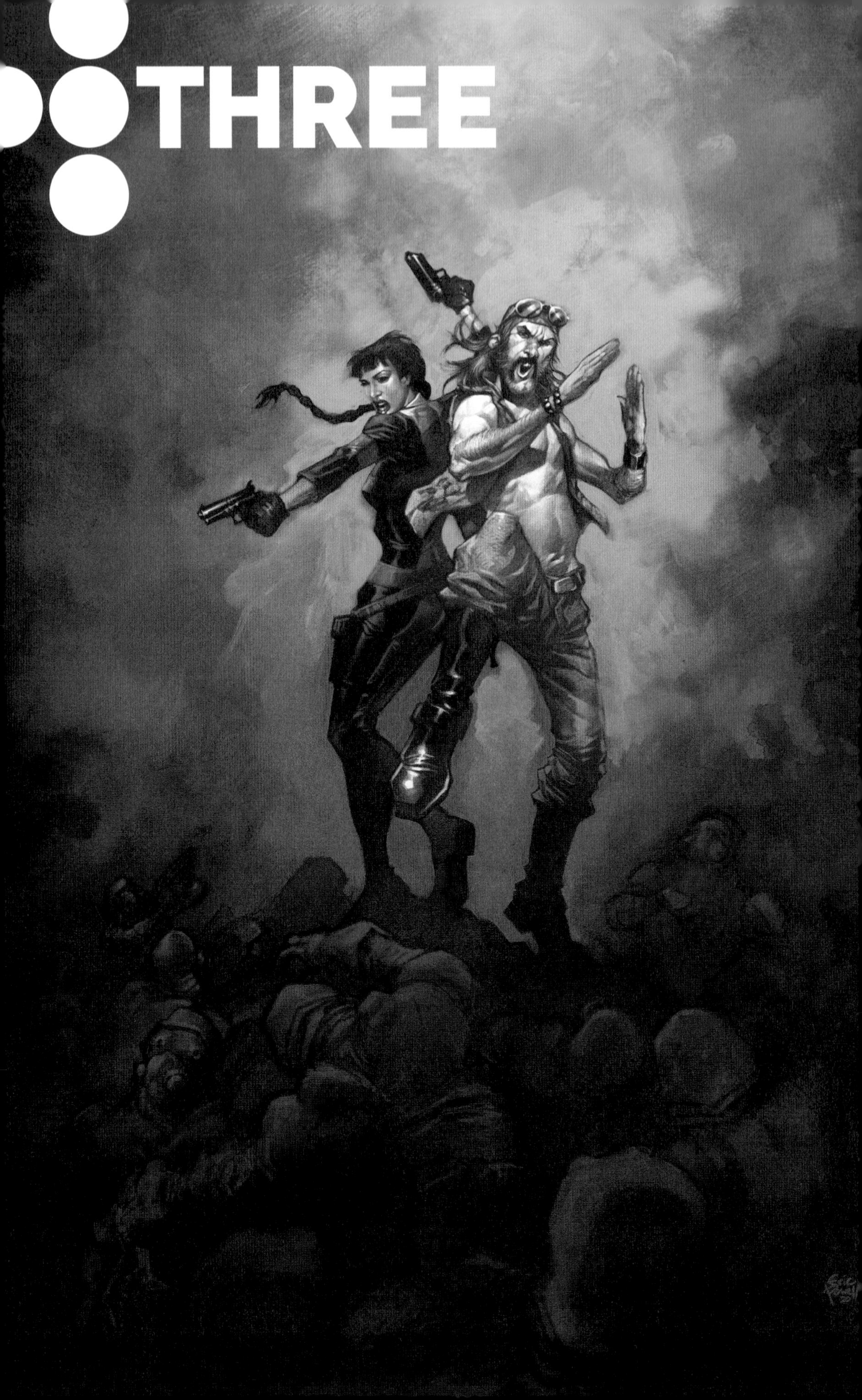

"THE *LIBERAL DRONES*
ARE *TRAINED* TO HEAR
NO VOICES BEYOND THOSE
IN THE SAFE SPACE OF
THEIR BLUE BUBBLES.

"THEY SELL THEMSELVES
AS LOVING AND INCLUSIVE,
WHILE USING *FEAR* TO
FORCE COMPLIANCE TO
THEIR WORLD VIEW.

"THEY WOULD HAVE US
THINK THAT THE ONLY WAY
TO *SURVIVE* THIS MOB
OUTRAGE IS TO *JOIN* IT..."

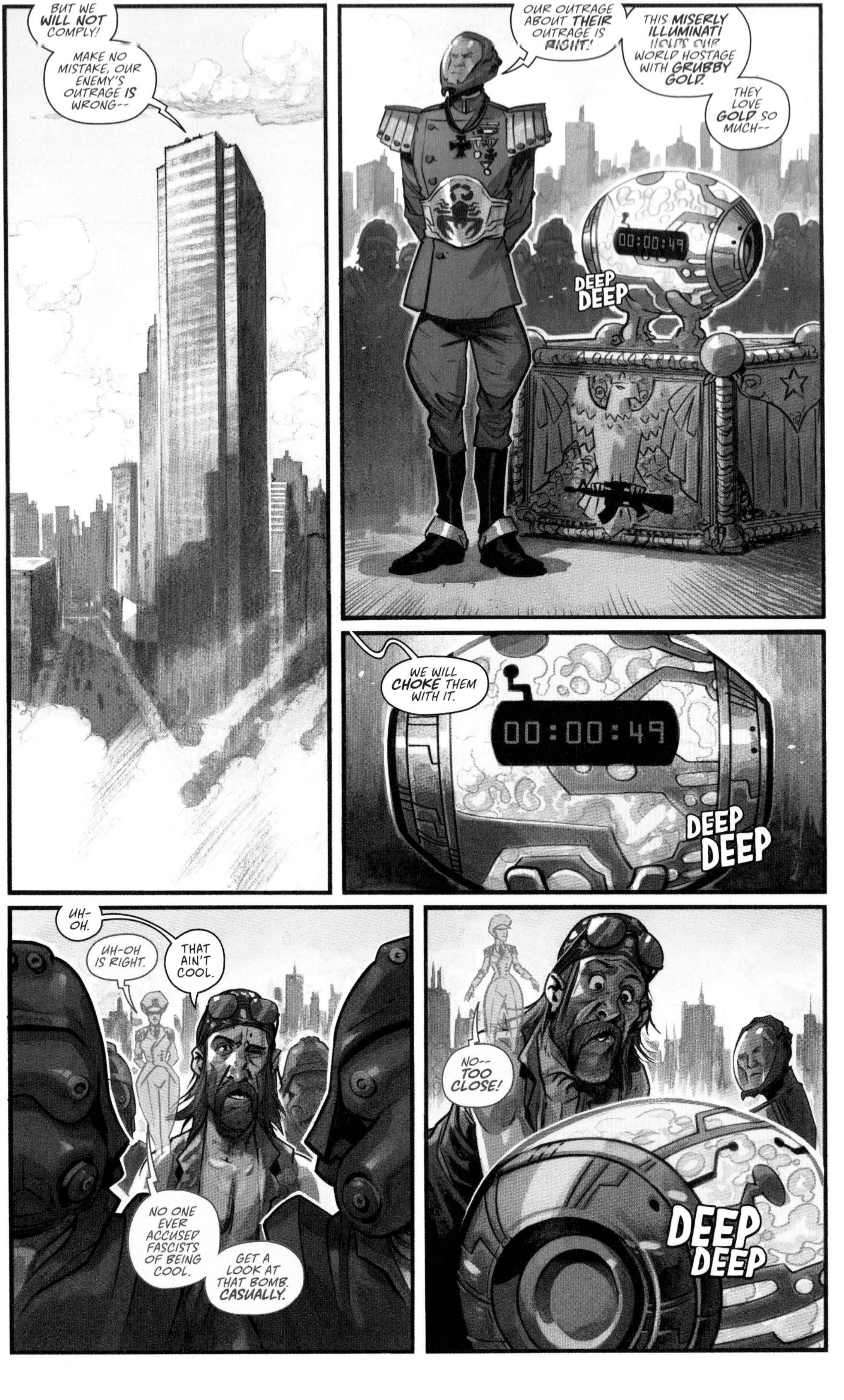
BUT WE **WILL NOT** COMPLY!
MAKE NO MISTAKE, OUR ENEMY'S OUTRAGE **IS** WRONG--
OUR OUTRAGE ABOUT **THEIR** OUTRAGE IS **RIGHT!**
THIS **MISERLY ILLUMINATI** HOLDS OUR WORLD HOSTAGE WITH **GRUBBY GOLD.**
THEY LOVE **GOLD** SO MUCH--
00:00:49
DEEP DEEP
WE WILL **CHOKE** THEM WITH IT.
00:00:49
DEEP DEEP
UH-OH.
UH-OH IS RIGHT.
THAT AIN'T COOL.
NO ONE EVER ACCUSED FASCISTS OF BEING COOL.
GET A LOOK AT THAT BOMB. **CASUALLY.**
NO-- TOO CLOSE!
DEEP DEEP

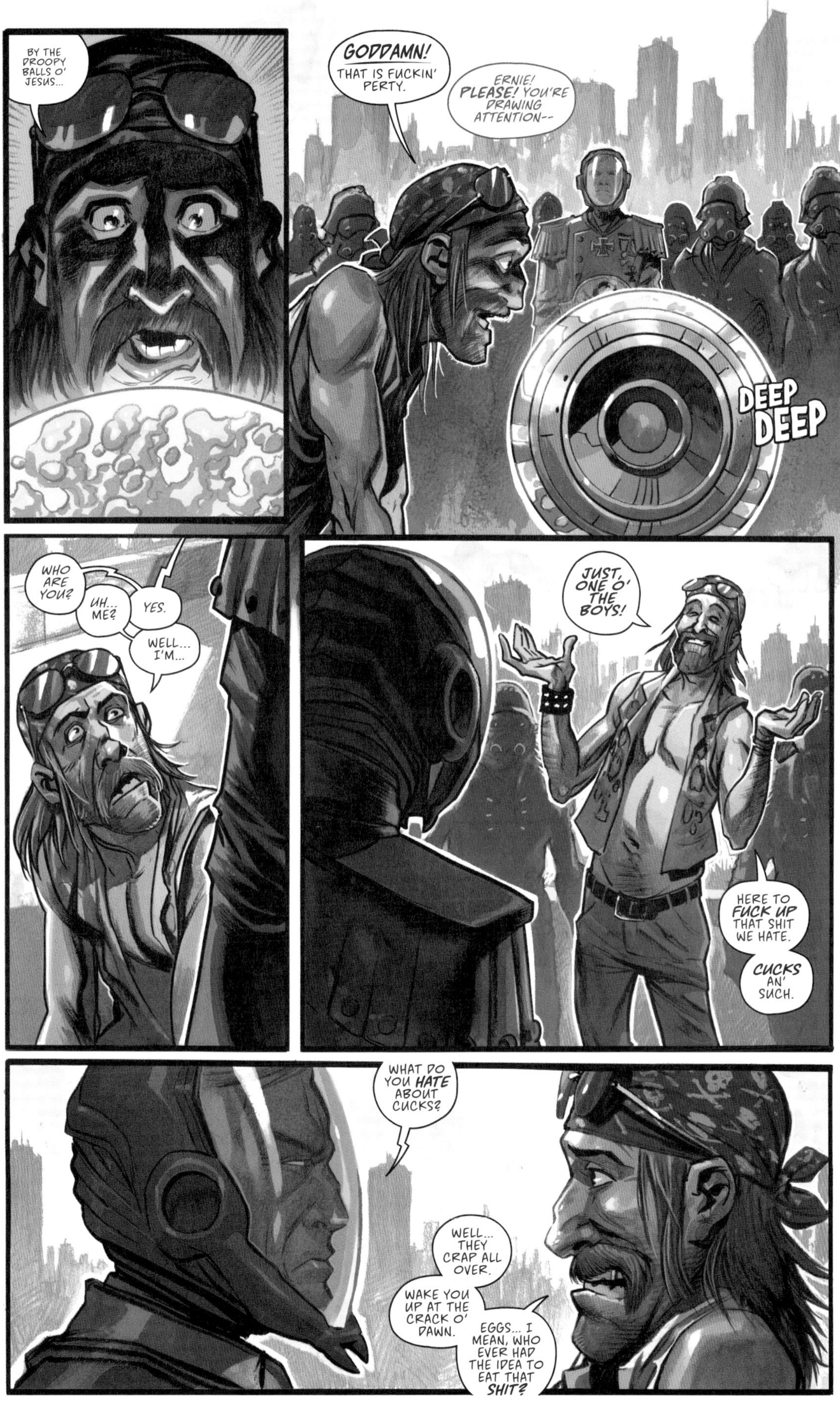
BY THE DROOPY BALLS O' JESUS...
GODDAMN! THAT IS FUCKIN' PERTY.
ERNIE! PLEASE! YOU'RE DRAWING ATTENTION--
DEEP DEEP
WHO ARE YOU?
UH... ME?
YES.
WELL... I'M...
JUST, ONE O' THE BOYS!
HERE TO FUCK UP THAT SHIT WE HATE.
CUCKS AN' SUCH.
WHAT DO YOU HATE ABOUT CUCKS?
WELL... THEY CRAP ALL OVER.
WAKE YOU UP AT THE CRACK O' DAWN.
EGGS... I MEAN, WHO EVER HAD THE IDEA TO EAT THAT SHIT?

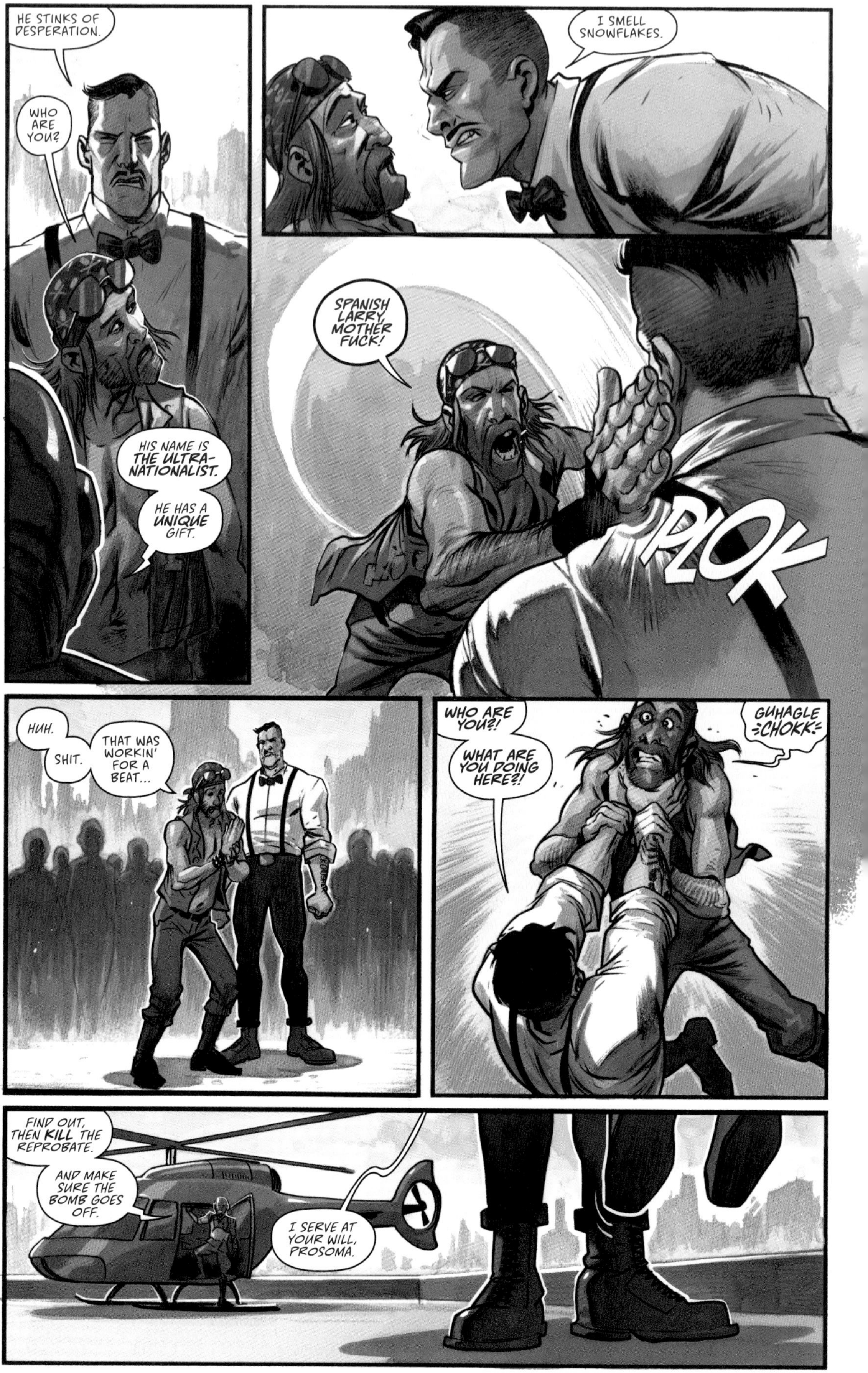
HE STINKS OF DESPERATION.
WHO ARE YOU?
I SMELL SNOWFLAKES.
HIS NAME IS **THE ULTRA-NATIONALIST.**
HE HAS A **UNIQUE** GIFT.
SPANISH LARRY, MOTHER FUCK!
PLOK
HUH.
SHIT.
THAT WAS WORKIN' FOR A BEAT...
WHO ARE YOU?!
WHAT ARE YOU DOING HERE?!
GUHAGLE CHOKK
FIND OUT, THEN **KILL** THE REPROBATE.
AND MAKE SURE THE BOMB GOES OFF.
I SERVE AT YOUR WILL, PROSOMA.

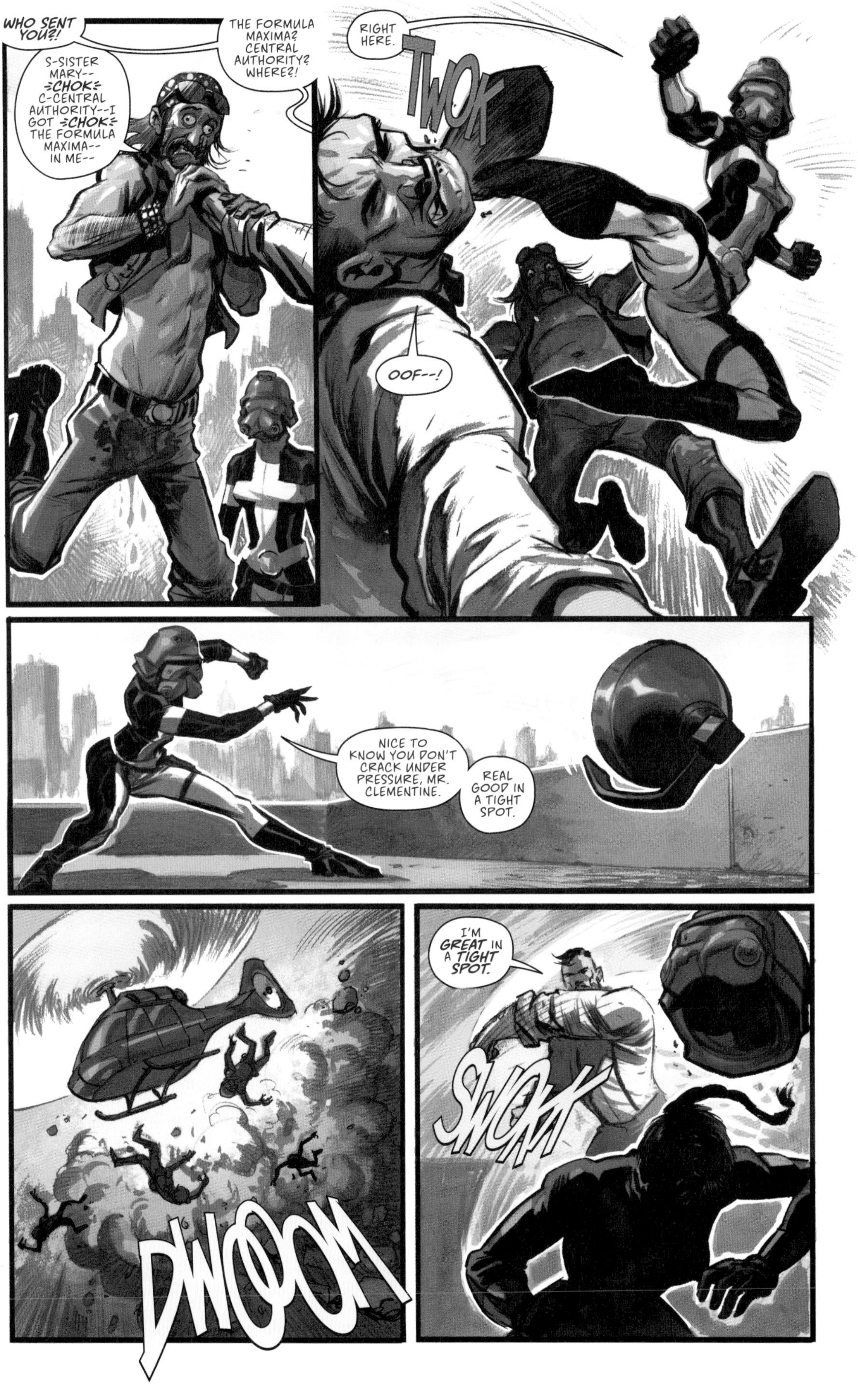
WHO SENT YOU?!
S-SISTER MARY-- ≈CHOK≈ C-CENTRAL AUTHORITY--I GOT ≈CHOK≈ THE FORMULA MAXIMA-- IN ME--
THE FORMULA MAXIMA? CENTRAL AUTHORITY? WHERE?!
RIGHT HERE.
TWOK
OOF--!
NICE TO KNOW YOU DON'T CRACK UNDER PRESSURE, MR. CLEMENTINE.
REAL GOOD IN A TIGHT SPOT.
DWOOOM
I'M GREAT IN A TIGHT SPOT.
SWOK

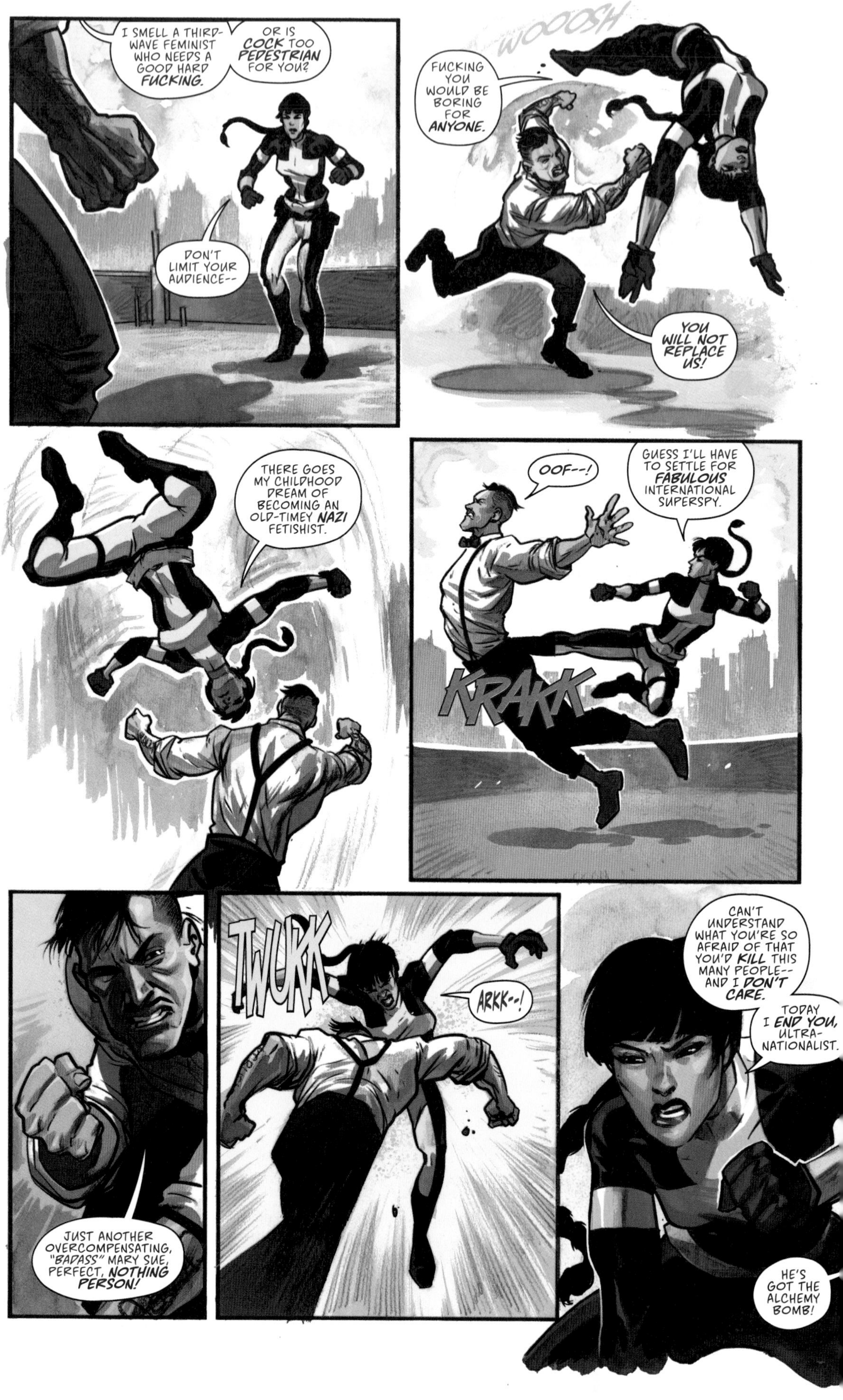

I SMELL A THIRD-WAVE FEMINIST WHO NEEDS A GOOD HARD FUCKING.
OR IS COCK TOO PEDESTRIAN FOR YOU?
DON'T LIMIT YOUR AUDIENCE--
WOOOSH
FUCKING YOU WOULD BE BORING FOR ANYONE.
YOU WILL NOT REPLACE US!
THERE GOES MY CHILDHOOD DREAM OF BECOMING AN OLD-TIMEY NAZI FETISHIST.
OOF--!
GUESS I'LL HAVE TO SETTLE FOR FABULOUS INTERNATIONAL SUPERSPY.
KRAKK
JUST ANOTHER OVERCOMPENSATING, "BADASS" MARY SUE, PERFECT, NOTHING PERSON!
TWUKK
ARKK--!
CAN'T UNDERSTAND WHAT YOU'RE SO AFRAID OF THAT YOU'D KILL THIS MANY PEOPLE-- AND I DON'T CARE.
TODAY I END YOU, ULTRA-NATIONALIST.
HE'S GOT THE ALCHEMY BOMB!

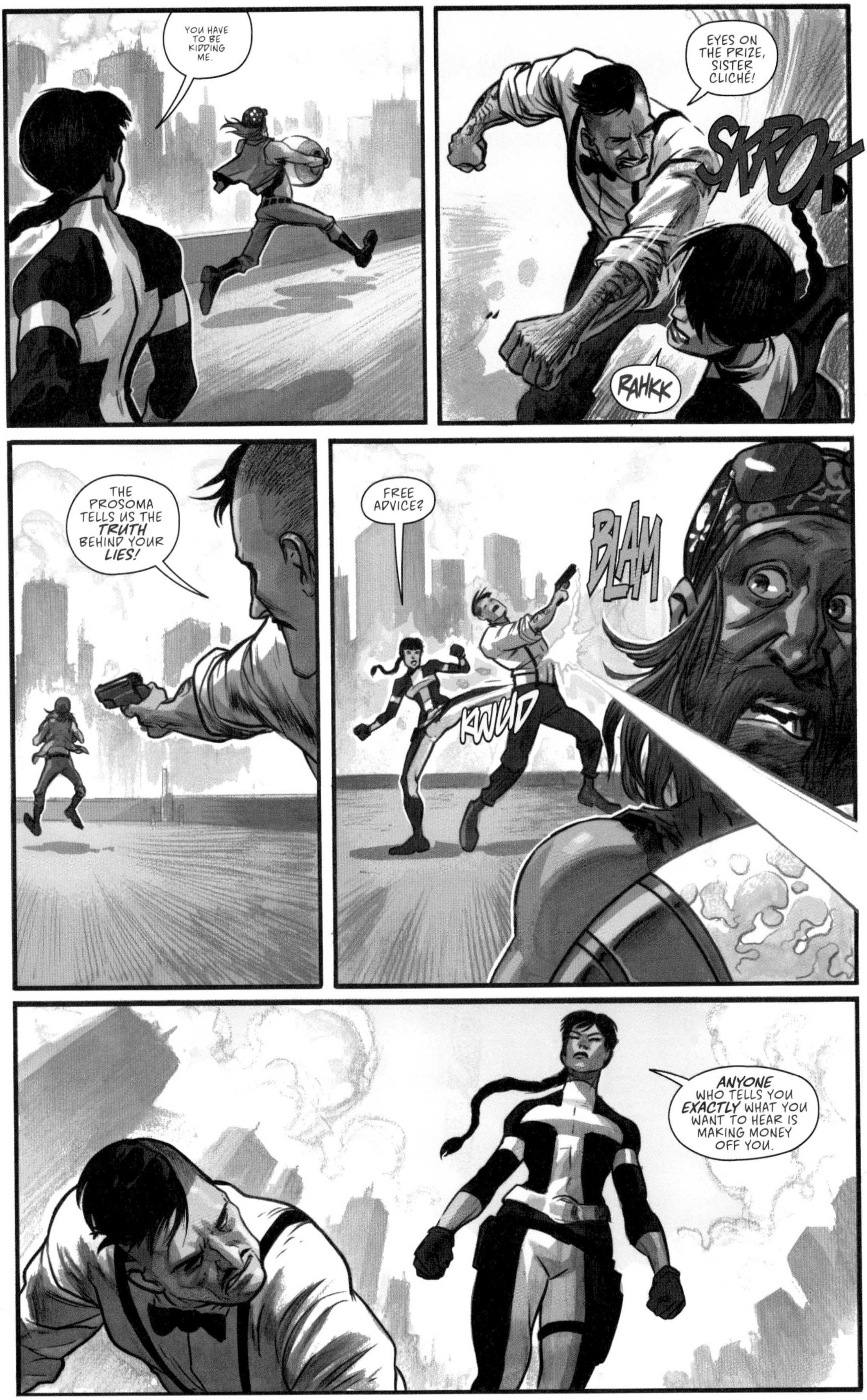
YOU HAVE TO BE KIDDING ME.
EYES ON THE PRIZE, SISTER CLICHÉ!
SKROK
RAHKK
THE PROSOMA TELLS US THE TRUTH BEHIND YOUR LIES!
FREE ADVICE?
BLAM
KWUD
ANYONE WHO TELLS YOU EXACTLY WHAT YOU WANT TO HEAR IS MAKING MONEY OFF YOU.

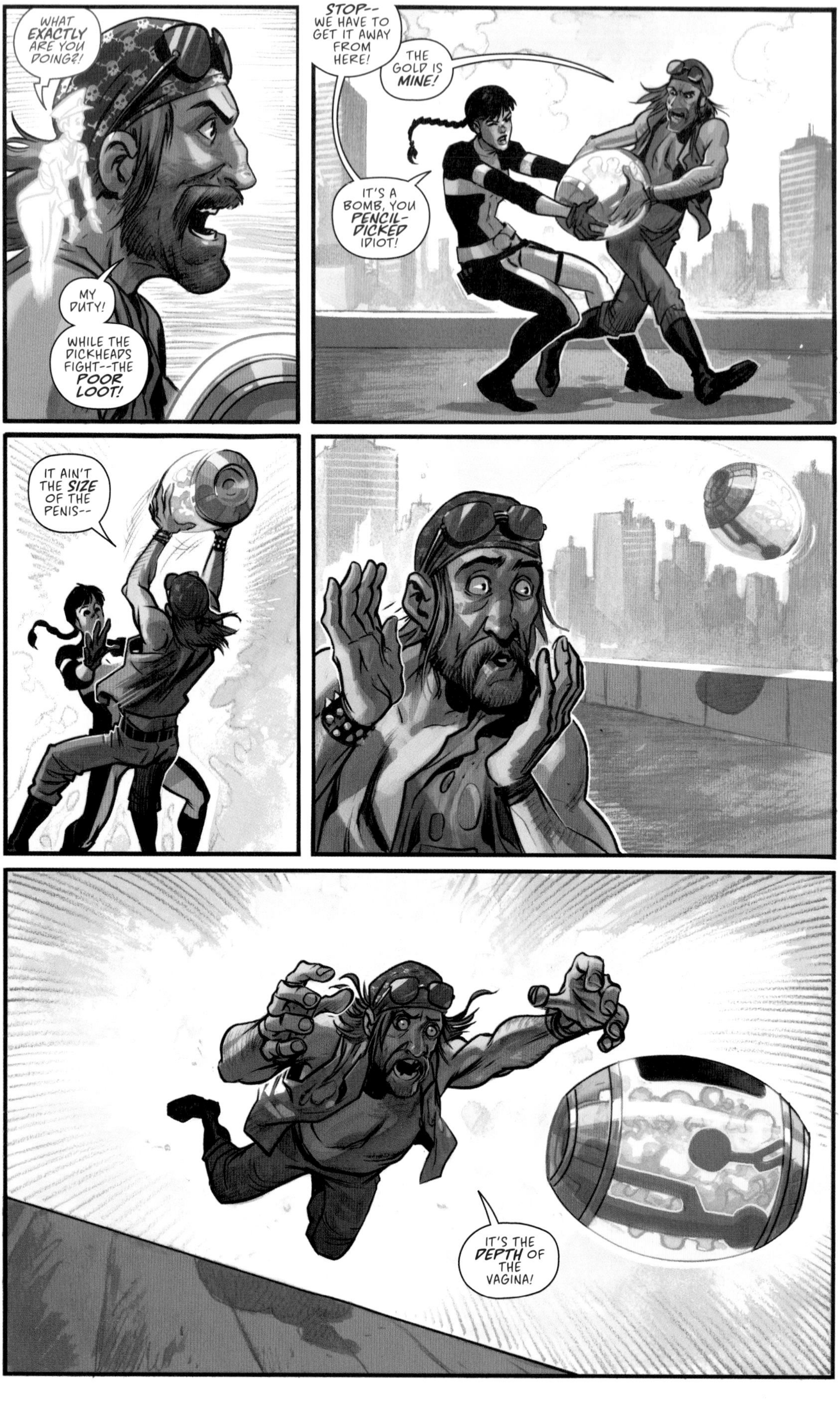
WHAT EXACTLY ARE YOU DOING?!
MY DUTY!
WHILE THE DICKHEADS FIGHT--THE POOR LOOT!
STOP-- WE HAVE TO GET IT AWAY FROM HERE!
THE GOLD IS MINE!
IT'S A BOMB, YOU PENCIL-DICKED IDIOT!
IT AIN'T THE SIZE OF THE PENIS--
IT'S THE DEPTH OF THE VAGINA!

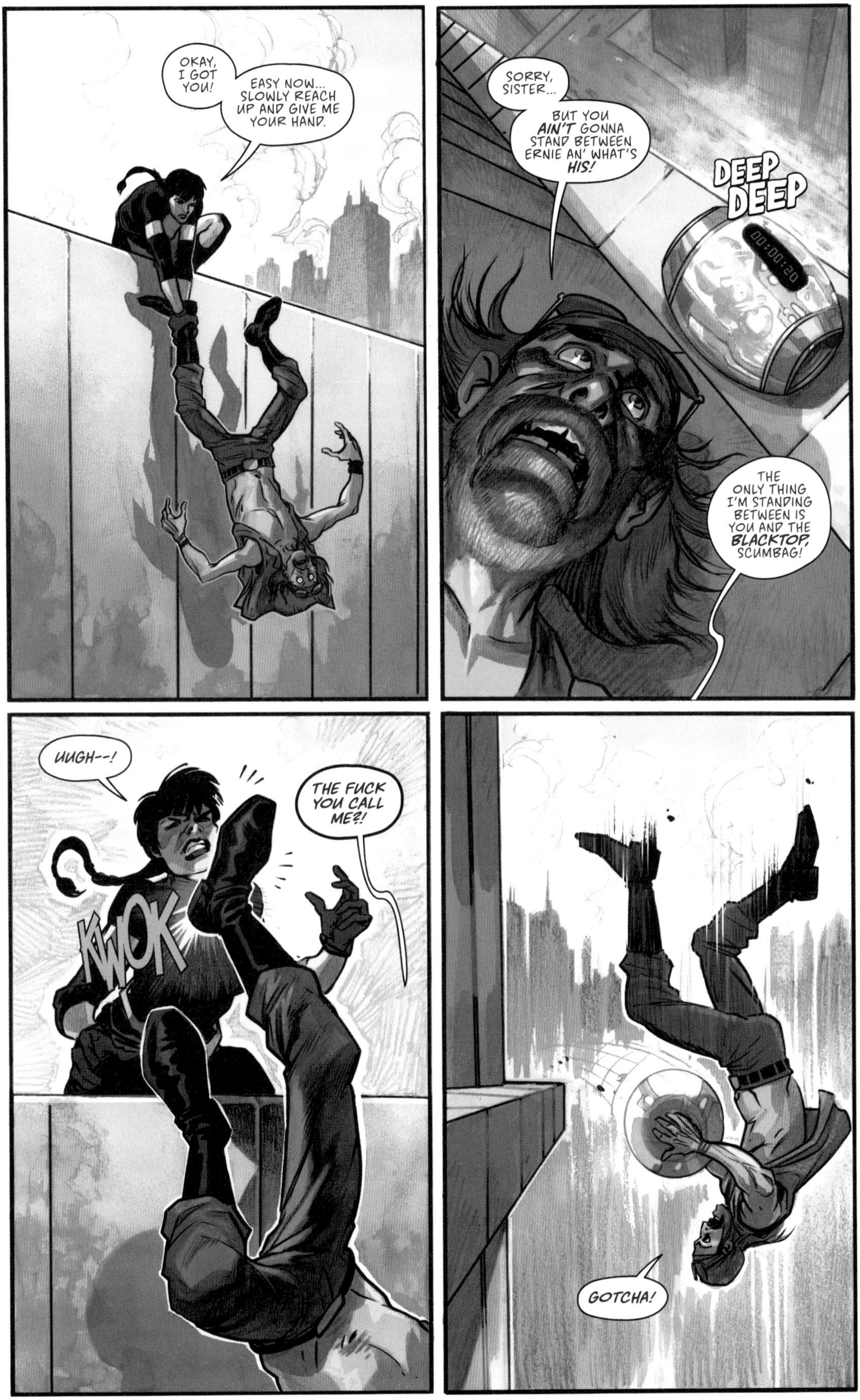
OKAY, I GOT YOU!
EASY NOW... SLOWLY REACH UP AND GIVE ME YOUR HAND.
SORRY, SISTER...
BUT YOU AIN'T GONNA STAND BETWEEN ERNIE AN' WHAT'S HIS!
DEEP DEEP
00:00:20
THE ONLY THING I'M STANDING BETWEEN IS YOU AND THE BLACKTOP, SCUMBAG!
UUGH--!
THE FUCK YOU CALL ME?!
KWOK
GOTCHA!

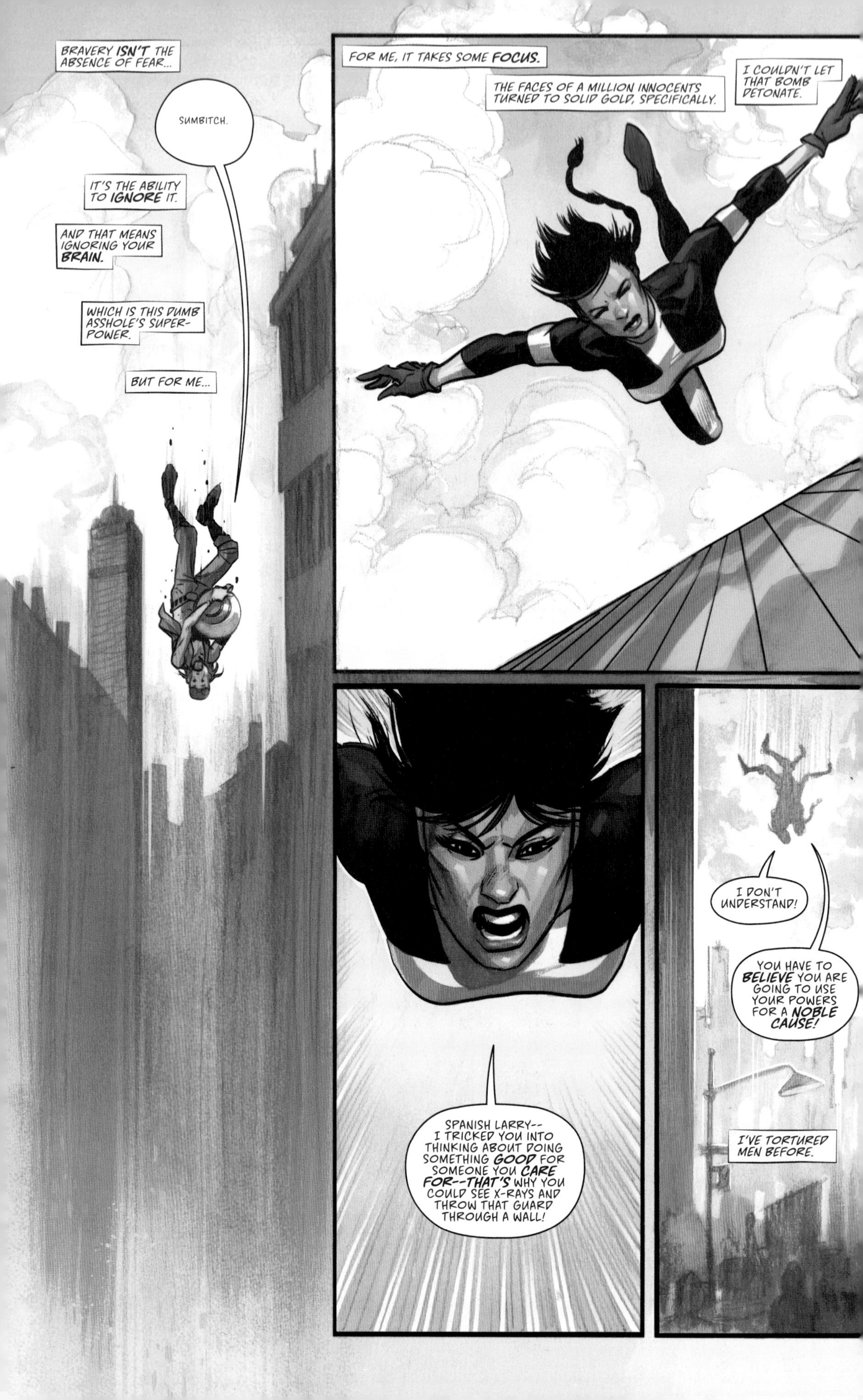
BRAVERY ISN'T THE ABSENCE OF FEAR...
SUMBITCH.
IT'S THE ABILITY TO IGNORE IT.
AND THAT MEANS IGNORING YOUR BRAIN.
WHICH IS THIS DUMB ASSHOLE'S SUPER-POWER.
BUT FOR ME...
FOR ME, IT TAKES SOME FOCUS.
THE FACES OF A MILLION INNOCENTS TURNED TO SOLID GOLD, SPECIFICALLY.
I COULDN'T LET THAT BOMB DETONATE.
SPANISH LARRY-- I TRICKED YOU INTO THINKING ABOUT DOING SOMETHING GOOD FOR SOMEONE YOU CARE FOR--THAT'S WHY YOU COULD SEE X-RAYS AND THROW THAT GUARD THROUGH A WALL!
I DON'T UNDERSTAND!
YOU HAVE TO BELIEVE YOU ARE GOING TO USE YOUR POWERS FOR A NOBLE CAUSE!
I'VE TORTURED MEN BEFORE.

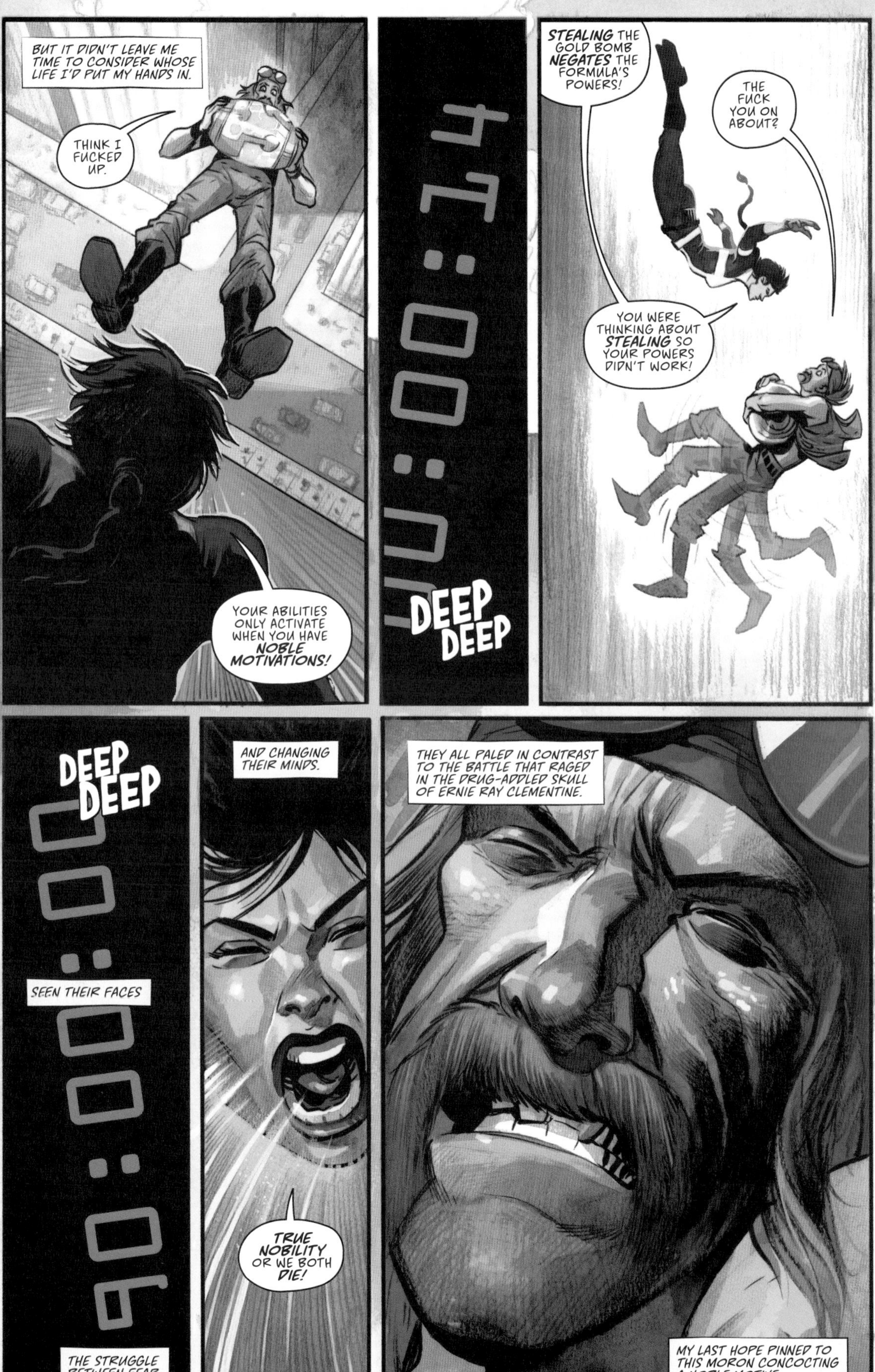

BUT IT DIDN'T LEAVE ME TIME TO CONSIDER WHOSE LIFE I'D PUT MY HANDS IN.
THINK I FUCKED UP.
YOUR ABILITIES ONLY ACTIVATE WHEN YOU HAVE NOBLE MOTIVATIONS!
DEEP DEEP
STEALING THE GOLD BOMB NEGATES THE FORMULA'S POWERS!
THE FUCK YOU ON ABOUT?
YOU WERE THINKING ABOUT STEALING SO YOUR POWERS DIDN'T WORK!
DEEP DEEP
SEEN THEIR FACES
THE STRUGGLE BETWEEN FEAR OF DEATH
AND CHANGING THEIR MINDS.
TRUE NOBILITY OR WE BOTH DIE!
THEY ALL PALED IN CONTRAST TO THE BATTLE THAT RAGED IN THE DRUG-ADDLED SKULL OF ERNIE RAY CLEMENTINE.
MY LAST HOPE PINNED TO THIS MORON CONCOCTING A NOBLE MOTIVE...

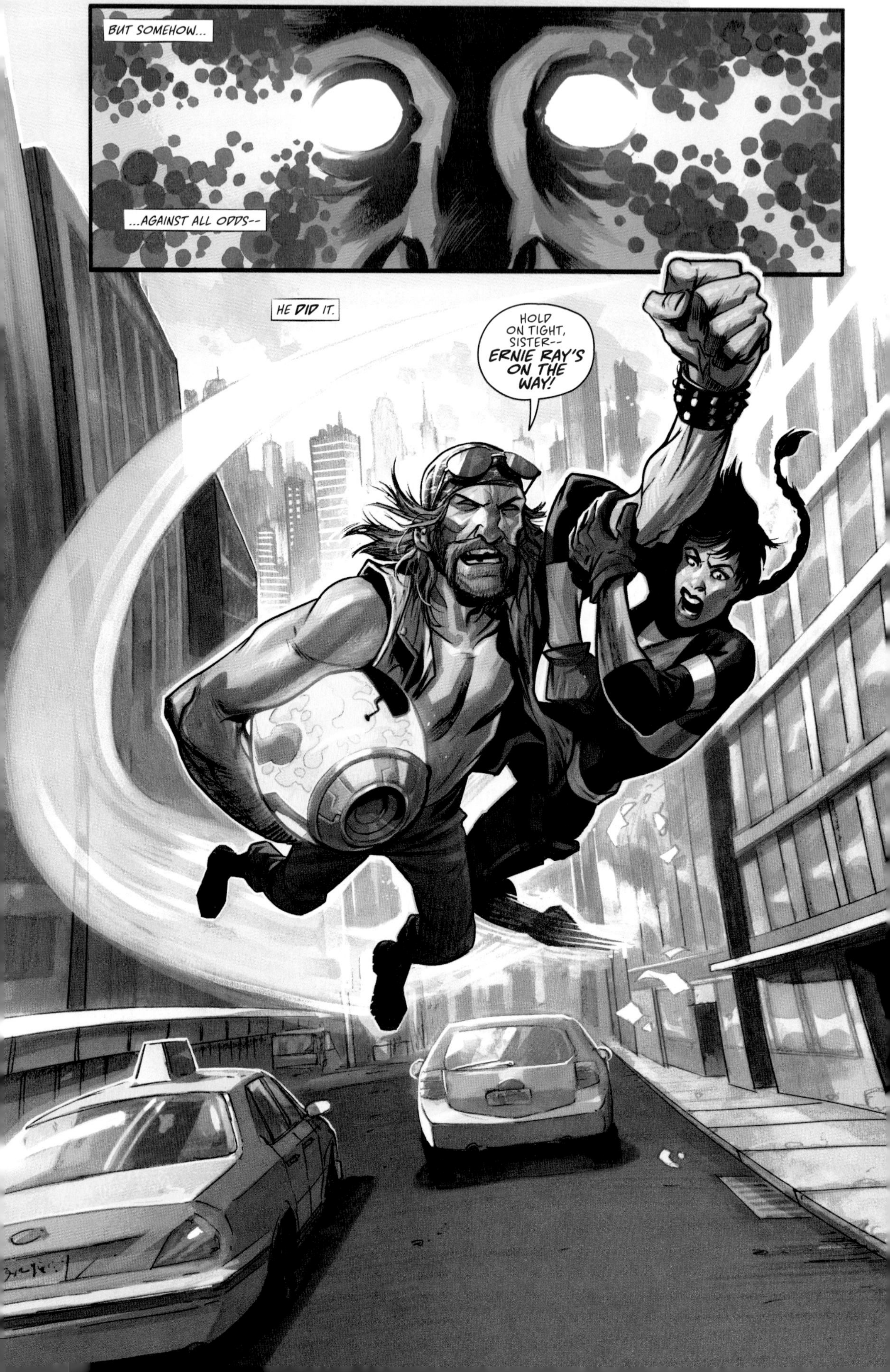
BUT SOMEHOW...
...AGAINST ALL ODDS--
HE DID IT.
HOLD ON TIGHT, SISTER-- ERNIE RAY'S ON THE WAY!

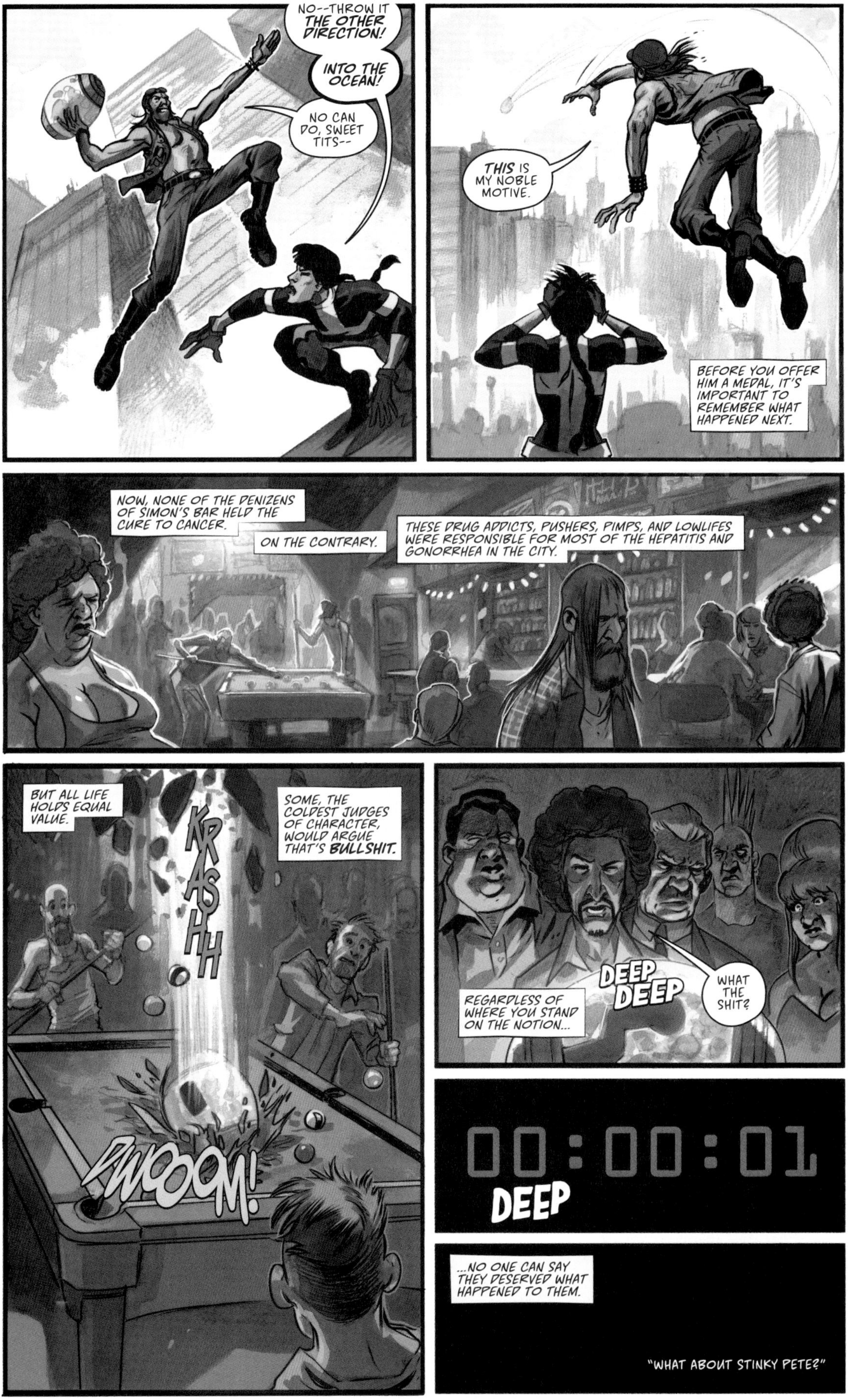
NO--THROW IT THE OTHER DIRECTION!
INTO THE OCEAN!
NO CAN DO, SWEET TITS--
THIS IS MY NOBLE MOTIVE.
BEFORE YOU OFFER HIM A MEDAL, IT'S IMPORTANT TO REMEMBER WHAT HAPPENED NEXT.
NOW, NONE OF THE DENIZENS OF SIMON'S BAR HELD THE CURE TO CANCER.
ON THE CONTRARY.
THESE DRUG ADDICTS, PUSHERS, PIMPS, AND LOWLIFES WERE RESPONSIBLE FOR MOST OF THE HEPATITIS AND GONORRHEA IN THE CITY.
BUT ALL LIFE HOLDS EQUAL VALUE.
SOME, THE COLDEST JUDGES OF CHARACTER, WOULD ARGUE THAT'S BULLSHIT.
KRASHH
DWOOOM!
DEEP DEEP
WHAT THE SHIT?
REGARDLESS OF WHERE YOU STAND ON THE NOTION...
00:00:01
DEEP
...NO ONE CAN SAY THEY DESERVED WHAT HAPPENED TO THEM.
"WHAT ABOUT STINKY PETE?"

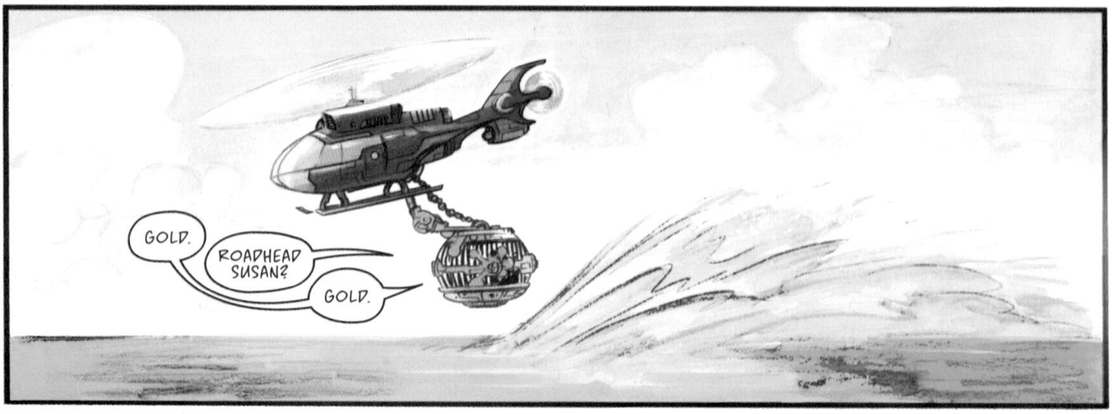
GOLD.
ROADHEAD SUSAN?
GOLD.

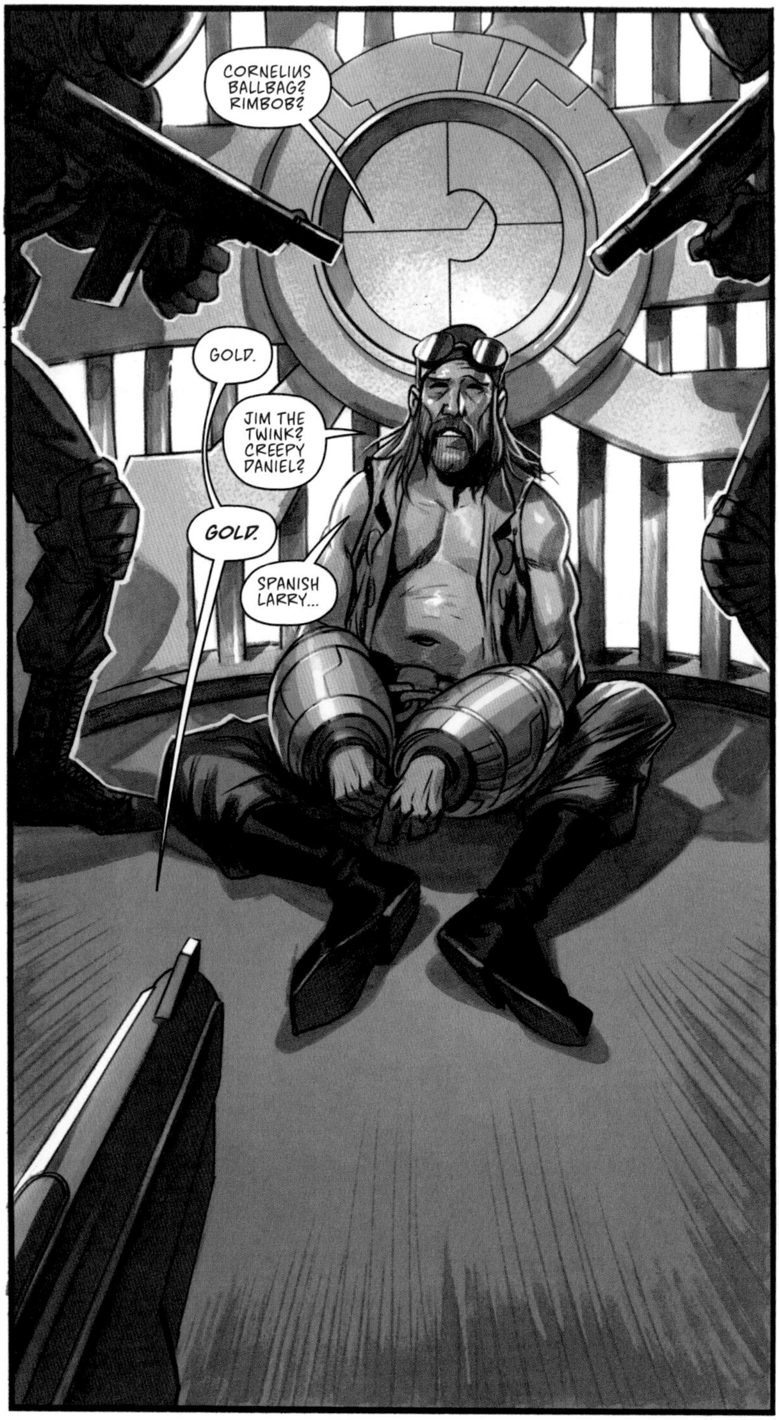
CORNELIUS BALLBAG? RIMBOB?
GOLD.
JIM THE TWINK? CREEPY DANIEL?
GOLD.
SPANISH LARRY...

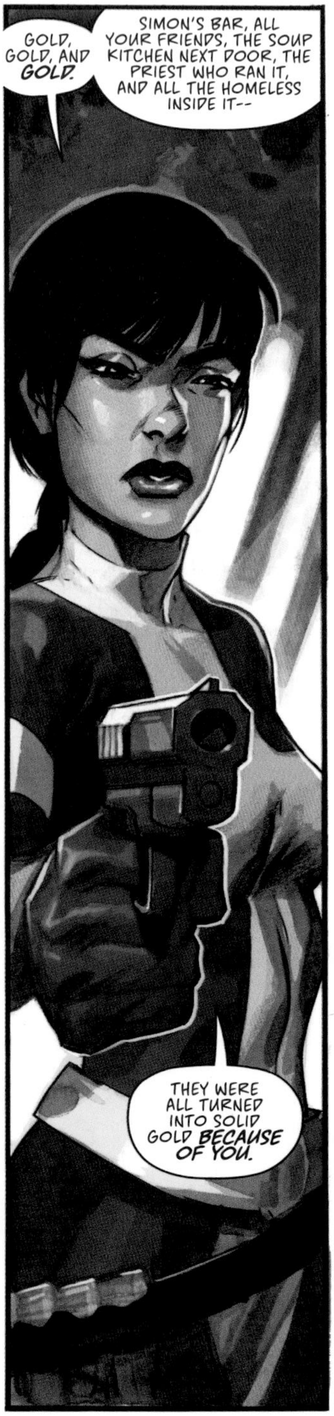
GOLD, GOLD, AND **GOLD.**
SIMON'S BAR, ALL YOUR FRIENDS, THE SOUP KITCHEN NEXT DOOR, THE PRIEST WHO RAN IT, AND ALL THE HOMELESS INSIDE IT--
THEY WERE ALL TURNED INTO SOLID GOLD **BECAUSE OF YOU.**

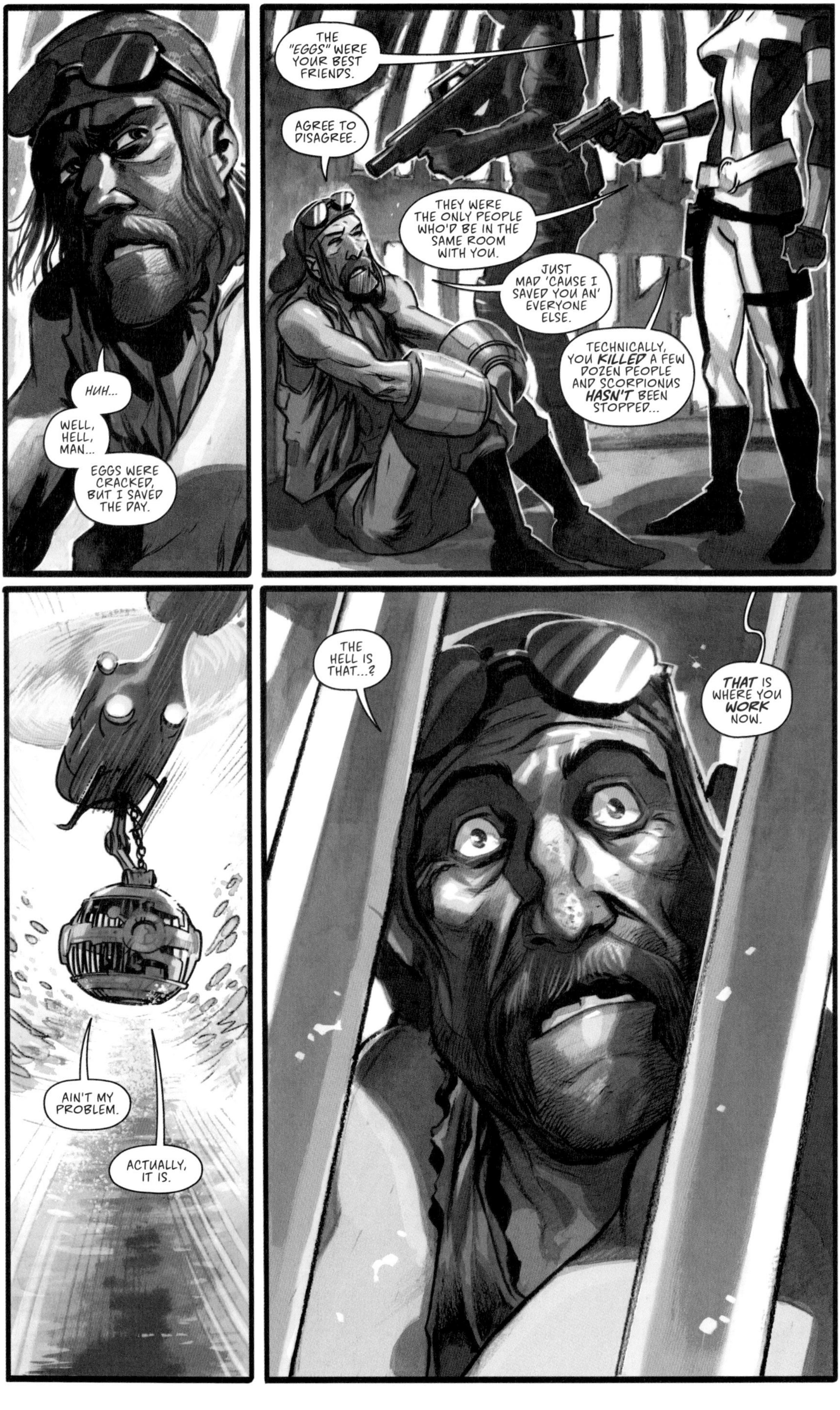
HUH...
WELL, HELL, MAN...
EGGS WERE CRACKED, BUT I SAVED THE DAY.
THE "EGGS" WERE YOUR BEST FRIENDS.
AGREE TO DISAGREE.
THEY WERE THE ONLY PEOPLE WHO'D BE IN THE SAME ROOM WITH YOU.
JUST MAD 'CAUSE I SAVED YOU AN' EVERYONE ELSE.
TECHNICALLY, YOU KILLED A FEW DOZEN PEOPLE AND SCORPIONUS HASN'T BEEN STOPPED...
AIN'T MY PROBLEM.
ACTUALLY, IT IS.
THE HELL IS THAT...?
THAT IS WHERE YOU WORK NOW.

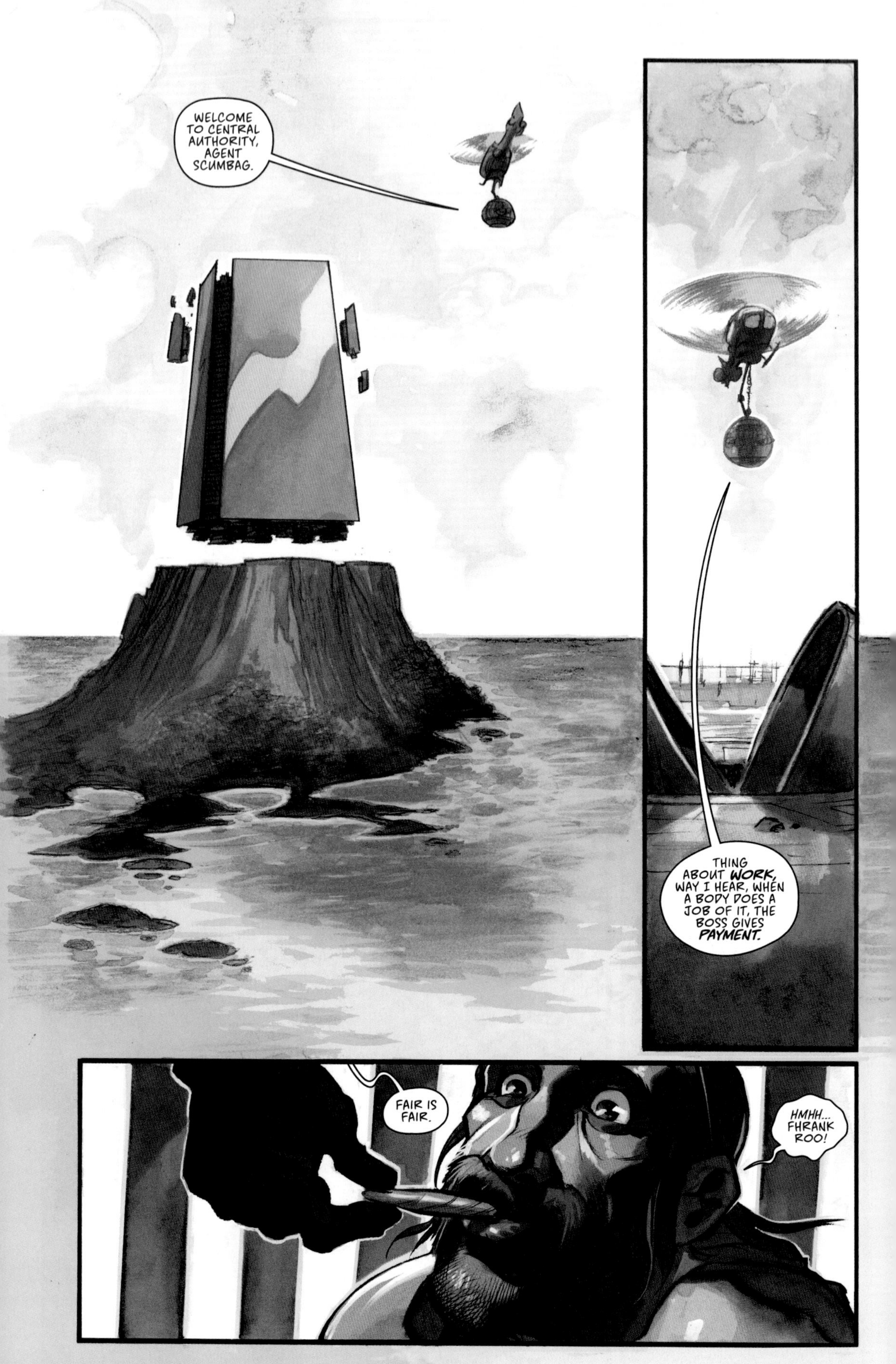
WELCOME TO CENTRAL AUTHORITY, AGENT SCUMBAG.
THING ABOUT WORK, WAY I HEAR, WHEN A BODY DOES A JOB OF IT, THE BOSS GIVES PAYMENT.
FAIR IS FAIR.
HMHH... FHRANK ROO!

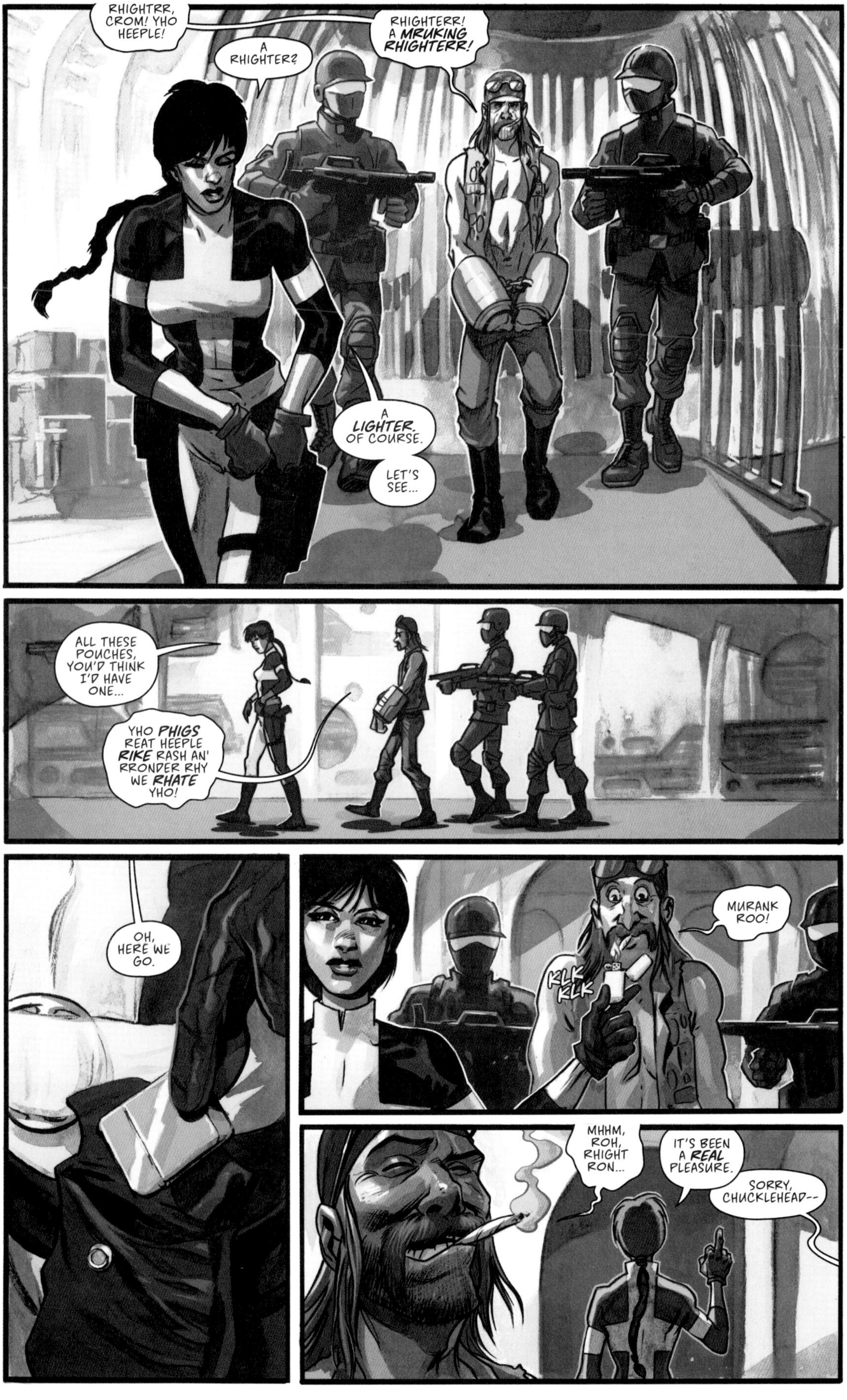
RHIGHTRR, CROM! YHO HEEPLE!
RHIGHTERR! A MRUKING RHIGHTERR!
A RHIGHTER?
A LIGHTER. OF COURSE.
LET'S SEE...
ALL THESE POUCHES, YOU'D THINK I'D HAVE ONE...
YHO PHIGS REAT HEEPLE RIKE RASH AN' RRONDER RHY WE RHATE YHO!
OH, HERE WE GO.
KLK KLK
MURANK ROO!
MHHM, ROH, RHIGHT RON...
IT'S BEEN A REAL PLEASURE.
SORRY, CHUCKLEHEAD--

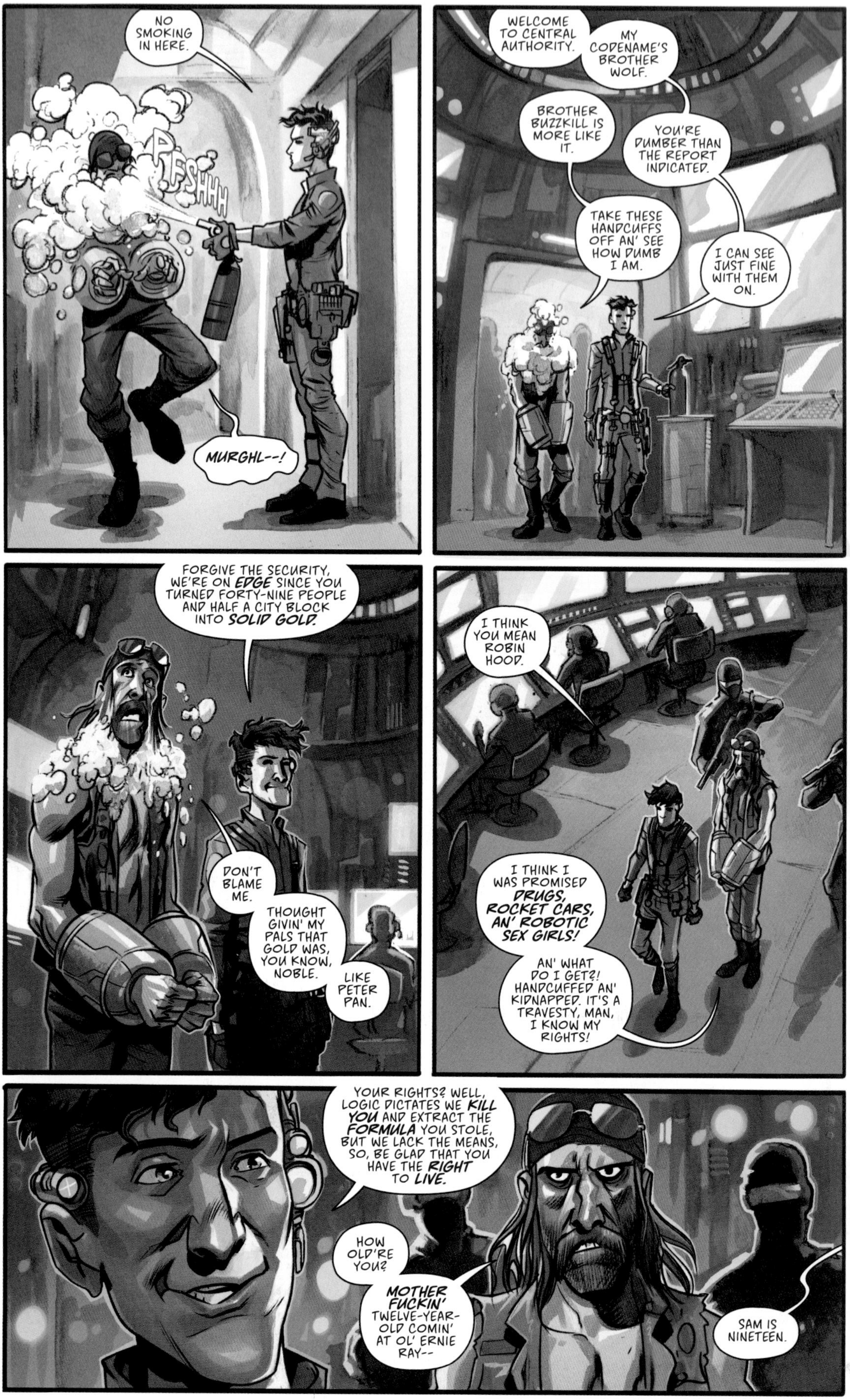
NO SMOKING IN HERE.
PFSHHH
MURGHL--!
WELCOME TO CENTRAL AUTHORITY.
MY CODENAME'S BROTHER WOLF.
BROTHER BUZZKILL IS MORE LIKE IT.
YOU'RE DUMBER THAN THE REPORT INDICATED.
TAKE THESE HANDCUFFS OFF AN' SEE HOW DUMB I AM.
I CAN SEE JUST FINE WITH THEM ON.
FORGIVE THE SECURITY, WE'RE ON EDGE SINCE YOU TURNED FORTY-NINE PEOPLE AND HALF A CITY BLOCK INTO SOLID GOLD.
DON'T BLAME ME.
THOUGHT GIVIN' MY PALS THAT GOLD WAS, YOU KNOW, NOBLE.
LIKE PETER PAN.
I THINK YOU MEAN ROBIN HOOD.
I THINK I WAS PROMISED DRUGS, ROCKET CARS, AN' ROBOTIC SEX GIRLS!
AN' WHAT DO I GET?! HANDCUFFED AN' KIDNAPPED. IT'S A TRAVESTY, MAN, I KNOW MY RIGHTS!
YOUR RIGHTS? WELL, LOGIC DICTATES WE KILL YOU AND EXTRACT THE FORMULA YOU STOLE, BUT WE LACK THE MEANS, SO, BE GLAD THAT YOU HAVE THE RIGHT TO LIVE.
HOW OLD'RE YOU?
MOTHER FUCKIN' TWELVE-YEAR-OLD COMIN' AT OL' ERNIE RAY--
SAM IS NINETEEN.

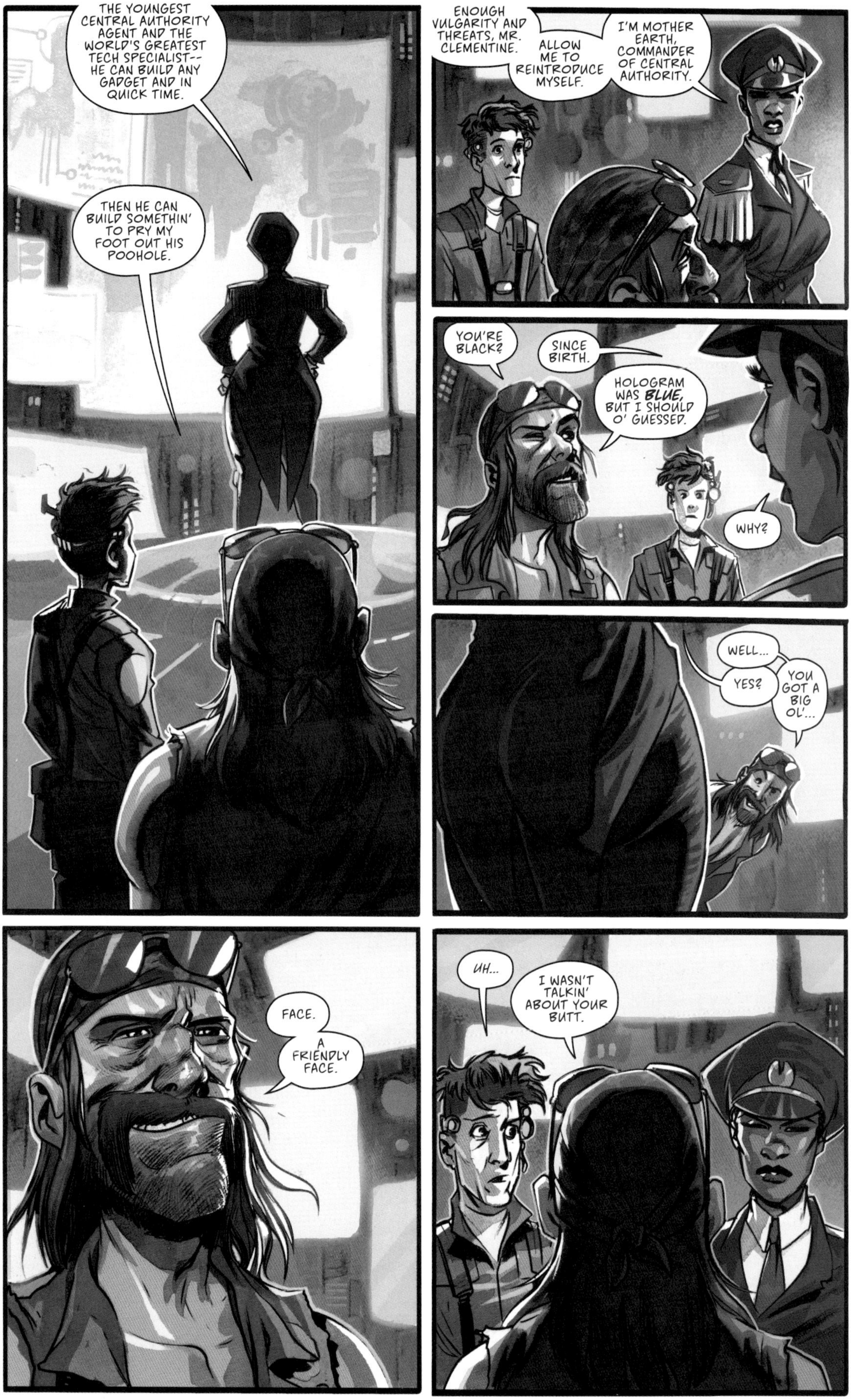
THE YOUNGEST CENTRAL AUTHORITY AGENT AND THE WORLD'S GREATEST TECH SPECIALIST-- HE CAN BUILD ANY GADGET AND IN QUICK TIME.
THEN HE CAN BUILD SOMETHIN' TO PRY MY FOOT OUT HIS POOHOLE.
ENOUGH VULGARITY AND THREATS, MR. CLEMENTINE.
ALLOW ME TO REINTRODUCE MYSELF.
I'M MOTHER EARTH, COMMANDER OF CENTRAL AUTHORITY.
YOU'RE BLACK?
SINCE BIRTH.
HOLOGRAM WAS **BLUE,** BUT I SHOULD O' GUESSED.
WHY?
WELL...
YES?
YOU GOT A BIG OL'...
FACE.
A FRIENDLY FACE.
UH...
I WASN'T TALKIN' ABOUT YOUR BUTT.

THE WORLD NEARS A **BREAKING** POINT, MR. CLEMENTINE.

EXTREME POLARIZATION, TRIBALISM, CLIMATE CHANGE, RACISM, FASCISM...

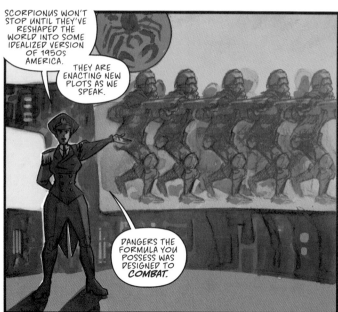

SCORPIONUS WON'T STOP UNTIL THEY'VE RESHAPED THE WORLD INTO SOME IDEALIZED VERSION OF 1950s AMERICA.

THEY ARE ENACTING NEW PLOTS AS WE SPEAK.

DANGERS THE FORMULA YOU POSSESS WAS DESIGNED TO **COMBAT.**

WELL... UGH-- YEAH. I HEAR YA.

THING IS, SINCE I WAS A BOY, PEOPLE ALWAYS TELLIN' ME I'M A PILE O' SHIT, SERVIN' **NO PURPOSE.**

BUT NOW, Y'ALL NEED OL' ERNIE RAY.

RITCHH

I KNEW I WAS DESTINED FER IMPORTANT GREATNESS.

FACT OF THE MATTER IS--I'M AN **INDIVIDUAL.** I MAKE MY CHOICES-- AN' HELL, THEY MAY NOT BE RIGHT, OR THOUGHT OUT, OR CONSIDER OTHER PEOPLE--

BUT THEY'RE **MINE.**

THAT'S THE AMERICAN WAY.

SO... YOU'LL HELP US PROTECT YOUR COUNTRY?

OH, **HELL NO.**

SOON AS I GET MY DRUGS, ROCKET CAR, AND SEX ROBOT, IT'S LATER DAYS AND ERNIE GOES TO CATCH SOME RAYS.

I'M **OUT.**

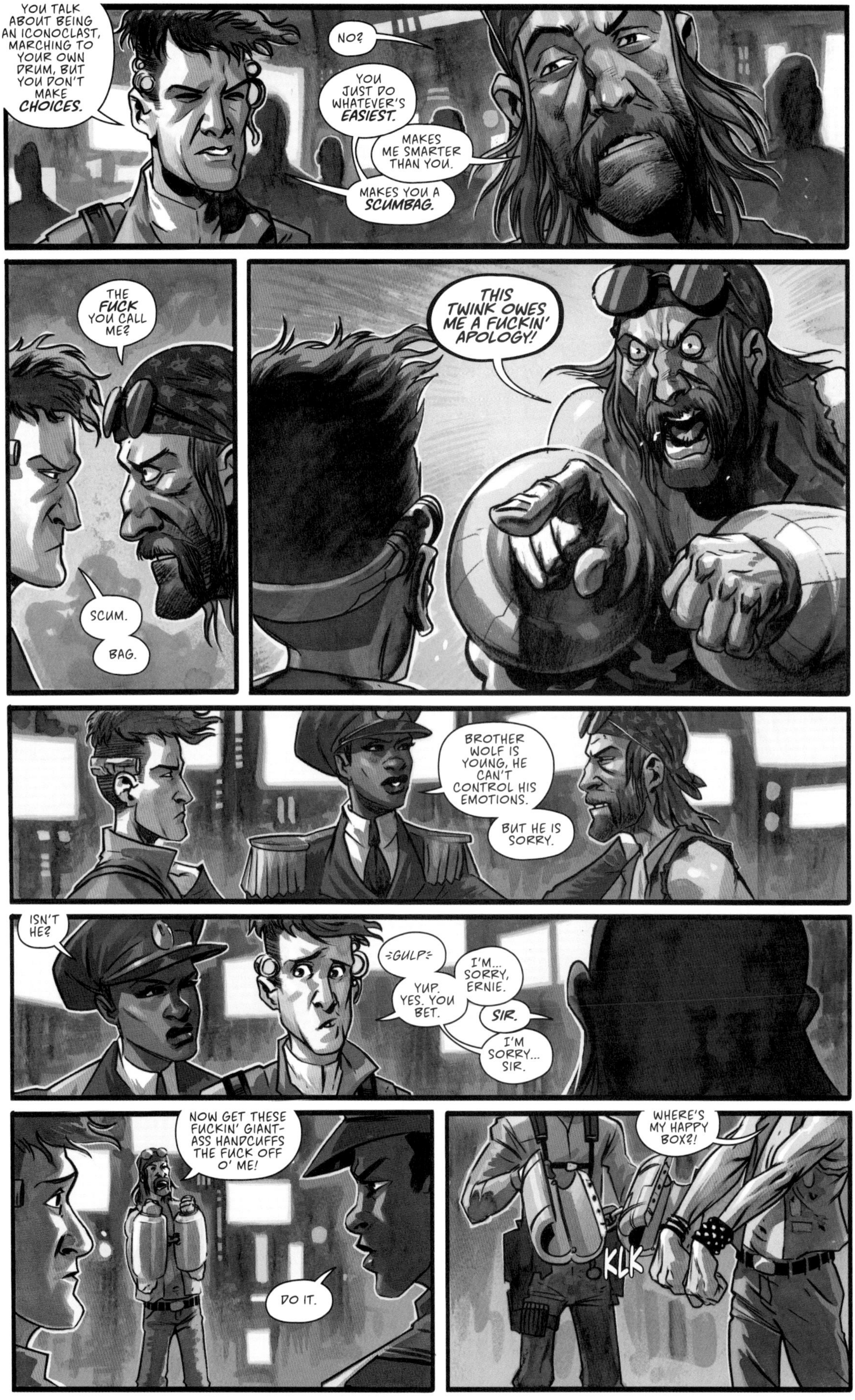
YOU TALK ABOUT BEING AN ICONOCLAST, MARCHING TO YOUR OWN DRUM, BUT YOU DON'T MAKE CHOICES.
NO?
YOU JUST DO WHATEVER'S EASIEST.
MAKES ME SMARTER THAN YOU.
MAKES YOU A SCUMBAG.
THE FUCK YOU CALL ME?
SCUM.
BAG.
THIS TWINK OWES ME A FUCKIN' APOLOGY!
BROTHER WOLF IS YOUNG, HE CAN'T CONTROL HIS EMOTIONS.
BUT HE IS SORRY.
ISN'T HE?
=GULP=
YUP. YES. YOU BET.
I'M... SORRY, ERNIE.
SIR.
I'M SORRY... SIR.
NOW GET THESE FUCKIN' GIANT-ASS HANDCUFFS THE FUCK OFF O' ME!
DO IT.
WHERE'S MY HAPPY BOX?!
KLK

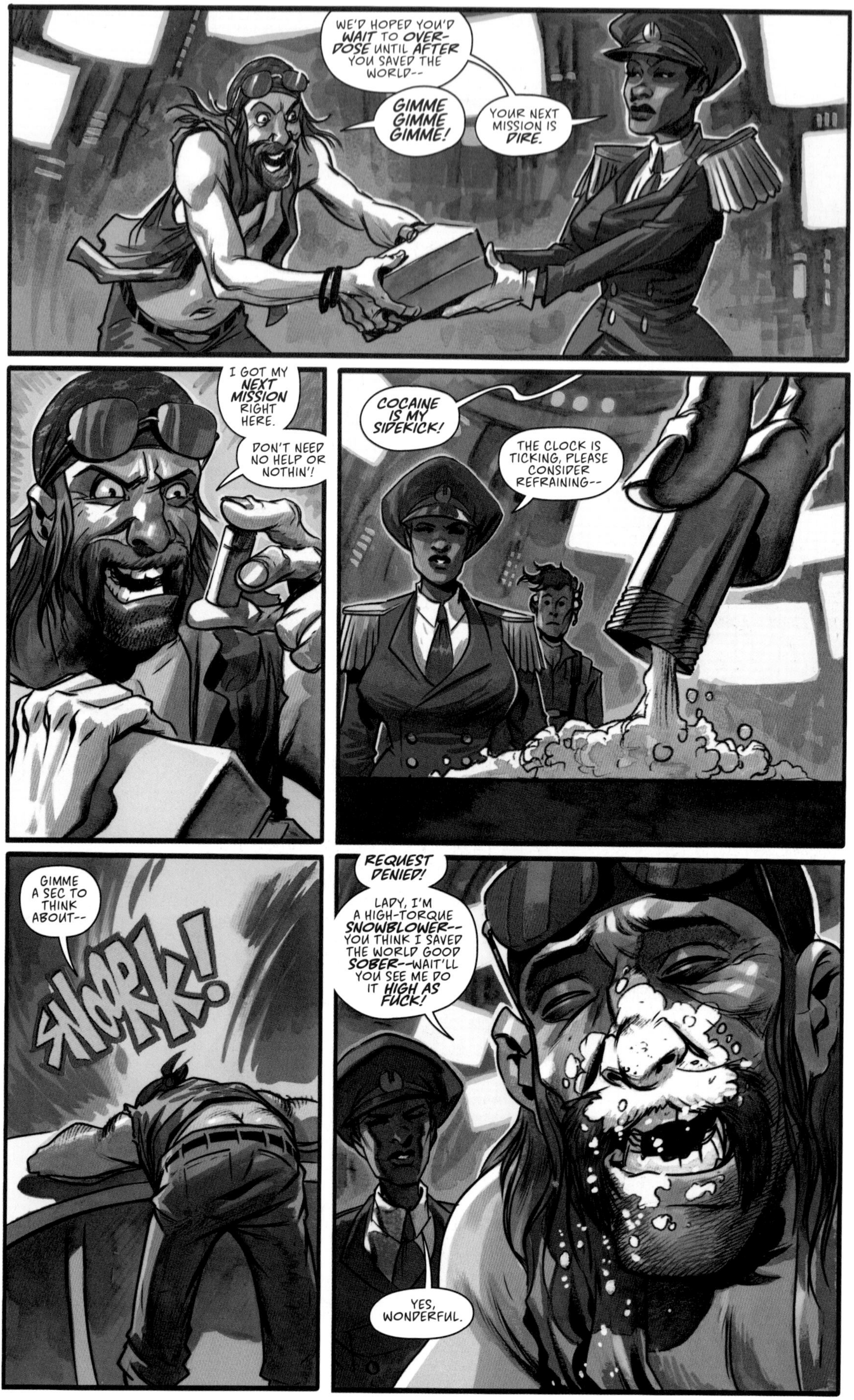
WE'D HOPED YOU'D WAIT TO OVER-DOSE UNTIL AFTER YOU SAVED THE WORLD--
GIMME GIMME GIMME!
YOUR NEXT MISSION IS DIRE.
I GOT MY NEXT MISSION RIGHT HERE.
DON'T NEED NO HELP OR NOTHIN'!
COCAINE IS MY SIDEKICK!
THE CLOCK IS TICKING, PLEASE CONSIDER REFRAINING--
GIMME A SEC TO THINK ABOUT--
SNORK!
REQUEST DENIED!
LADY, I'M A HIGH-TORQUE SNOWBLOWER--YOU THINK I SAVED THE WORLD GOOD SOBER--WAIT'LL YOU SEE ME DO IT HIGH AS FUCK!
YES, WONDERFUL.

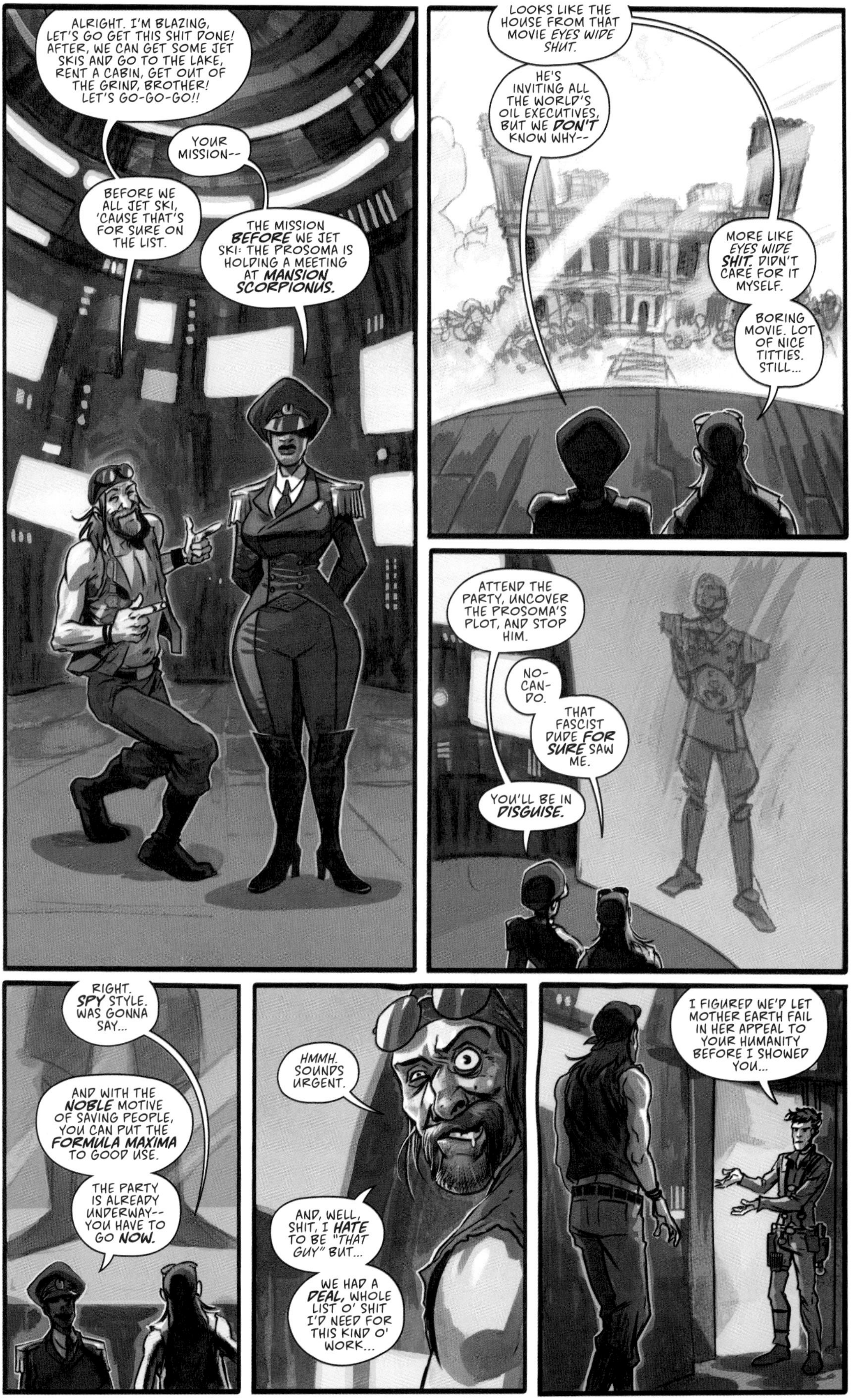
ALRIGHT. I'M BLAZING, LET'S GO GET THIS SHIT DONE! AFTER, WE CAN GET SOME JET SKIS AND GO TO THE LAKE, RENT A CABIN, GET OUT OF THE GRIND, BROTHER! LET'S GO-GO-GO!!
YOUR MISSION--
BEFORE WE ALL JET SKI, 'CAUSE THAT'S FOR SURE ON THE LIST.
THE MISSION BEFORE WE JET SKI: THE PROSOMA IS HOLDING A MEETING AT MANSION SCORPIONUS.
LOOKS LIKE THE HOUSE FROM THAT MOVIE EYES WIDE SHUT.
HE'S INVITING ALL THE WORLD'S OIL EXECUTIVES, BUT WE DON'T KNOW WHY--
MORE LIKE EYES WIDE SHIT. DIDN'T CARE FOR IT MYSELF.
BORING MOVIE. LOT OF NICE TITTIES. STILL...
ATTEND THE PARTY, UNCOVER THE PROSOMA'S PLOT, AND STOP HIM.
NO-CAN-DO.
THAT FASCIST DUDE FOR SURE SAW ME.
YOU'LL BE IN DISGUISE.
RIGHT. SPY STYLE. WAS GONNA SAY...
AND WITH THE NOBLE MOTIVE OF SAVING PEOPLE, YOU CAN PUT THE FORMULA MAXIMA TO GOOD USE.
THE PARTY IS ALREADY UNDERWAY-- YOU HAVE TO GO NOW.
HMMH. SOUNDS URGENT.
AND, WELL, SHIT, I HATE TO BE "THAT GUY" BUT...
WE HAD A DEAL, WHOLE LIST O' SHIT I'D NEED FOR THIS KIND O' WORK...
I FIGURED WE'D LET MOTHER EARTH FAIL IN HER APPEAL TO YOUR HUMANITY BEFORE I SHOWED YOU...

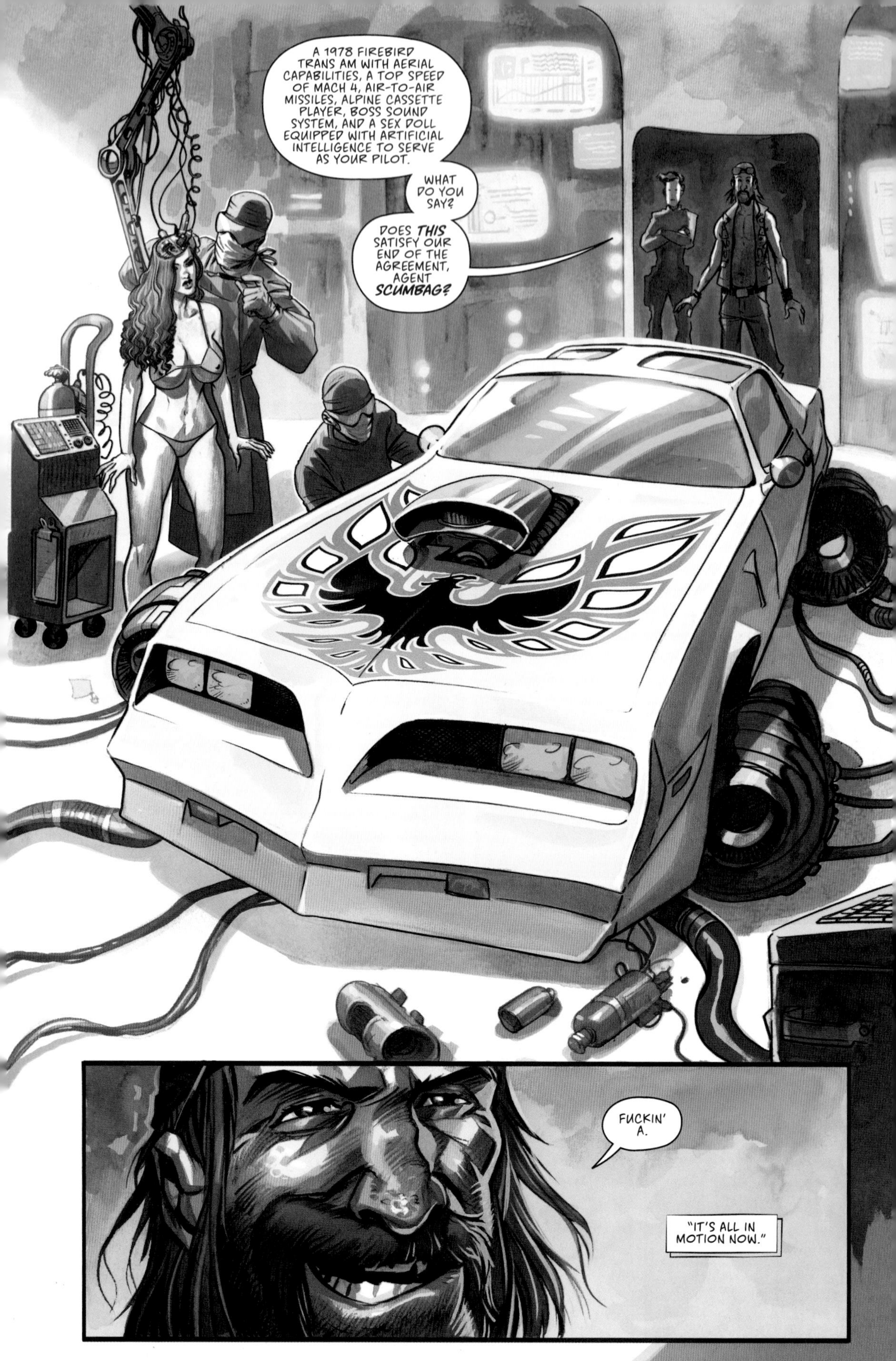
A 1978 FIREBIRD TRANS AM WITH AERIAL CAPABILITIES, A TOP SPEED OF MACH 4, AIR-TO-AIR MISSILES, ALPINE CASSETTE PLAYER, BOSS SOUND SYSTEM, AND A SEX DOLL EQUIPPED WITH ARTIFICIAL INTELLIGENCE TO SERVE AS YOUR PILOT.
WHAT DO YOU SAY?
DOES THIS SATISFY OUR END OF THE AGREEMENT, AGENT SCUMBAG?
FUCKIN' A.
"IT'S ALL IN MOTION NOW."

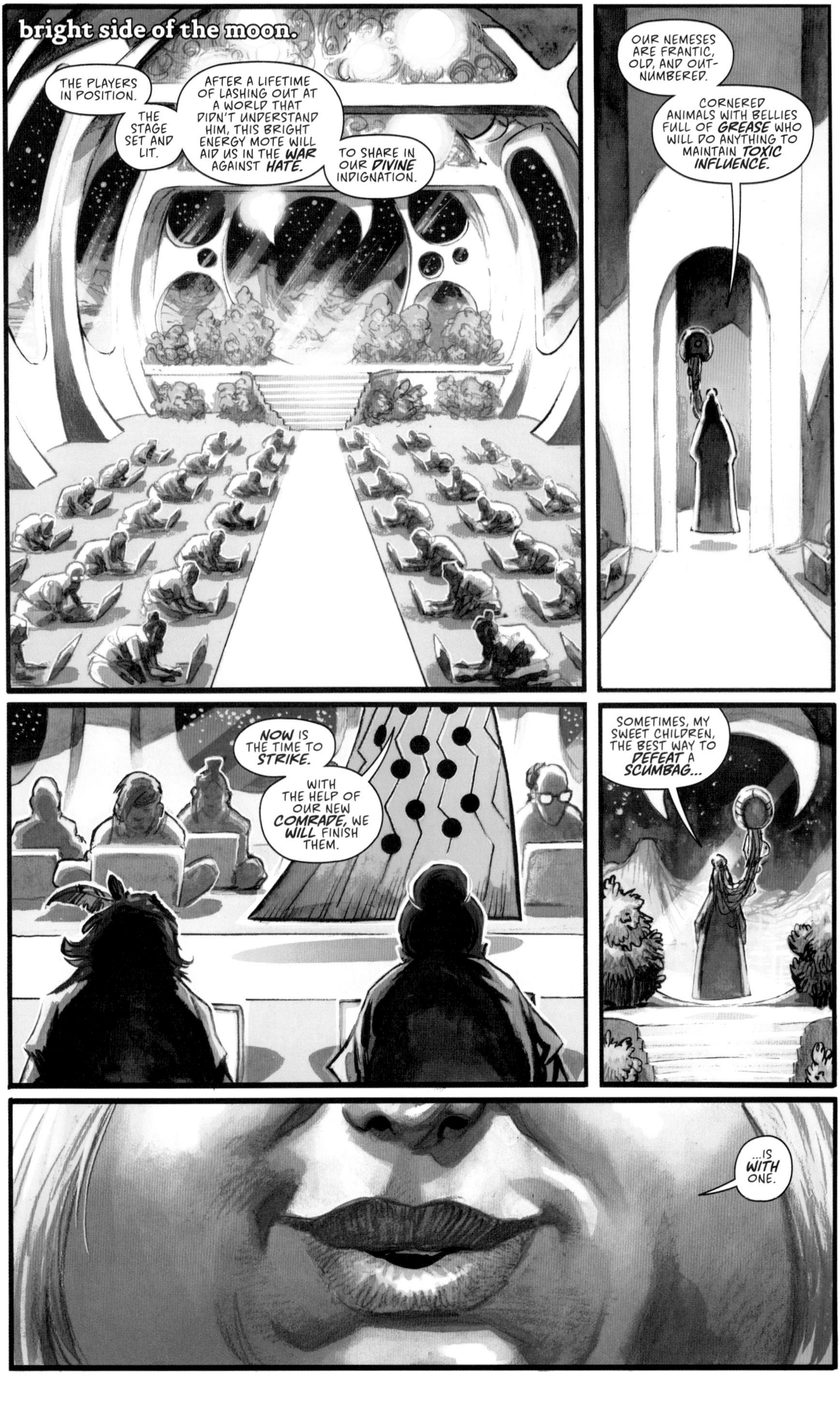
bright side of the moon.
THE PLAYERS IN POSITION.
THE STAGE SET AND LIT.
AFTER A LIFETIME OF LASHING OUT AT A WORLD THAT DIDN'T UNDERSTAND HIM, THIS BRIGHT ENERGY MOTE WILL AID US IN THE WAR AGAINST HATE.
TO SHARE IN OUR DIVINE INDIGNATION.
OUR NEMESES ARE FRANTIC, OLD, AND OUT-NUMBERED.
CORNERED ANIMALS WITH BELLIES FULL OF GREASE WHO WILL DO ANYTHING TO MAINTAIN TOXIC INFLUENCE.
NOW IS THE TIME TO STRIKE.
WITH THE HELP OF OUR NEW COMRADE, WE WILL FINISH THEM.
SOMETIMES, MY SWEET CHILDREN, THE BEST WAY TO DEFEAT A SCUMBAG...
...IS WITH ONE.

FOUR

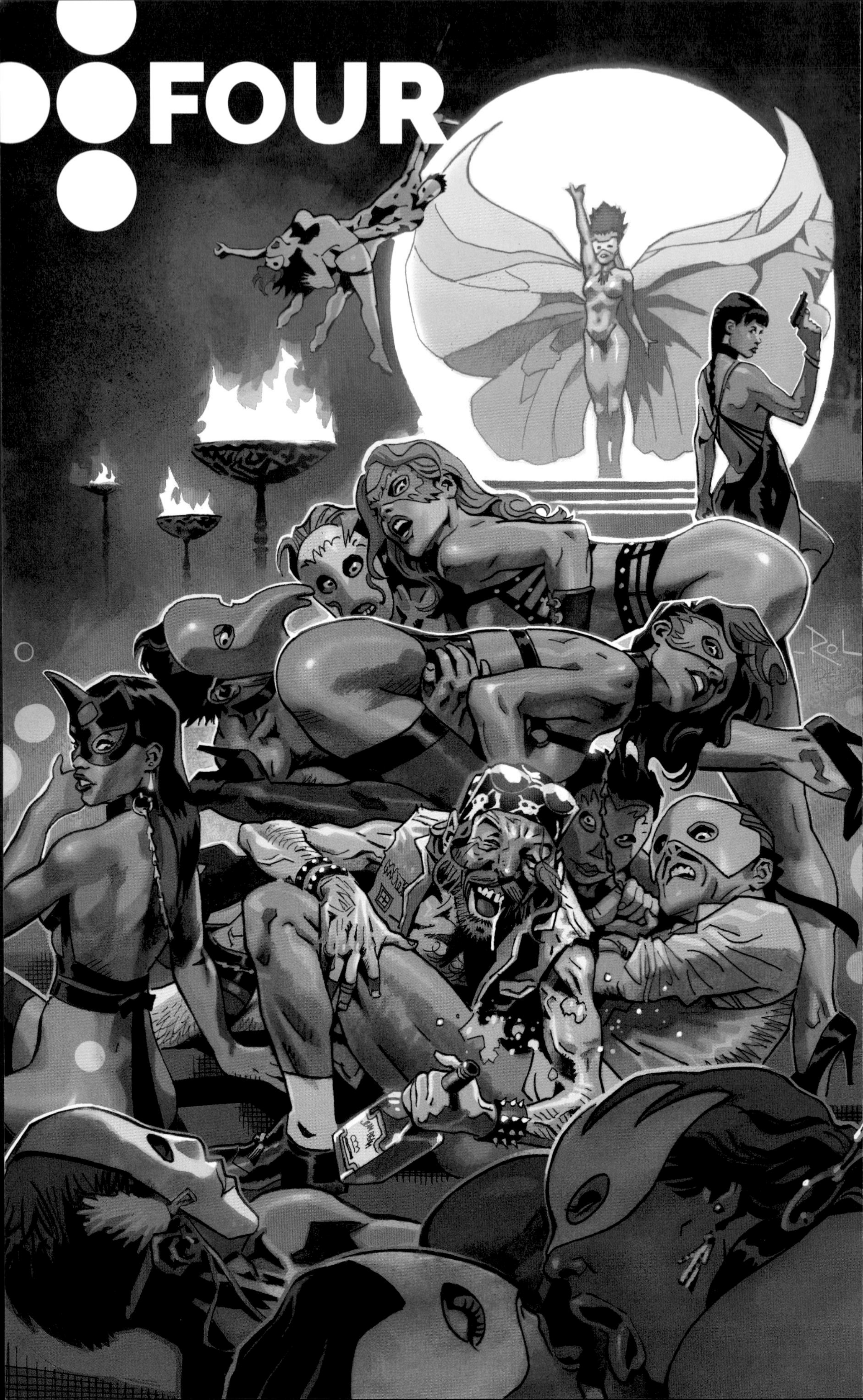

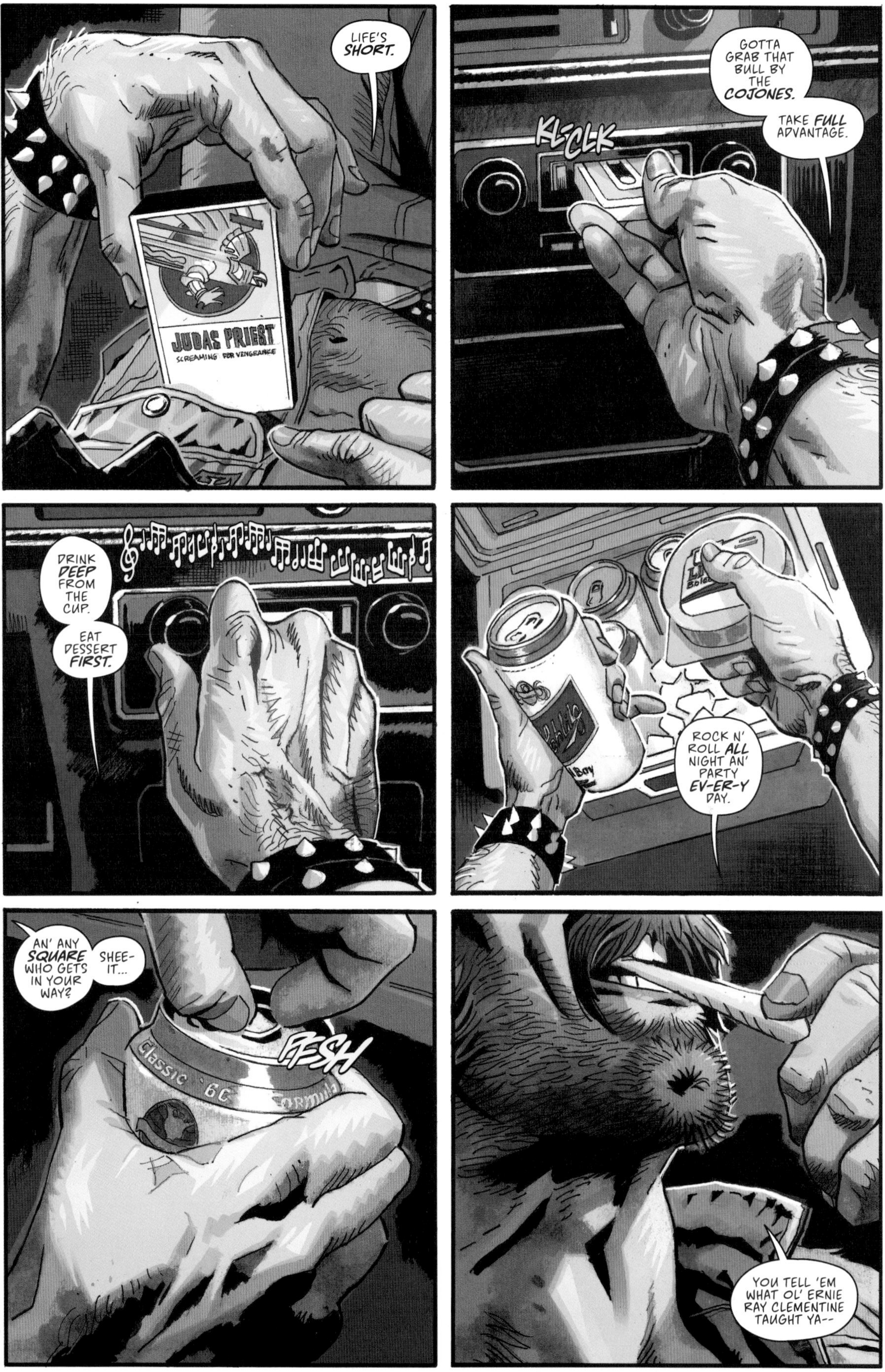

LIFE'S SHORT.
JUDAS PRIEST
SCREAMING FOR VENGEANCE
GOTTA GRAB THAT BULL BY THE COJONES.
TAKE FULL ADVANTAGE.
KL-CLK
DRINK DEEP FROM THE CUP.
EAT DESSERT FIRST.
ROCK N' ROLL ALL NIGHT AN' PARTY EV-ER-Y DAY.
AN' ANY SQUARE WHO GETS IN YOUR WAY?
SHEE-IT...
FFSH
Classic '60 Formula
YOU TELL 'EM WHAT OL' ERNIE RAY CLEMENTINE TAUGHT YA--

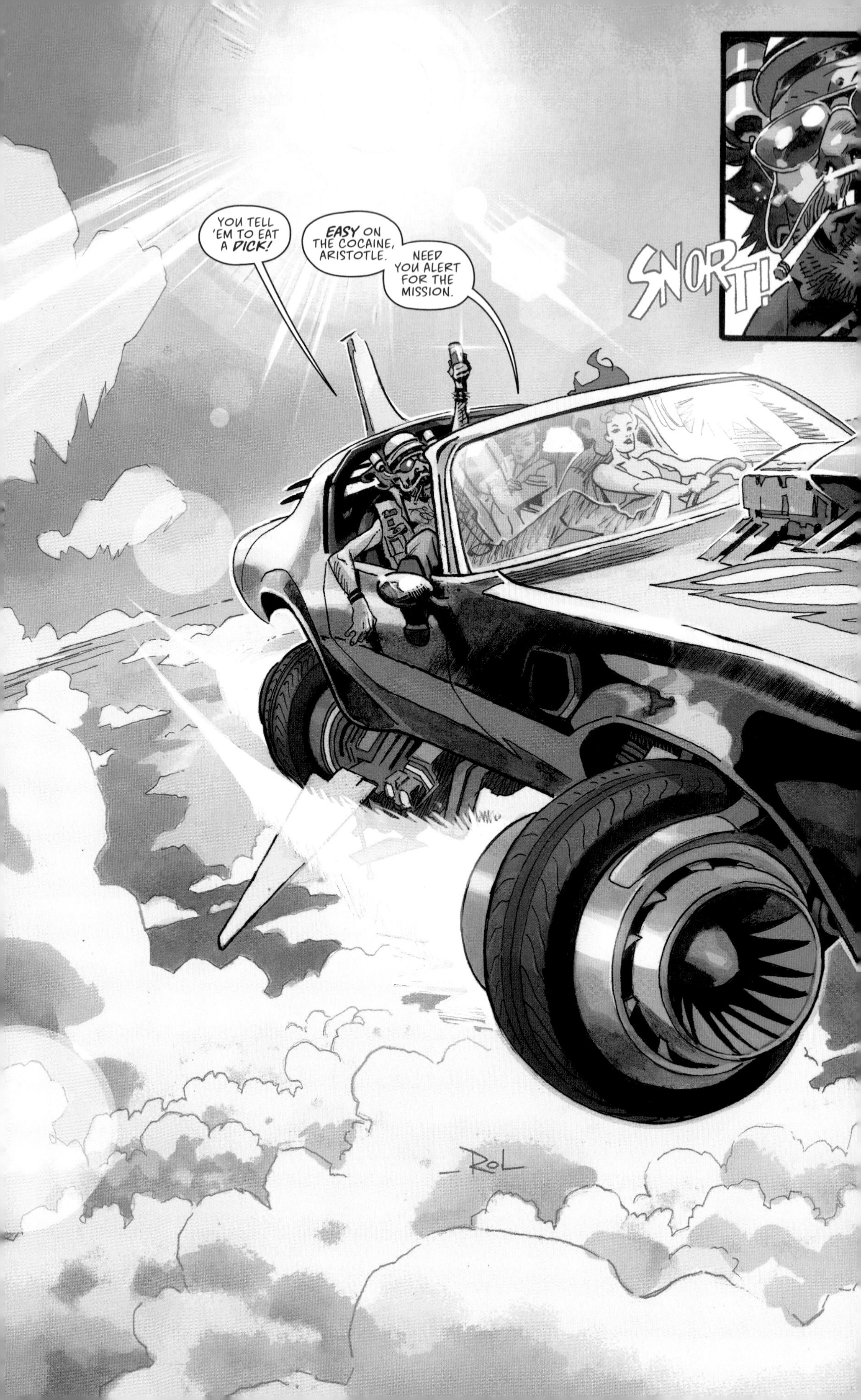
YOU TELL 'EM TO EAT A DICK!
EASY ON THE COCAINE, ARISTOTLE.
NEED YOU ALERT FOR THE MISSION.
SNORT!
ROL

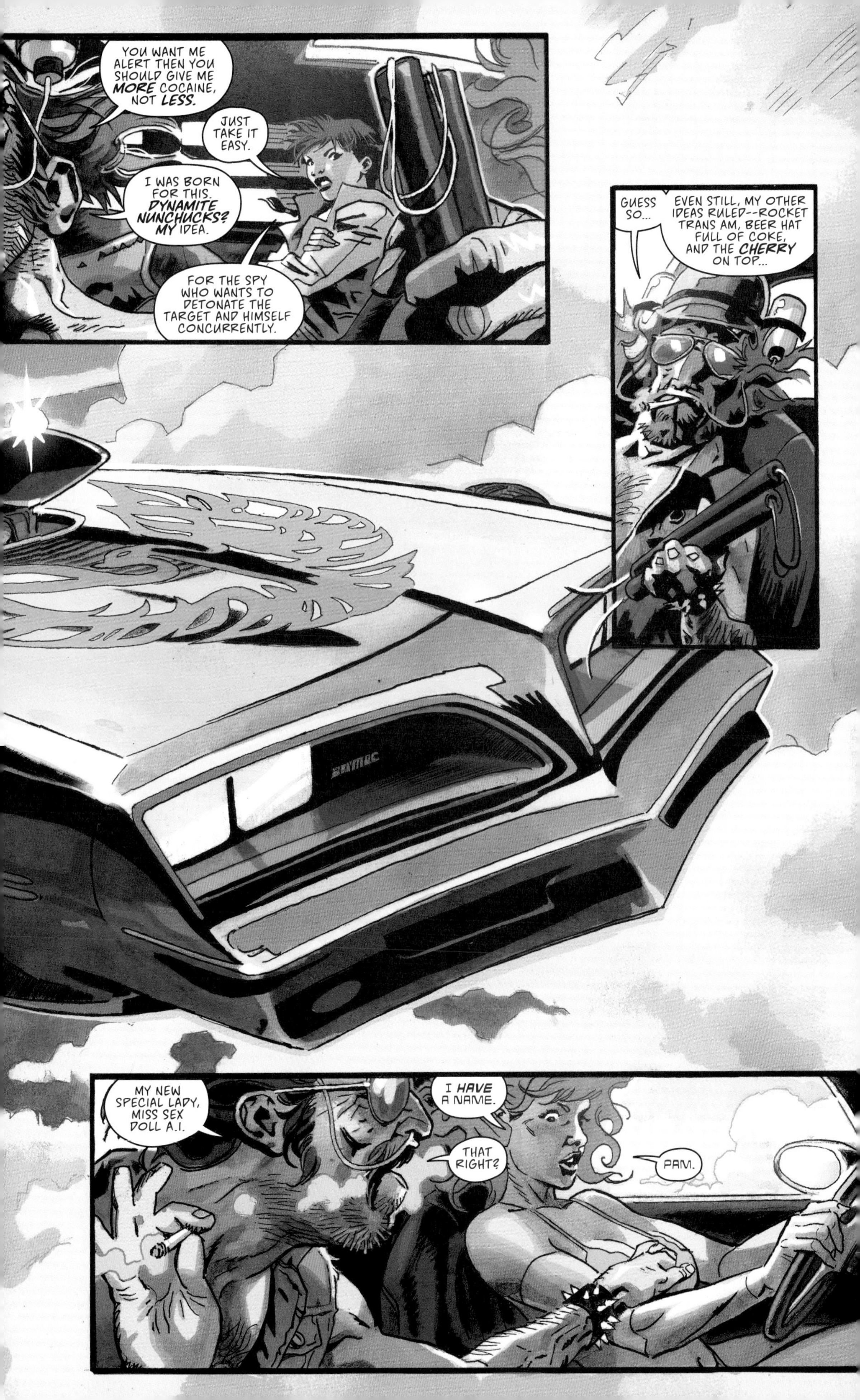
YOU WANT ME ALERT THEN YOU SHOULD GIVE ME MORE COCAINE, NOT LESS.
JUST TAKE IT EASY.
I WAS BORN FOR THIS. DYNAMITE NUNCHUCKS? MY IDEA.
FOR THE SPY WHO WANTS TO DETONATE THE TARGET AND HIMSELF CONCURRENTLY.
GUESS SO...
EVEN STILL, MY OTHER IDEAS RULED--ROCKET TRANS AM, BEER HAT FULL OF COKE, AND THE CHERRY ON TOP...
MY NEW SPECIAL LADY, MISS SEX DOLL A.I.
I HAVE A NAME.
THAT RIGHT?
PAM.

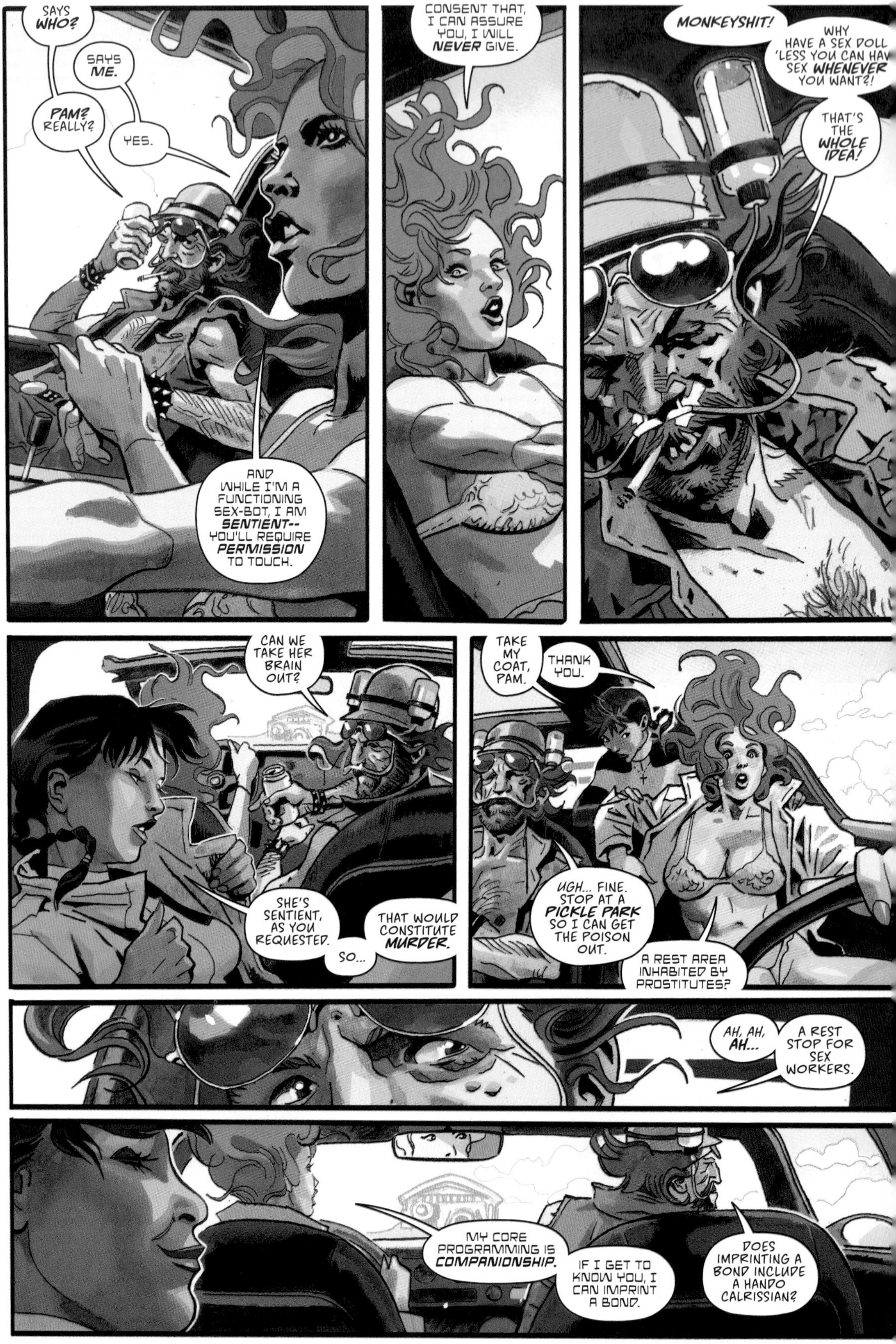
SAYS WHO?
SAYS ME.
PAM? REALLY?
YES.
AND WHILE I'M A FUNCTIONING SEX-BOT, I AM SENTIENT-- YOU'LL REQUIRE PERMISSION TO TOUCH.
CONSENT THAT, I CAN ASSURE YOU, I WILL NEVER GIVE.
MONKEYSHIT!
WHY HAVE A SEX DOLL 'LESS YOU CAN HAV SEX WHENEVER YOU WANT?!
THAT'S THE WHOLE IDEA!
CAN WE TAKE HER BRAIN OUT?
SHE'S SENTIENT, AS YOU REQUESTED.
SO...
THAT WOULD CONSTITUTE MURDER.
TAKE MY COAT, PAM.
THANK YOU.
UGH... FINE. STOP AT A PICKLE PARK SO I CAN GET THE POISON OUT.
A REST AREA INHABITED BY PROSTITUTES?
AH, AH, AH...
A REST STOP FOR SEX WORKERS.
MY CORE PROGRAMMING IS COMPANIONSHIP.
IF I GET TO KNOW YOU, I CAN IMPRINT A BOND.
DOES IMPRINTING A BOND INCLUDE A HANDO CALRISSIAN?

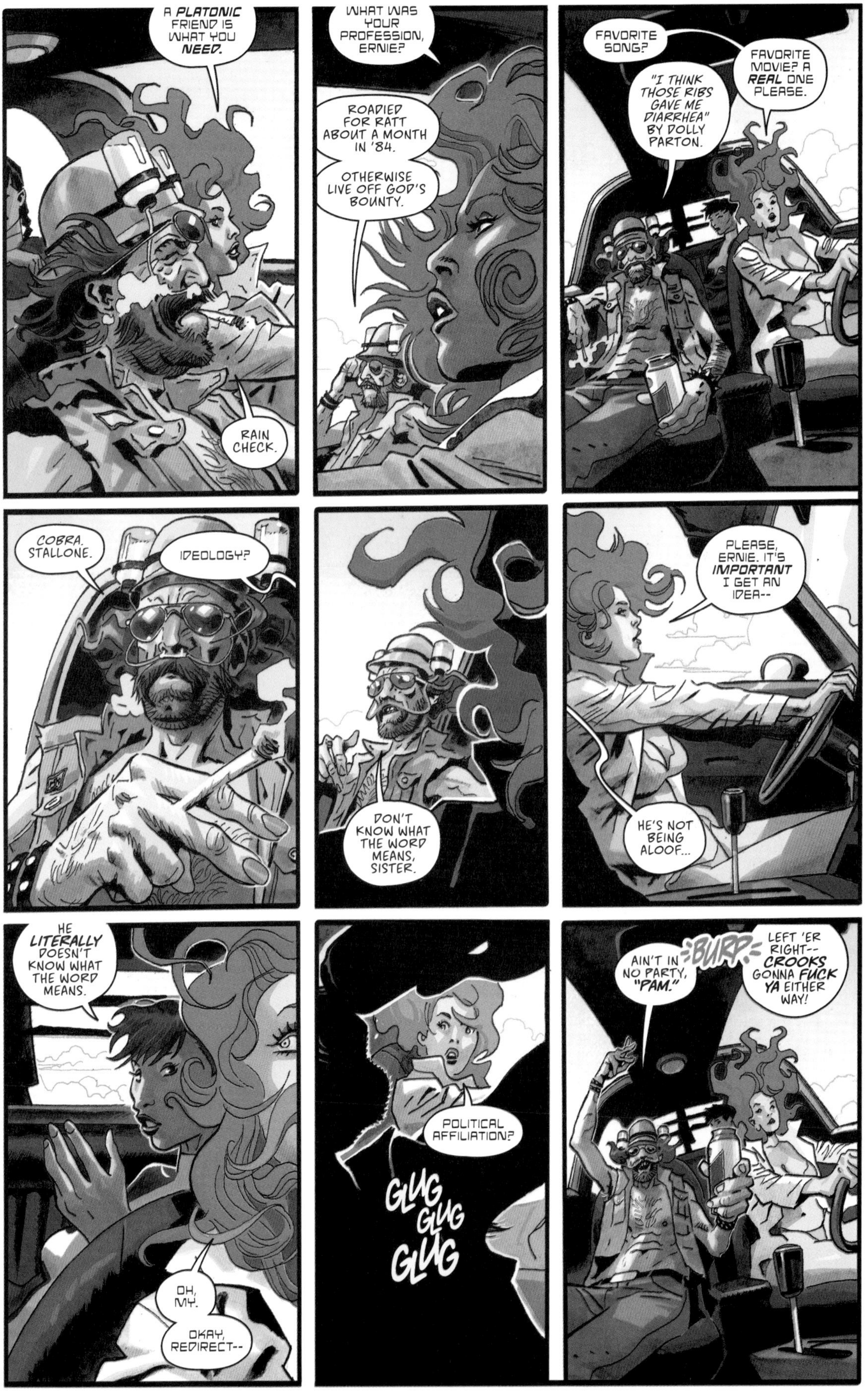
A PLATONIC FRIEND IS WHAT YOU NEED.
RAIN CHECK.
WHAT WAS YOUR PROFESSION, ERNIE?
ROADIED FOR RATT ABOUT A MONTH IN '84.
OTHERWISE LIVE OFF GOD'S BOUNTY.
FAVORITE SONG?
"I THINK THOSE RIBS GAVE ME DIARRHEA" BY DOLLY PARTON.
FAVORITE MOVIE? A REAL ONE PLEASE.
COBRA. STALLONE.
IDEOLOGY?
DON'T KNOW WHAT THE WORD MEANS, SISTER.
PLEASE, ERNIE. IT'S IMPORTANT I GET AN IDEA--
HE'S NOT BEING ALOOF...
HE LITERALLY DOESN'T KNOW WHAT THE WORD MEANS.
OH, MY.
OKAY, REDIRECT--
POLITICAL AFFILIATION?
GLUG GLUG GLUG
AIN'T IN NO PARTY, "PAM."
BURP
LEFT 'ER RIGHT-- CROOKS GONNA FUCK YA EITHER WAY!

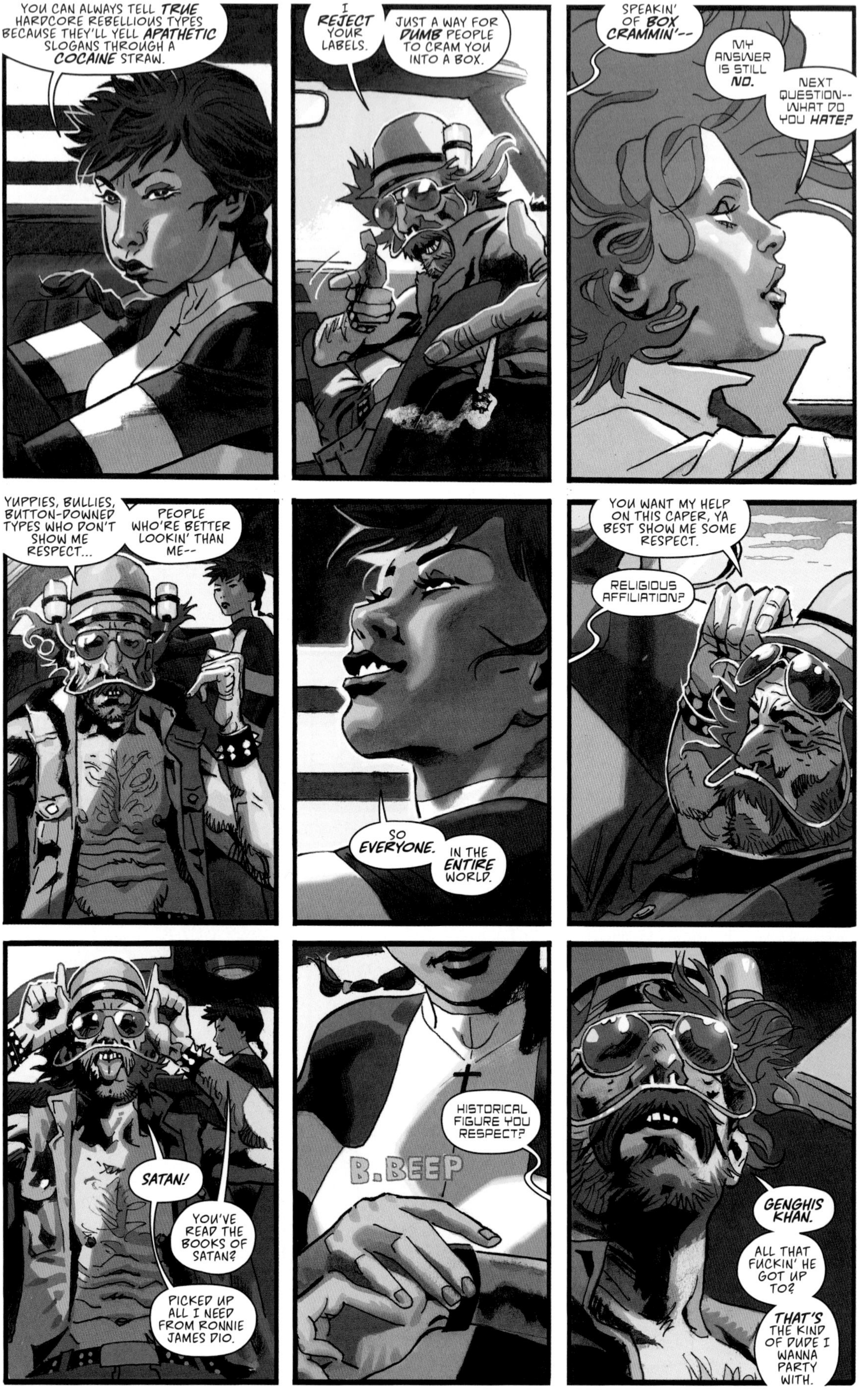
YOU CAN ALWAYS TELL TRUE HARDCORE REBELLIOUS TYPES BECAUSE THEY'LL YELL APATHETIC SLOGANS THROUGH A COCAINE STRAW.
I REJECT YOUR LABELS.
JUST A WAY FOR DUMB PEOPLE TO CRAM YOU INTO A BOX.
SPEAKIN' OF BOX CRAMMIN'--
MY ANSWER IS STILL NO.
NEXT QUESTION-- WHAT DO YOU HATE?
YUPPIES, BULLIES, BUTTON-DOWNED TYPES WHO DON'T SHOW ME RESPECT...
PEOPLE WHO'RE BETTER LOOKIN' THAN ME--
SO EVERYONE.
IN THE ENTIRE WORLD.
YOU WANT MY HELP ON THIS CAPER, YA BEST SHOW ME SOME RESPECT.
RELIGIOUS AFFILIATION?
SATAN!
YOU'VE READ THE BOOKS OF SATAN?
PICKED UP ALL I NEED FROM RONNIE JAMES DIO.
HISTORICAL FIGURE YOU RESPECT?
B.BEEP
GENGHIS KHAN.
ALL THAT FUCKIN' HE GOT UP TO?
THAT'S THE KIND OF DUDE I WANNA PARTY WITH.

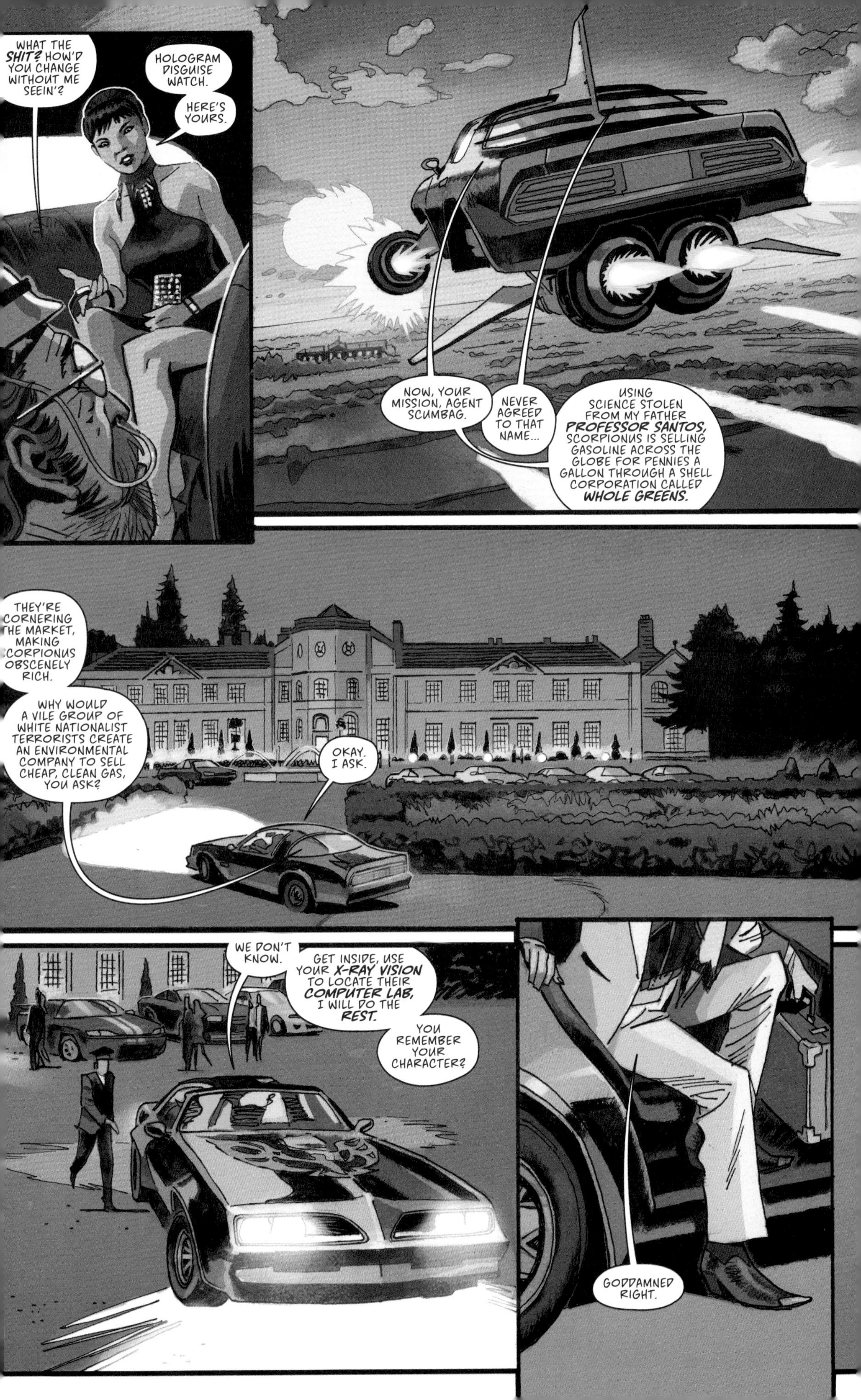
WHAT THE SHIT? HOW'D YOU CHANGE WITHOUT ME SEEIN'?
HOLOGRAM DISGUISE WATCH.
HERE'S YOURS.
NOW, YOUR MISSION, AGENT SCUMBAG.
NEVER AGREED TO THAT NAME...
USING SCIENCE STOLEN FROM MY FATHER PROFESSOR SANTOS, SCORPIONUS IS SELLING GASOLINE ACROSS THE GLOBE FOR PENNIES A GALLON THROUGH A SHELL CORPORATION CALLED WHOLE GREENS.
THEY'RE CORNERING THE MARKET, MAKING SCORPIONUS OBSCENELY RICH.
WHY WOULD A VILE GROUP OF WHITE NATIONALIST TERRORISTS CREATE AN ENVIRONMENTAL COMPANY TO SELL CHEAP, CLEAN GAS, YOU ASK?
OKAY. I ASK.
WE DON'T KNOW.
GET INSIDE, USE YOUR X-RAY VISION TO LOCATE THEIR COMPUTER LAB, I WILL DO THE REST.
YOU REMEMBER YOUR CHARACTER?
GODDAMNED RIGHT.

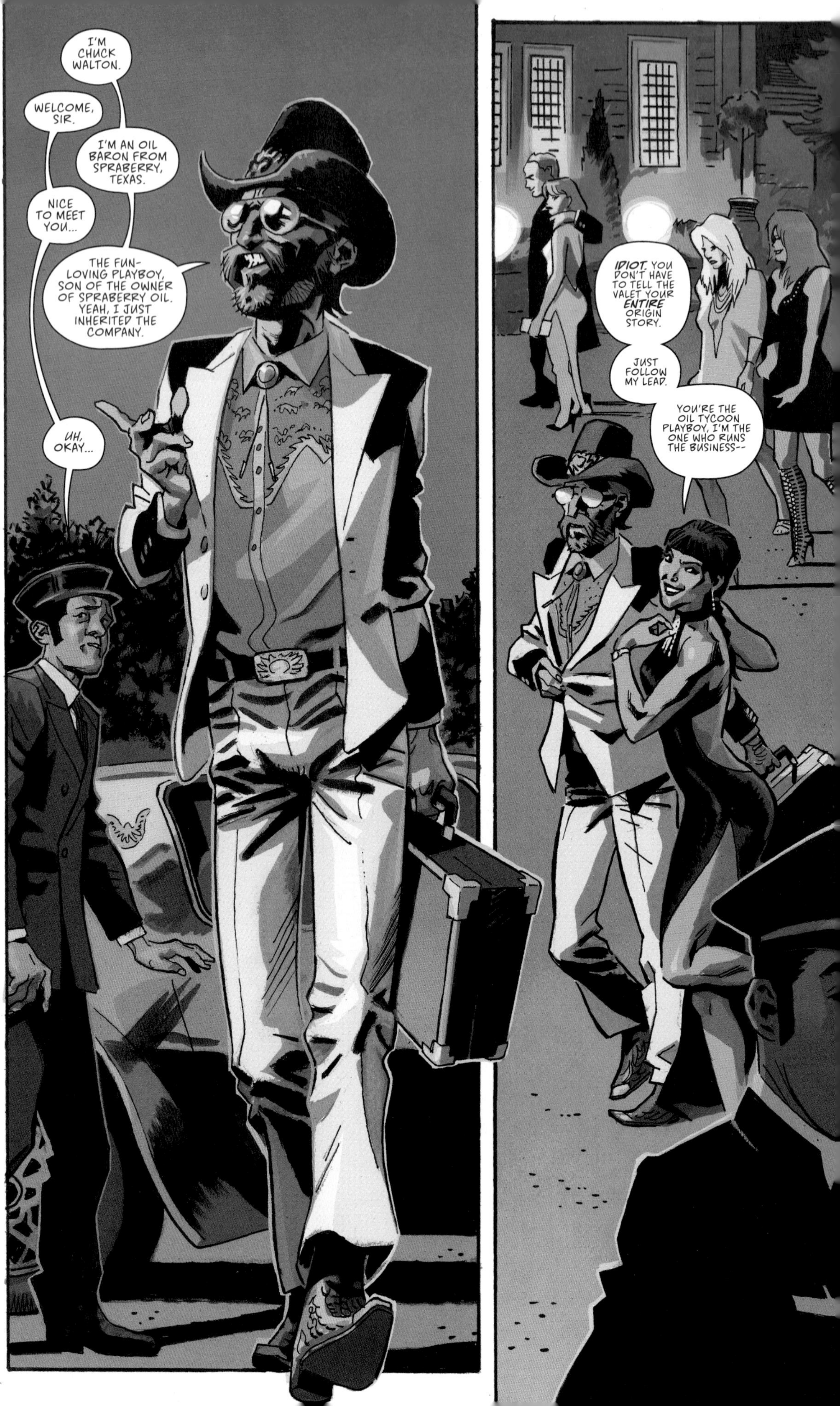

I'M CHUCK WALTON.
WELCOME, SIR.
I'M AN OIL BARON FROM SPRABERRY, TEXAS.
NICE TO MEET YOU...
THE FUN-LOVING PLAYBOY, SON OF THE OWNER OF SPRABERRY OIL. YEAH, I JUST INHERITED THE COMPANY.
UH, OKAY...
IDIOT. YOU DON'T HAVE TO TELL THE VALET YOUR ENTIRE ORIGIN STORY.
JUST FOLLOW MY LEAD.
YOU'RE THE OIL TYCOON PLAYBOY, I'M THE ONE WHO RUNS THE BUSINESS--

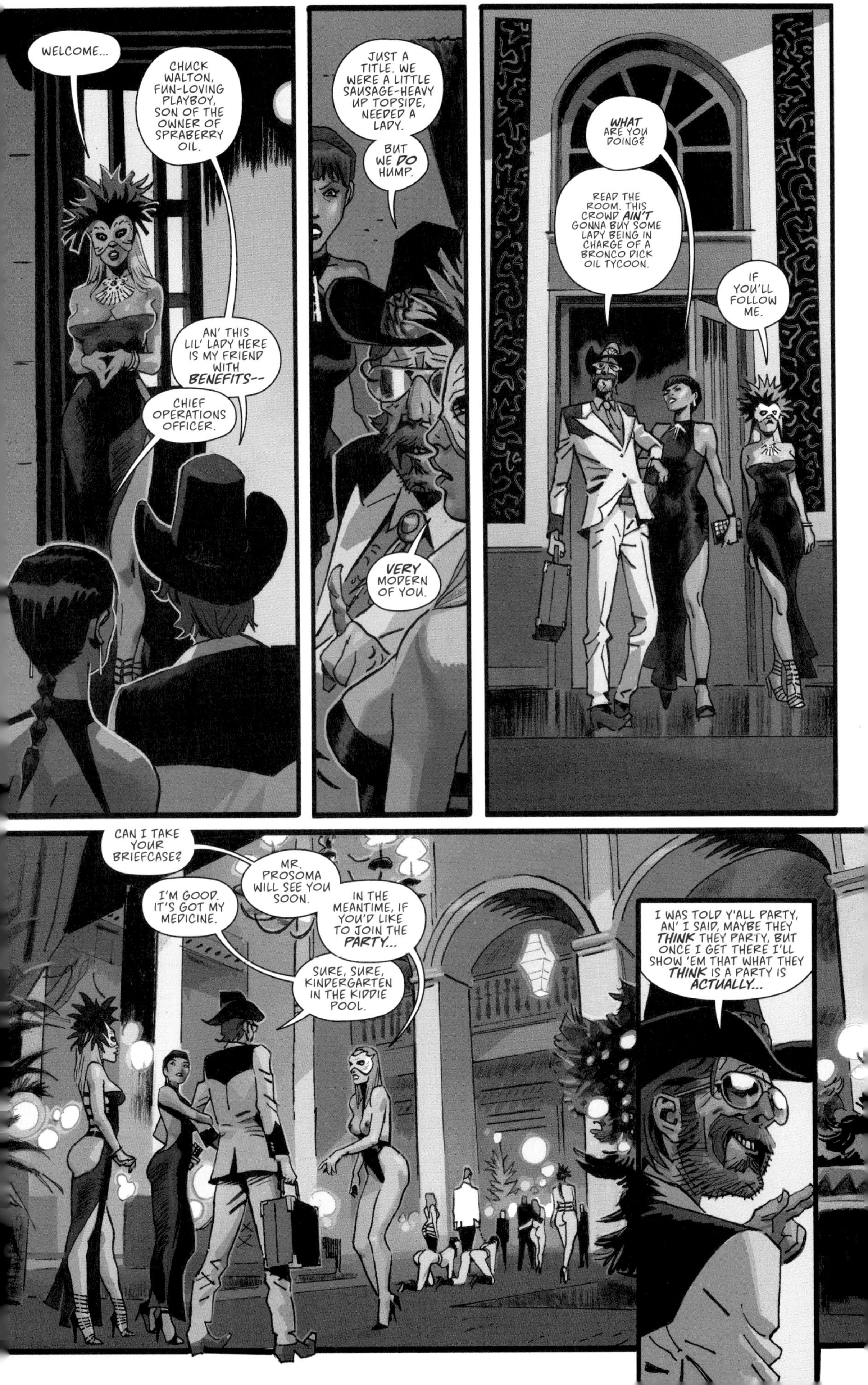
WELCOME...
CHUCK WALTON, FUN-LOVING PLAYBOY, SON OF THE OWNER OF SPRABERRY OIL.
AN' THIS LIL' LADY HERE IS MY FRIEND WITH BENEFITS--
CHIEF OPERATIONS OFFICER.
JUST A TITLE. WE WERE A LITTLE SAUSAGE-HEAVY UP TOPSIDE, NEEDED A LADY.
BUT WE DO HUMP.
VERY MODERN OF YOU.
WHAT ARE YOU DOING?
READ THE ROOM. THIS CROWD AIN'T GONNA BUY SOME LADY BEING IN CHARGE OF A BRONCO DICK OIL TYCOON.
IF YOU'LL FOLLOW ME.
CAN I TAKE YOUR BRIEFCASE?
I'M GOOD. IT'S GOT MY MEDICINE.
MR. PROSOMA WILL SEE YOU SOON.
IN THE MEANTIME, IF YOU'D LIKE TO JOIN THE PARTY...
SURE, SURE, KINDERGARTEN IN THE KIDDIE POOL.
I WAS TOLD Y'ALL PARTY, AN' I SAID, MAYBE THEY THINK THEY PARTY, BUT ONCE I GET THERE I'LL SHOW 'EM THAT WHAT THEY THINK IS A PARTY IS ACTUALLY...

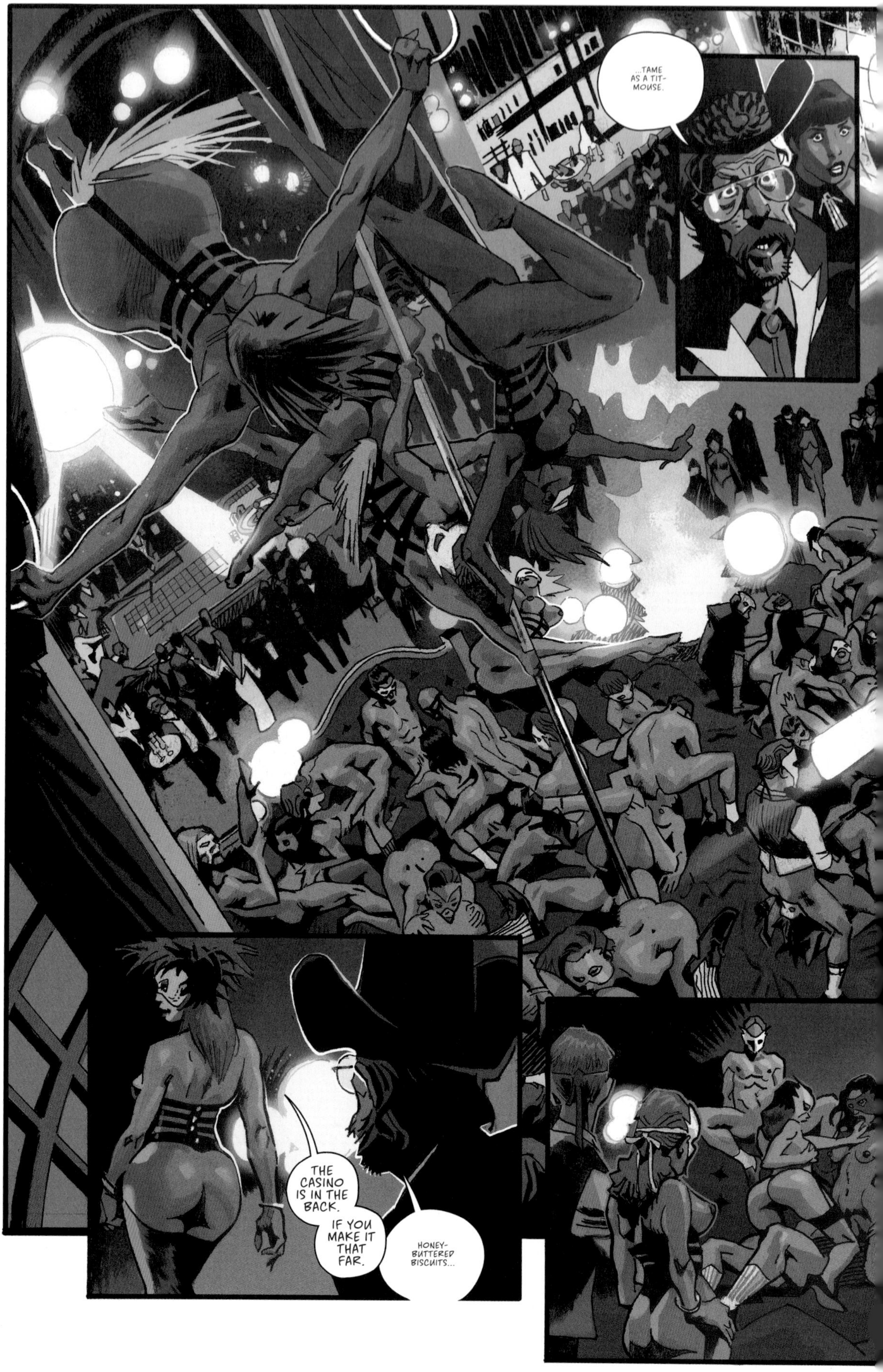
...TAME AS A TIT-MOUSE.
THE CASINO IS IN THE BACK.
IF YOU MAKE IT THAT FAR.
HONEY-BUTTERED BISCUITS...

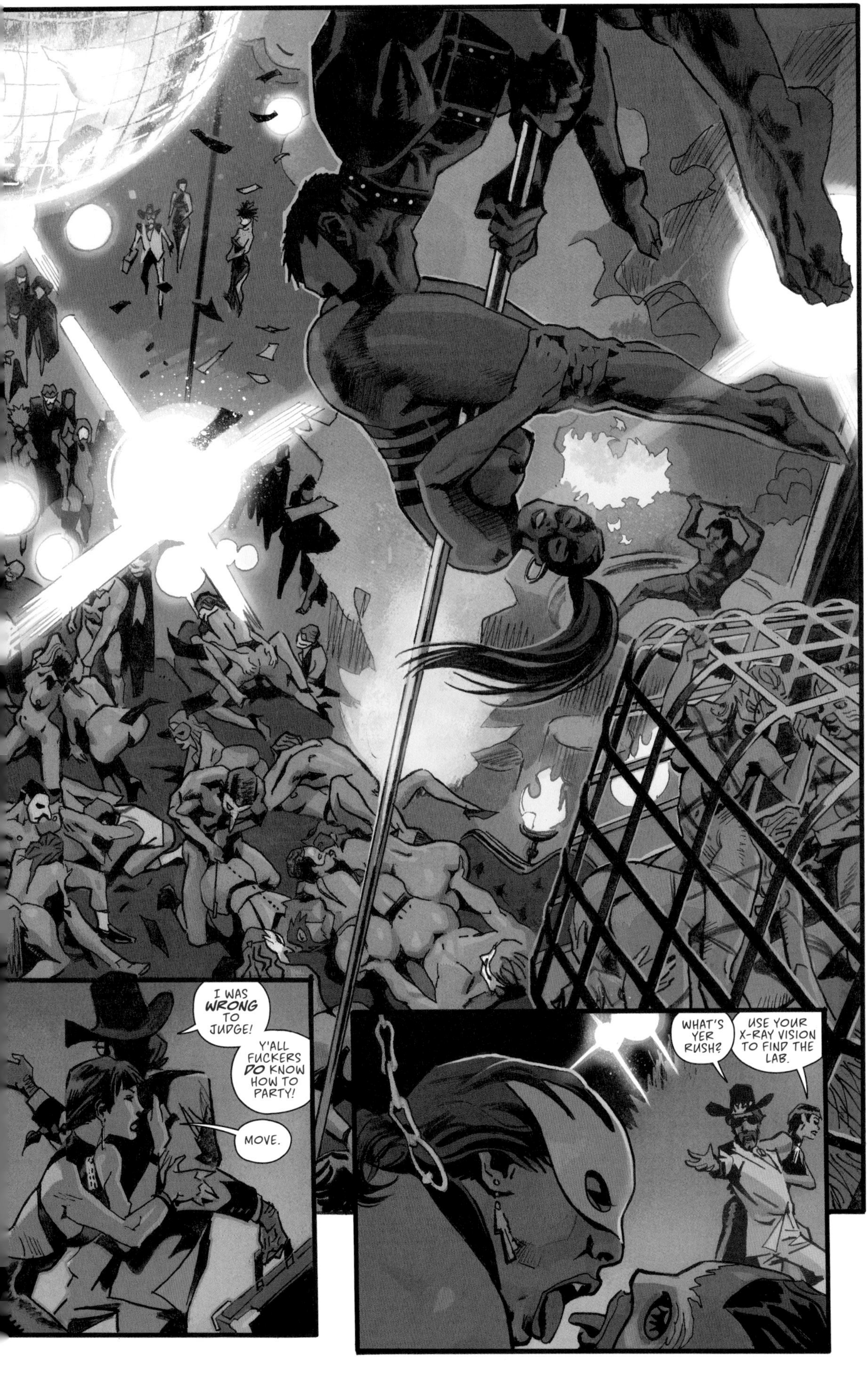
I WAS **WRONG** TO JUDGE!
Y'ALL FUCKERS **DO** KNOW HOW TO PARTY!
MOVE.
WHAT'S YER RUSH?
USE YOUR X-RAY VISION TO FIND THE LAB.

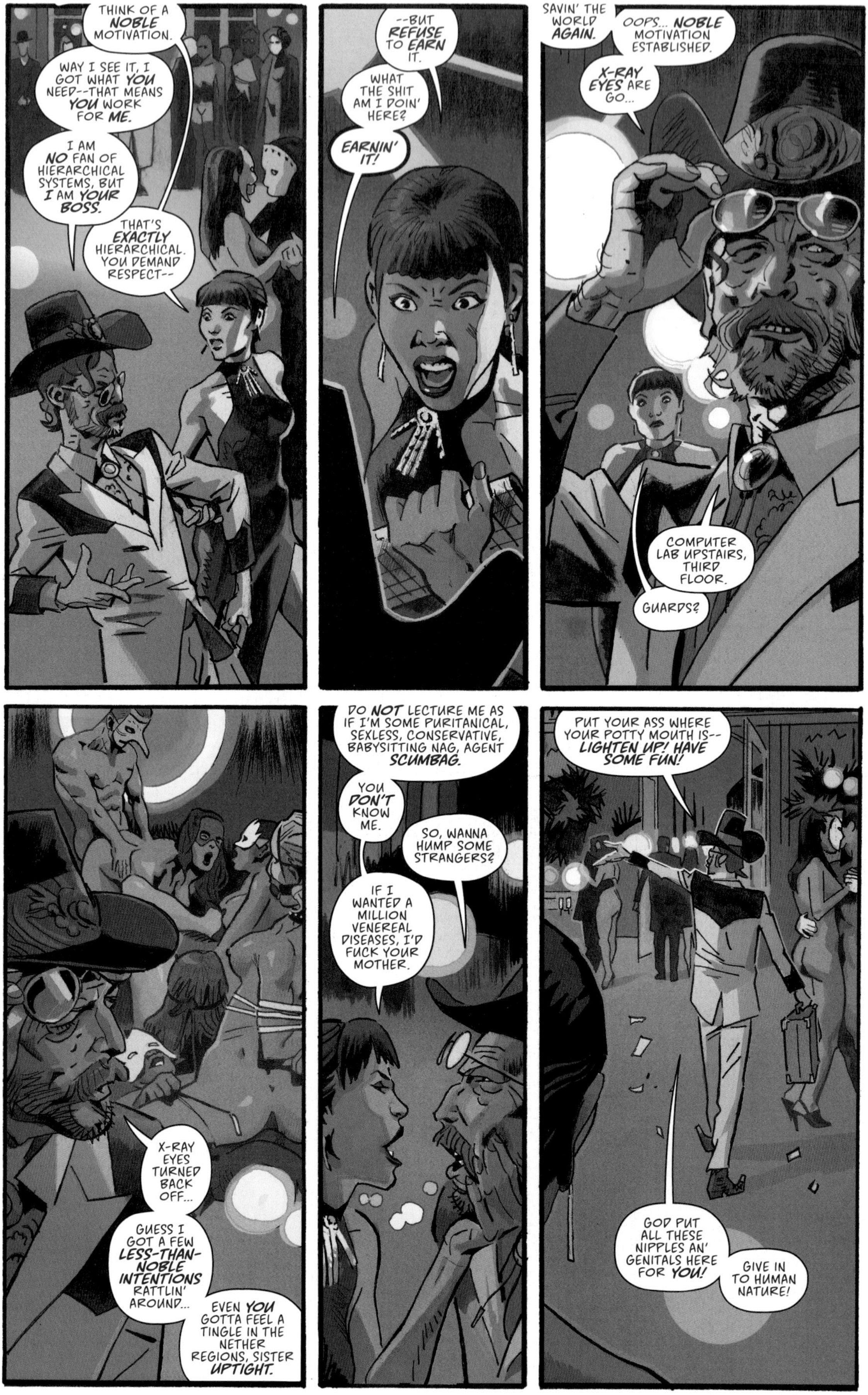
THINK OF A NOBLE MOTIVATION.
WAY I SEE IT, I GOT WHAT YOU NEED--THAT MEANS YOU WORK FOR ME.
I AM NO FAN OF HIERARCHICAL SYSTEMS, BUT I AM YOUR BOSS.
THAT'S EXACTLY HIERARCHICAL. YOU DEMAND RESPECT--
--BUT REFUSE TO EARN IT.
WHAT THE SHIT AM I DOIN' HERE?
EARNIN' IT!
SAVIN' THE WORLD AGAIN.
OOPS... NOBLE MOTIVATION ESTABLISHED.
X-RAY EYES ARE GO...
COMPUTER LAB UPSTAIRS, THIRD FLOOR.
GUARDS?
X-RAY EYES TURNED BACK OFF...
GUESS I GOT A FEW LESS-THAN-NOBLE INTENTIONS RATTLIN' AROUND...
EVEN YOU GOTTA FEEL A TINGLE IN THE NETHER REGIONS, SISTER UPTIGHT.
DO NOT LECTURE ME AS IF I'M SOME PURITANICAL, SEXLESS, CONSERVATIVE, BABYSITTING NAG, AGENT SCUMBAG.
YOU DON'T KNOW ME.
SO, WANNA HUMP SOME STRANGERS?
IF I WANTED A MILLION VENEREAL DISEASES, I'D FUCK YOUR MOTHER.
PUT YOUR ASS WHERE YOUR POTTY MOUTH IS-- LIGHTEN UP! HAVE SOME FUN!
GOD PUT ALL THESE NIPPLES AN' GENITALS HERE FOR YOU!
GIVE IN TO HUMAN NATURE!

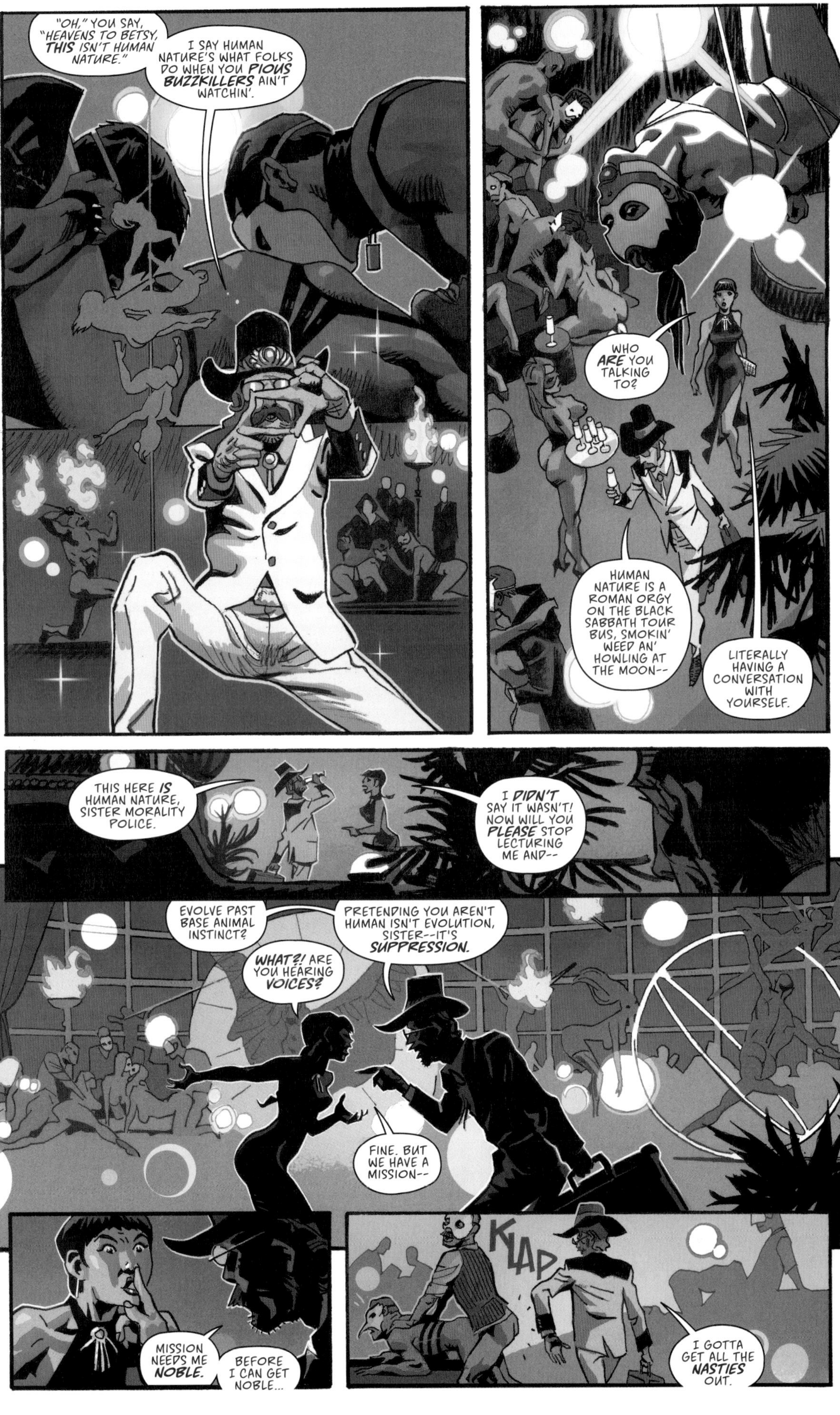
"OH," YOU SAY, "HEAVENS TO BETSY, THIS ISN'T HUMAN NATURE."
I SAY HUMAN NATURE'S WHAT FOLKS DO WHEN YOU PIOUS BUZZKILLERS AIN'T WATCHIN'.
WHO ARE YOU TALKING TO?
HUMAN NATURE IS A ROMAN ORGY ON THE BLACK SABBATH TOUR BUS, SMOKIN' WEED AN' HOWLING AT THE MOON--
LITERALLY HAVING A CONVERSATION WITH YOURSELF.
THIS HERE IS HUMAN NATURE, SISTER MORALITY POLICE.
I DIDN'T SAY IT WASN'T! NOW WILL YOU PLEASE STOP LECTURING ME AND--
EVOLVE PAST BASE ANIMAL INSTINCT?
PRETENDING YOU AREN'T HUMAN ISN'T EVOLUTION, SISTER--IT'S SUPPRESSION.
WHAT?! ARE YOU HEARING VOICES?
FINE. BUT WE HAVE A MISSION--
MISSION NEEDS ME NOBLE.
BEFORE I CAN GET NOBLE...
KLAP
I GOTTA GET ALL THE NASTIES OUT.

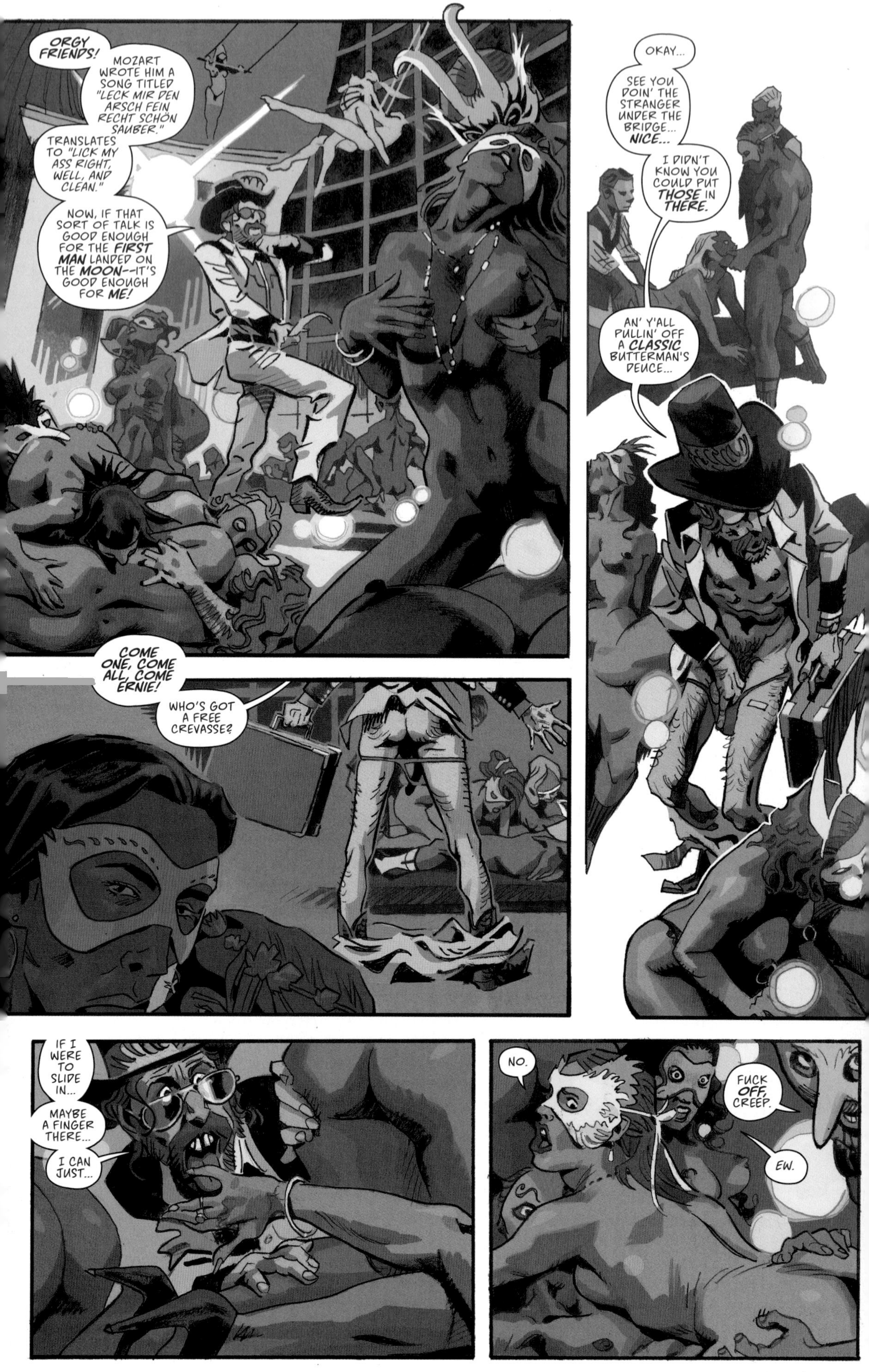

ORGY FRIENDS!
MOZART WROTE HIM A SONG TITLED "LECK MIR DEN ARSCH FEIN RECHT SCHÖN SAUBER."
TRANSLATES TO "LICK MY ASS RIGHT, WELL, AND CLEAN."
NOW, IF THAT SORT OF TALK IS GOOD ENOUGH FOR THE **FIRST MAN** LANDED ON THE **MOON**--IT'S GOOD ENOUGH FOR **ME!**
OKAY...
SEE YOU DOIN' THE STRANGER UNDER THE BRIDGE... **NICE...**
I DIDN'T KNOW YOU COULD PUT **THOSE** IN **THERE.**
AN' Y'ALL PULLIN' OFF A **CLASSIC** BUTTERMAN'S DEUCE...
COME ONE, COME ALL, COME ERNIE!
WHO'S GOT A FREE CREVASSE?
IF I WERE TO SLIDE IN...
MAYBE A FINGER THERE...
I CAN JUST...
NO.
FUCK **OFF,** CREEP.
EW.

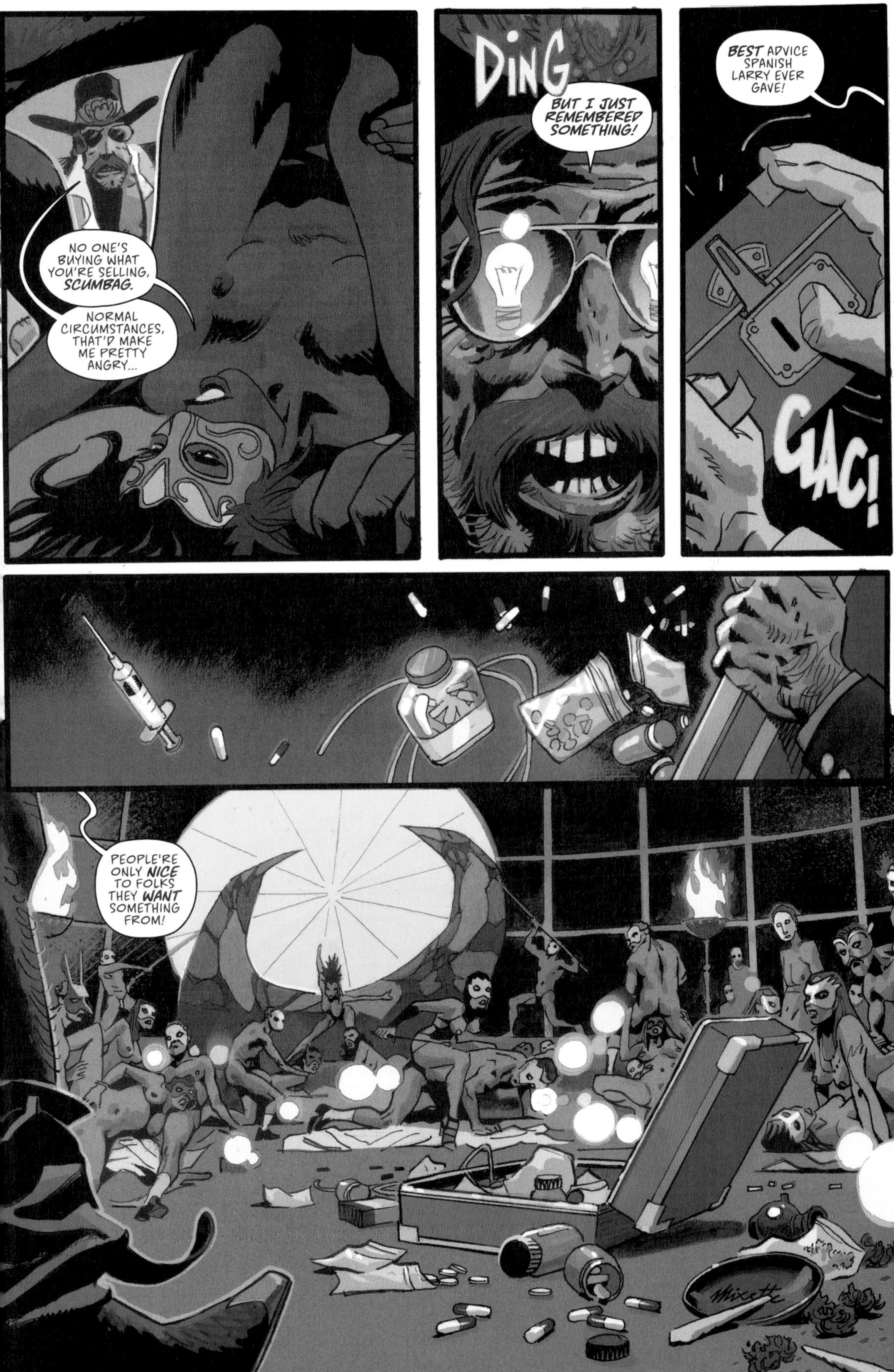
NO ONE'S BUYING WHAT YOU'RE SELLING, SCUMBAG.
NORMAL CIRCUMSTANCES, THAT'D MAKE ME PRETTY ANGRY...
DING
BUT I JUST REMEMBERED SOMETHING!
BEST ADVICE SPANISH LARRY EVER GAVE!
GLAC!
PEOPLE'RE ONLY NICE TO FOLKS THEY WANT SOMETHING FROM!

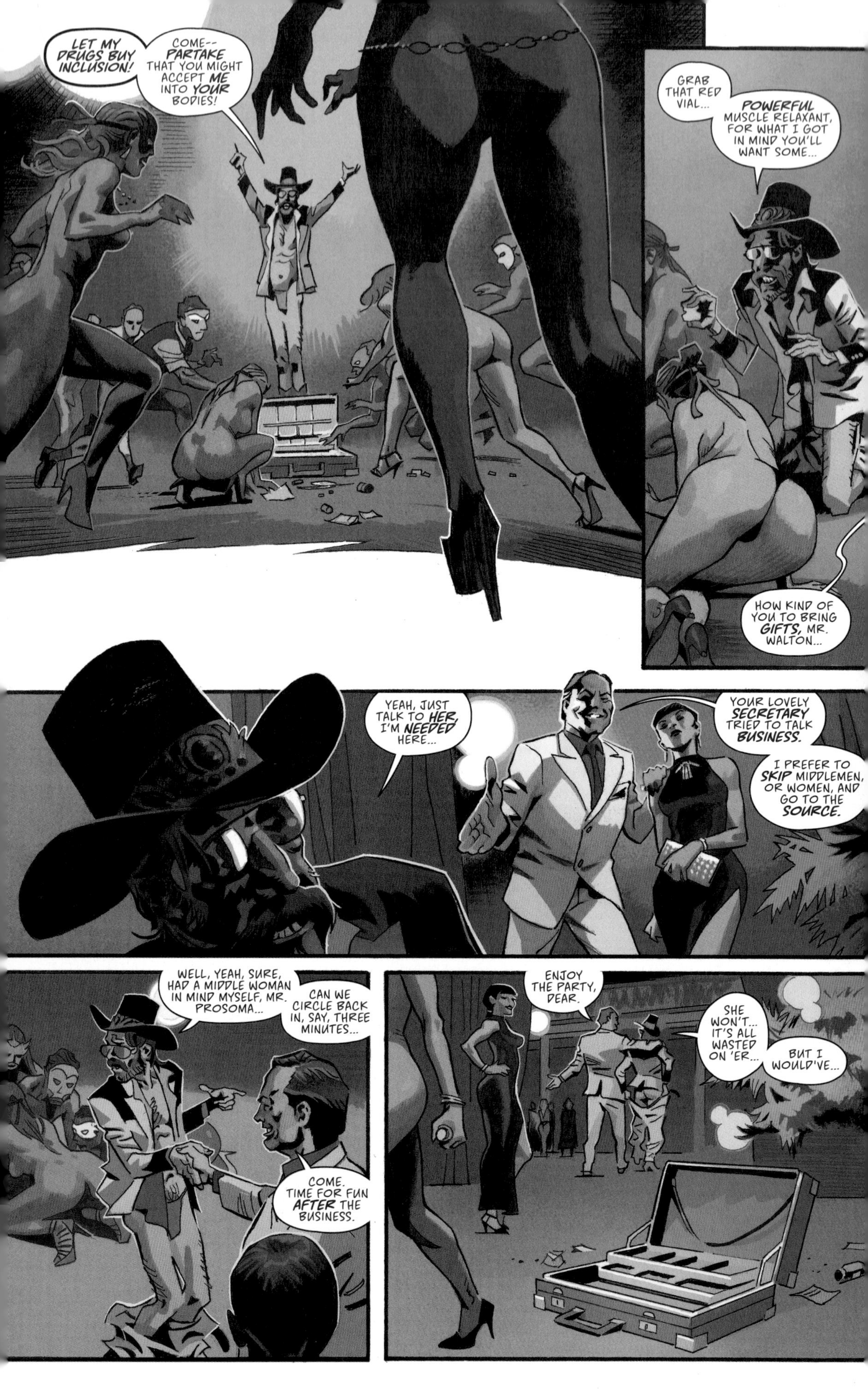
LET MY DRUGS BUY INCLUSION!
COME-- PARTAKE THAT YOU MIGHT ACCEPT ME INTO YOUR BODIES!
GRAB THAT RED VIAL...
POWERFUL MUSCLE RELAXANT, FOR WHAT I GOT IN MIND YOU'LL WANT SOME...
HOW KIND OF YOU TO BRING GIFTS, MR. WALTON...
YEAH, JUST TALK TO HER, I'M NEEDED HERE...
YOUR LOVELY SECRETARY TRIED TO TALK BUSINESS.
I PREFER TO SKIP MIDDLEMEN, OR WOMEN, AND GO TO THE SOURCE.
WELL, YEAH, SURE, HAD A MIDDLE WOMAN IN MIND MYSELF, MR. PROSOMA...
CAN WE CIRCLE BACK IN, SAY, THREE MINUTES...
COME. TIME FOR FUN AFTER THE BUSINESS.
ENJOY THE PARTY, DEAR.
SHE WON'T... IT'S ALL WASTED ON 'ER...
BUT I WOULD'VE...

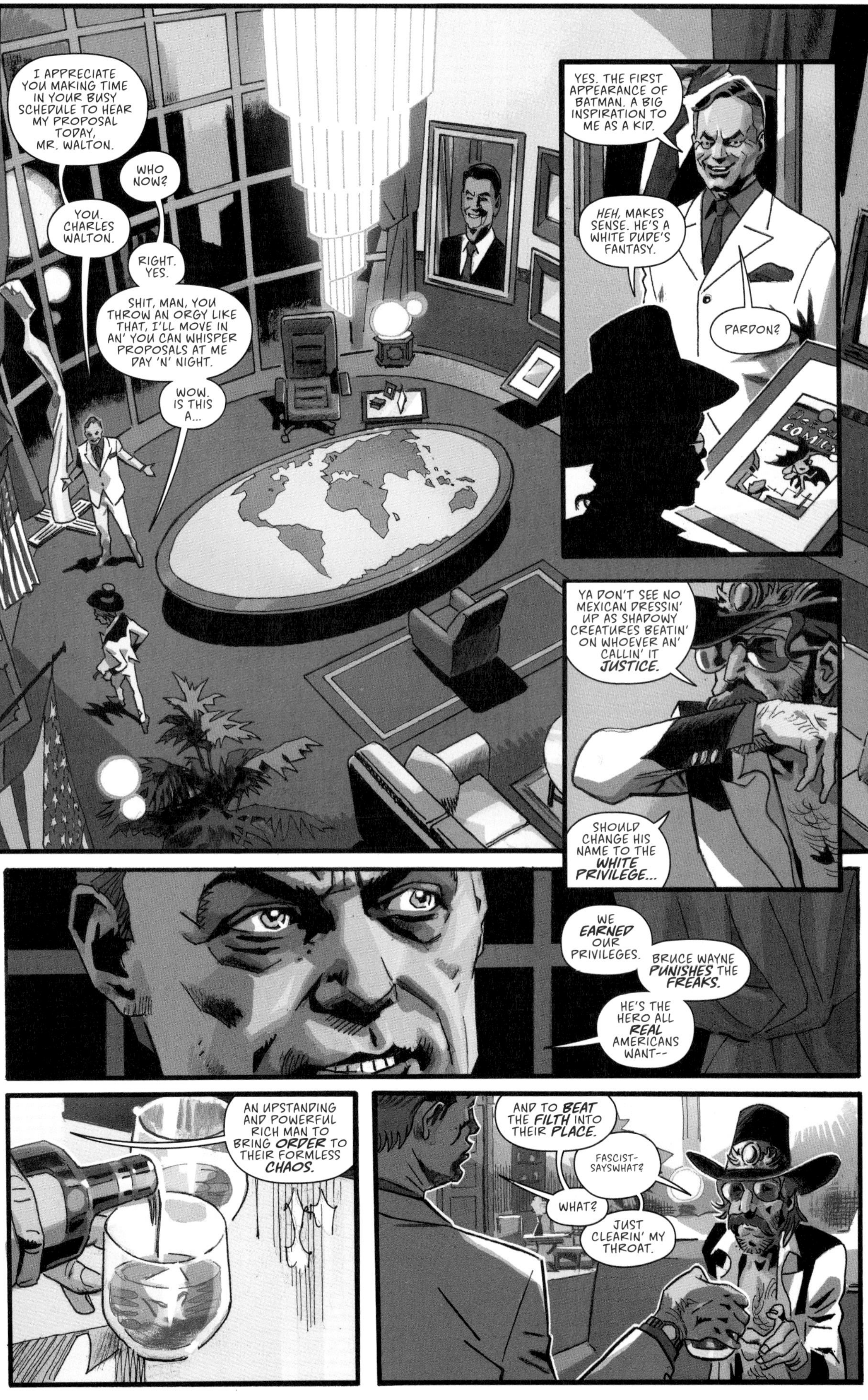
I APPRECIATE YOU MAKING TIME IN YOUR BUSY SCHEDULE TO HEAR MY PROPOSAL TODAY, MR. WALTON.
WHO NOW?
YOU. CHARLES WALTON.
RIGHT. YES.
SHIT, MAN, YOU THROW AN ORGY LIKE THAT, I'LL MOVE IN AN' YOU CAN WHISPER PROPOSALS AT ME DAY 'N' NIGHT.
WOW. IS THIS A...
YES. THE FIRST APPEARANCE OF BATMAN. A BIG INSPIRATION TO ME AS A KID.
HEH, MAKES SENSE. HE'S A WHITE DUDE'S FANTASY.
PARDON?
YA DON'T SEE NO MEXICAN DRESSIN' UP AS SHADOWY CREATURES BEATIN' ON WHOEVER AN' CALLIN' IT JUSTICE.
SHOULD CHANGE HIS NAME TO THE WHITE PRIVILEGE...
WE EARNED OUR PRIVILEGES.
BRUCE WAYNE PUNISHES THE FREAKS.
HE'S THE HERO ALL REAL AMERICANS WANT--
AN UPSTANDING AND POWERFUL RICH MAN TO BRING ORDER TO THEIR FORMLESS CHAOS.
AND TO BEAT THE FILTH INTO THEIR PLACE.
FASCIST-SAYSWHAT?
WHAT?
JUST CLEARIN' MY THROAT.

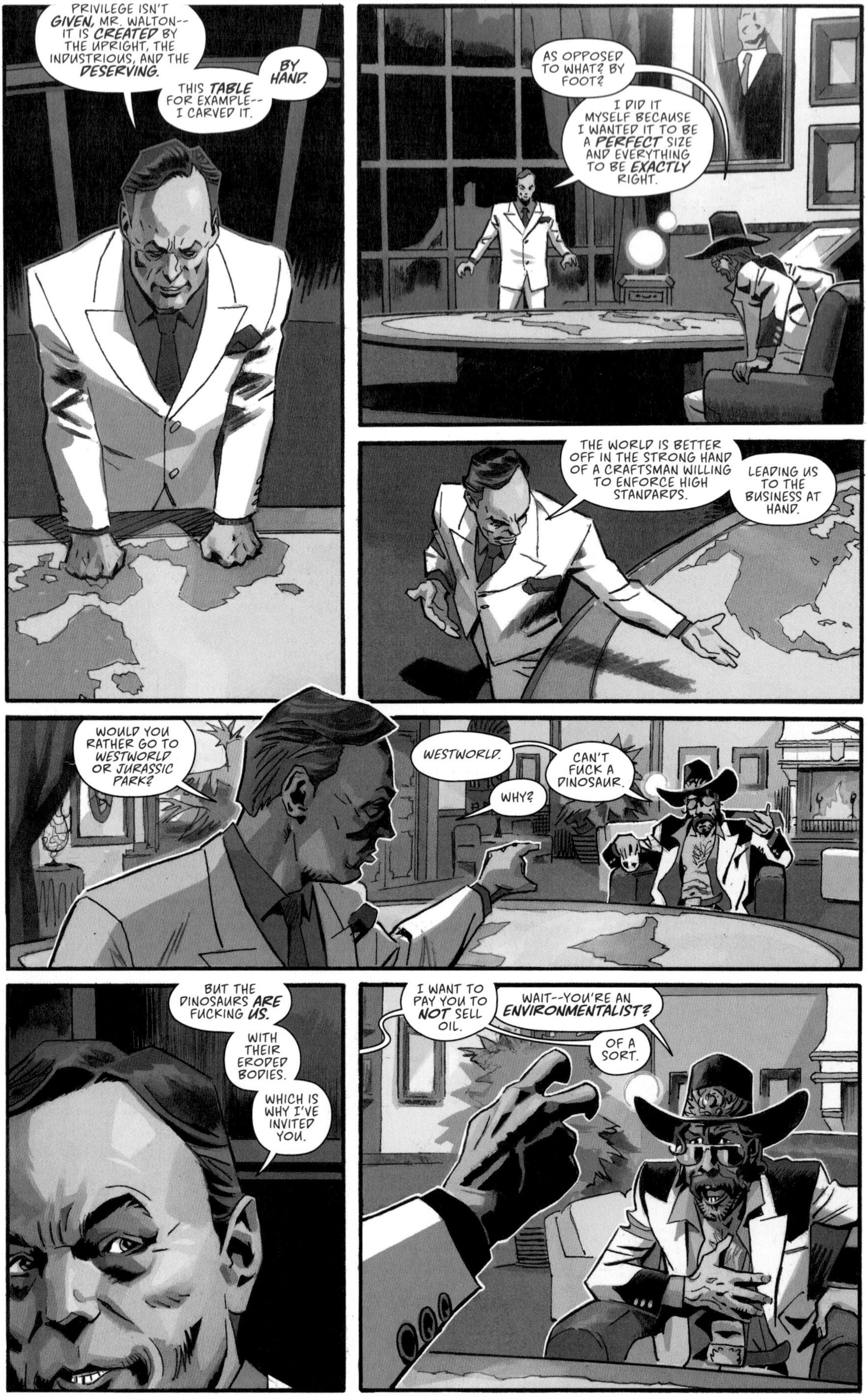
PRIVILEGE ISN'T GIVEN, MR. WALTON--IT IS CREATED BY THE UPRIGHT, THE INDUSTRIOUS, AND THE DESERVING.
THIS TABLE FOR EXAMPLE--I CARVED IT.
BY HAND.
AS OPPOSED TO WHAT? BY FOOT?
I DID IT MYSELF BECAUSE I WANTED IT TO BE A PERFECT SIZE AND EVERYTHING TO BE EXACTLY RIGHT.
THE WORLD IS BETTER OFF IN THE STRONG HAND OF A CRAFTSMAN WILLING TO ENFORCE HIGH STANDARDS.
LEADING US TO THE BUSINESS AT HAND.
WOULD YOU RATHER GO TO WESTWORLD OR JURASSIC PARK?
WESTWORLD.
WHY?
CAN'T FUCK A DINOSAUR.
BUT THE DINOSAURS ARE FUCKING US.
WITH THEIR ERODED BODIES.
WHICH IS WHY I'VE INVITED YOU.
I WANT TO PAY YOU TO NOT SELL OIL.
WAIT--YOU'RE AN ENVIRONMENTALIST?
OF A SORT.

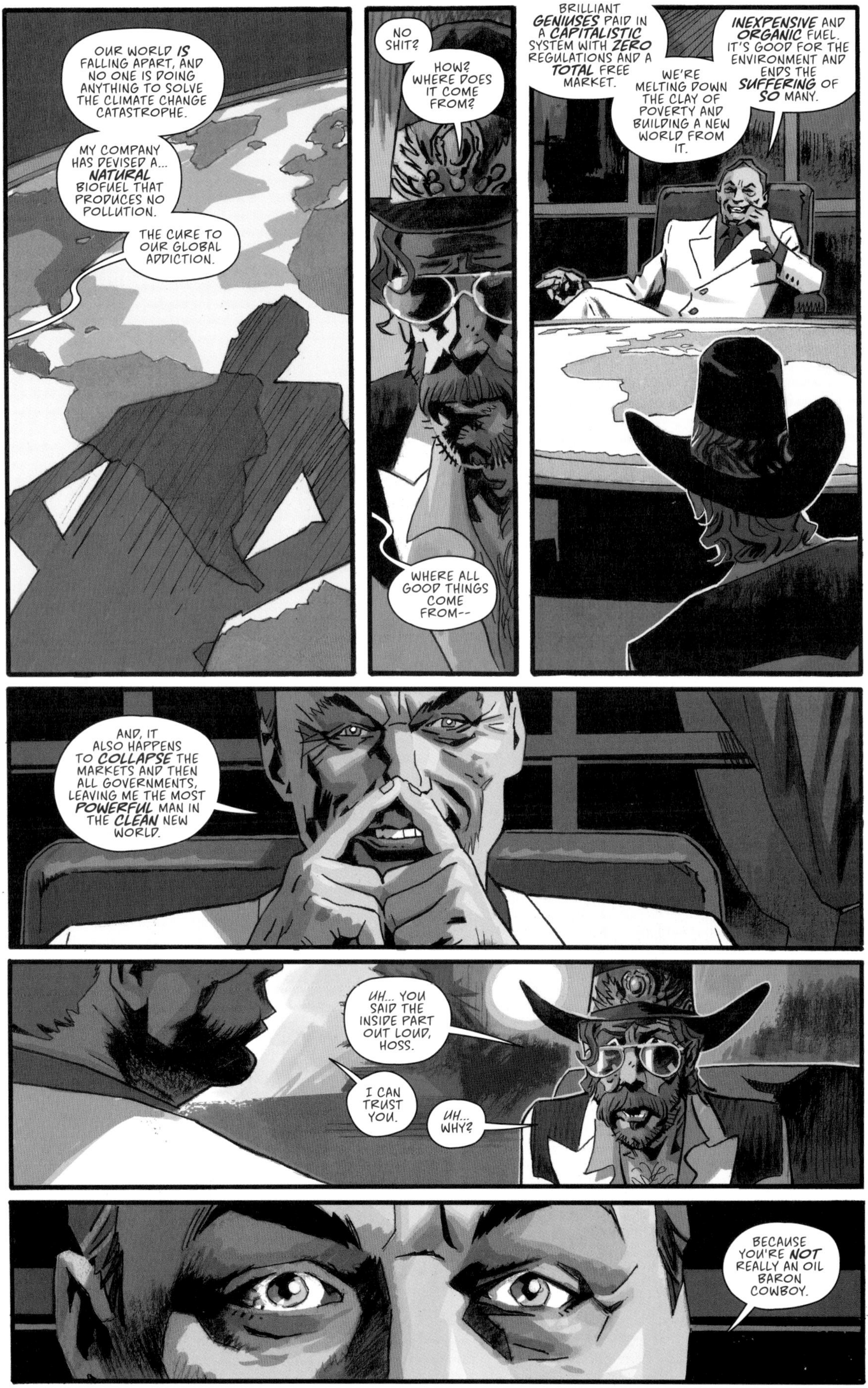
OUR WORLD IS FALLING APART, AND NO ONE IS DOING ANYTHING TO SOLVE THE CLIMATE CHANGE CATASTROPHE.
MY COMPANY HAS DEVISED A... NATURAL BIOFUEL THAT PRODUCES NO POLLUTION.
THE CURE TO OUR GLOBAL ADDICTION.
NO SHIT?
HOW? WHERE DOES IT COME FROM?
WHERE ALL GOOD THINGS COME FROM--
BRILLIANT GENIUSES PAID IN A CAPITALISTIC SYSTEM WITH ZERO REGULATIONS AND A TOTAL FREE MARKET.
INEXPENSIVE AND ORGANIC FUEL. IT'S GOOD FOR THE ENVIRONMENT AND ENDS THE SUFFERING OF SO MANY.
WE'RE MELTING DOWN THE CLAY OF POVERTY AND BUILDING A NEW WORLD FROM IT.
AND, IT ALSO HAPPENS TO COLLAPSE THE MARKETS AND THEN ALL GOVERNMENTS, LEAVING ME THE MOST POWERFUL MAN IN THE CLEAN NEW WORLD.
UH... YOU SAID THE INSIDE PART OUT LOUD, HOSS.
I CAN TRUST YOU.
UH... WHY?
BECAUSE YOU'RE NOT REALLY AN OIL BARON COWBOY.

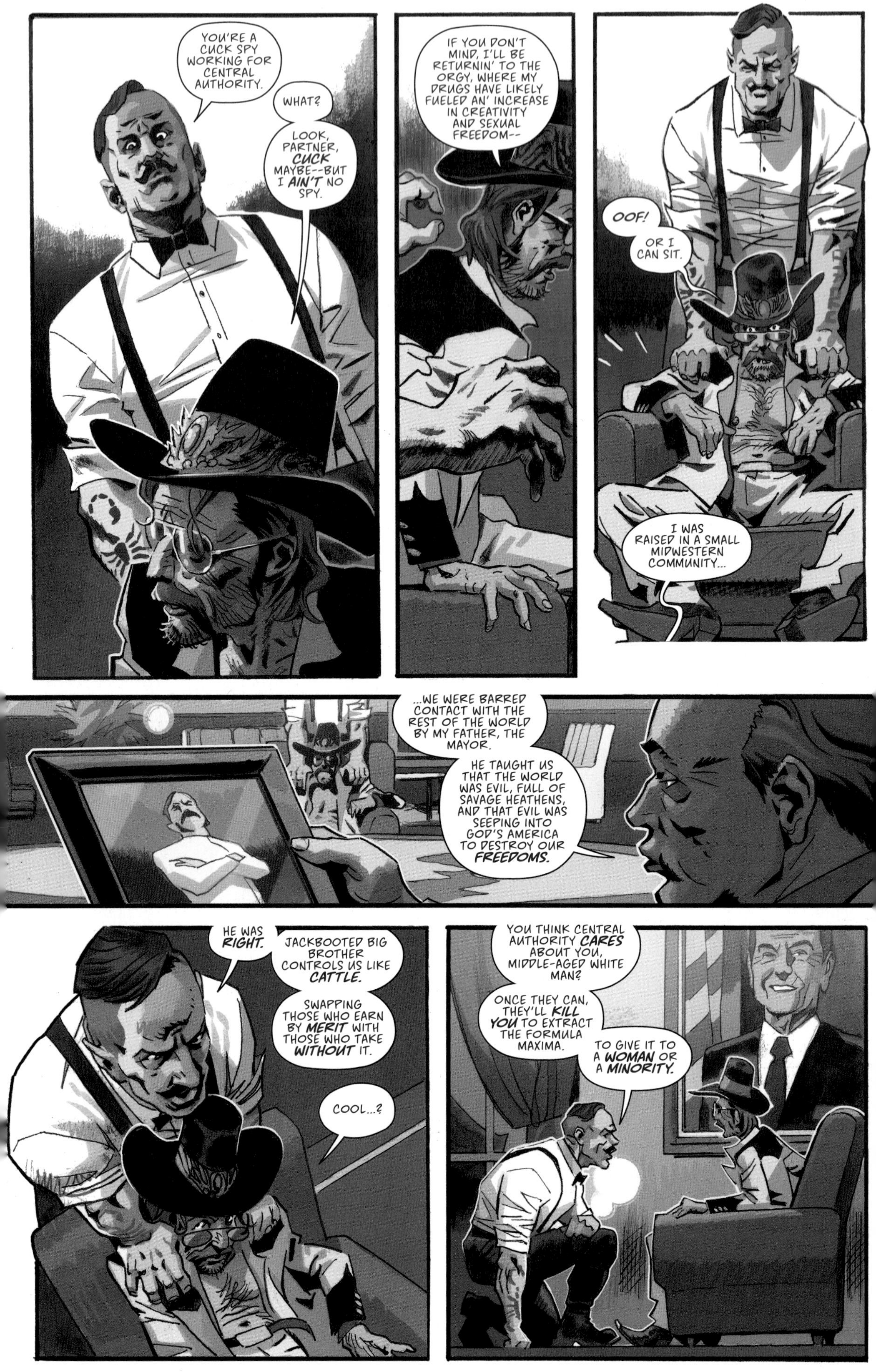
YOU'RE A CUCK SPY WORKING FOR CENTRAL AUTHORITY.
WHAT?
LOOK, PARTNER, CUCK MAYBE--BUT I AIN'T NO SPY.
IF YOU DON'T MIND, I'LL BE RETURNIN' TO THE ORGY, WHERE MY DRUGS HAVE LIKELY FUELED AN' INCREASE IN CREATIVITY AND SEXUAL FREEDOM--
OOF!
OR I CAN SIT.
I WAS RAISED IN A SMALL MIDWESTERN COMMUNITY...
...WE WERE BARRED CONTACT WITH THE REST OF THE WORLD BY MY FATHER, THE MAYOR.
HE TAUGHT US THAT THE WORLD WAS EVIL, FULL OF SAVAGE HEATHENS, AND THAT EVIL WAS SEEPING INTO GOD'S AMERICA TO DESTROY OUR FREEDOMS.
HE WAS RIGHT.
JACKBOOTED BIG BROTHER CONTROLS US LIKE CATTLE.
SWAPPING THOSE WHO EARN BY MERIT WITH THOSE WHO TAKE WITHOUT IT.
COOL...?
YOU THINK CENTRAL AUTHORITY CARES ABOUT YOU, MIDDLE-AGED WHITE MAN?
ONCE THEY CAN, THEY'LL KILL YOU TO EXTRACT THE FORMULA MAXIMA.
TO GIVE IT TO A WOMAN OR A MINORITY.

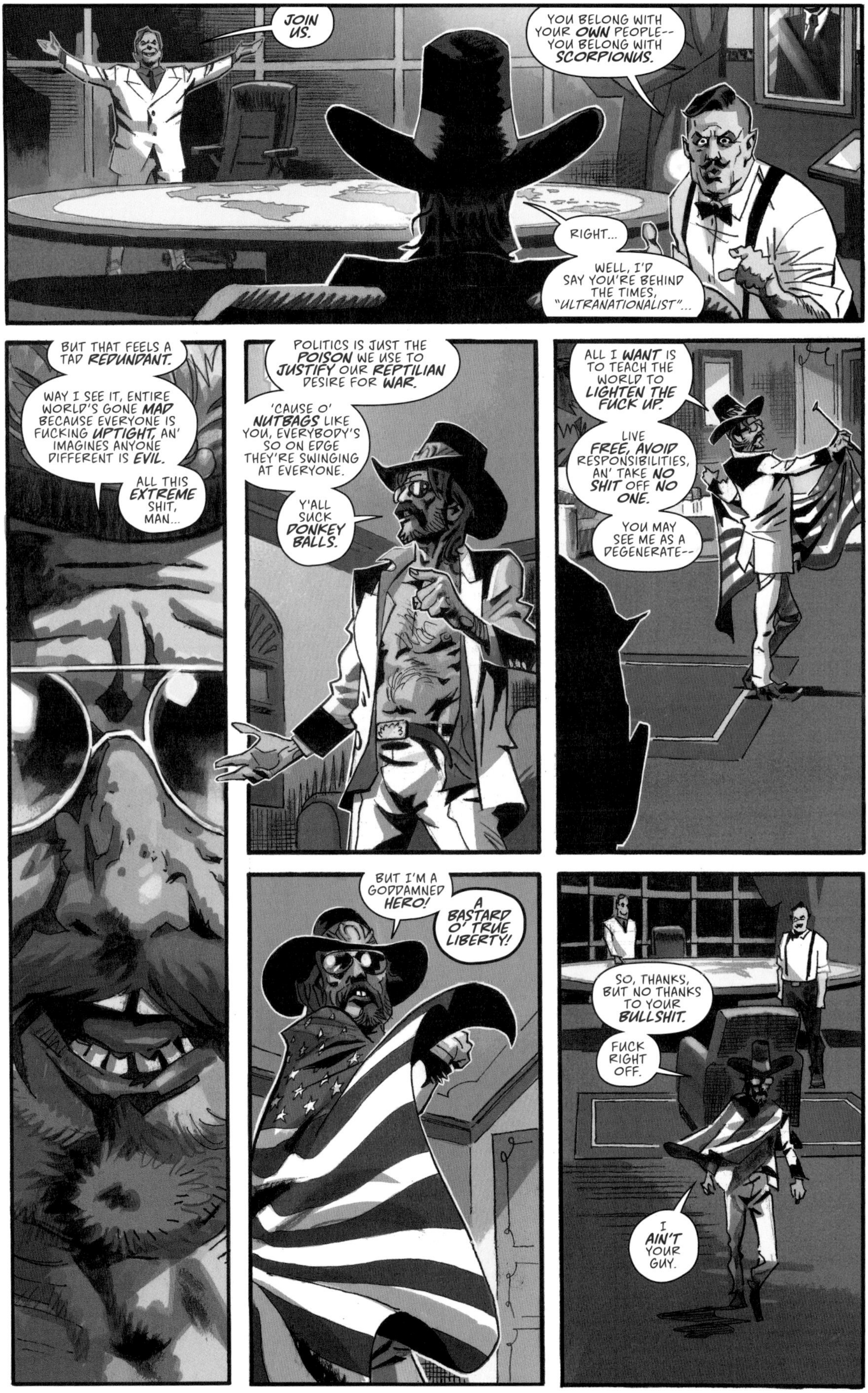
JOIN US.
YOU BELONG WITH YOUR OWN PEOPLE-- YOU BELONG WITH SCORPIONUS.
RIGHT...
WELL, I'D SAY YOU'RE BEHIND THE TIMES, "ULTRANATIONALIST"...
BUT THAT FEELS A TAD REDUNDANT.
WAY I SEE IT, ENTIRE WORLD'S GONE MAD BECAUSE EVERYONE IS FUCKING UPTIGHT, AN' IMAGINES ANYONE DIFFERENT IS EVIL.
ALL THIS EXTREME SHIT, MAN...
POLITICS IS JUST THE POISON WE USE TO JUSTIFY OUR REPTILIAN DESIRE FOR WAR.
'CAUSE O' NUTBAGS LIKE YOU, EVERYBODY'S SO ON EDGE THEY'RE SWINGING AT EVERYONE.
Y'ALL SUCK DONKEY BALLS.
ALL I WANT IS TO TEACH THE WORLD TO LIGHTEN THE FUCK UP.
LIVE FREE, AVOID RESPONSIBILITIES, AN' TAKE NO SHIT OFF NO ONE.
YOU MAY SEE ME AS A DEGENERATE--
BUT I'M A GODDAMNED HERO!
A BASTARD O' TRUE LIBERTY!
SO, THANKS, BUT NO THANKS TO YOUR BULLSHIT.
FUCK RIGHT OFF.
I AIN'T YOUR GUY.

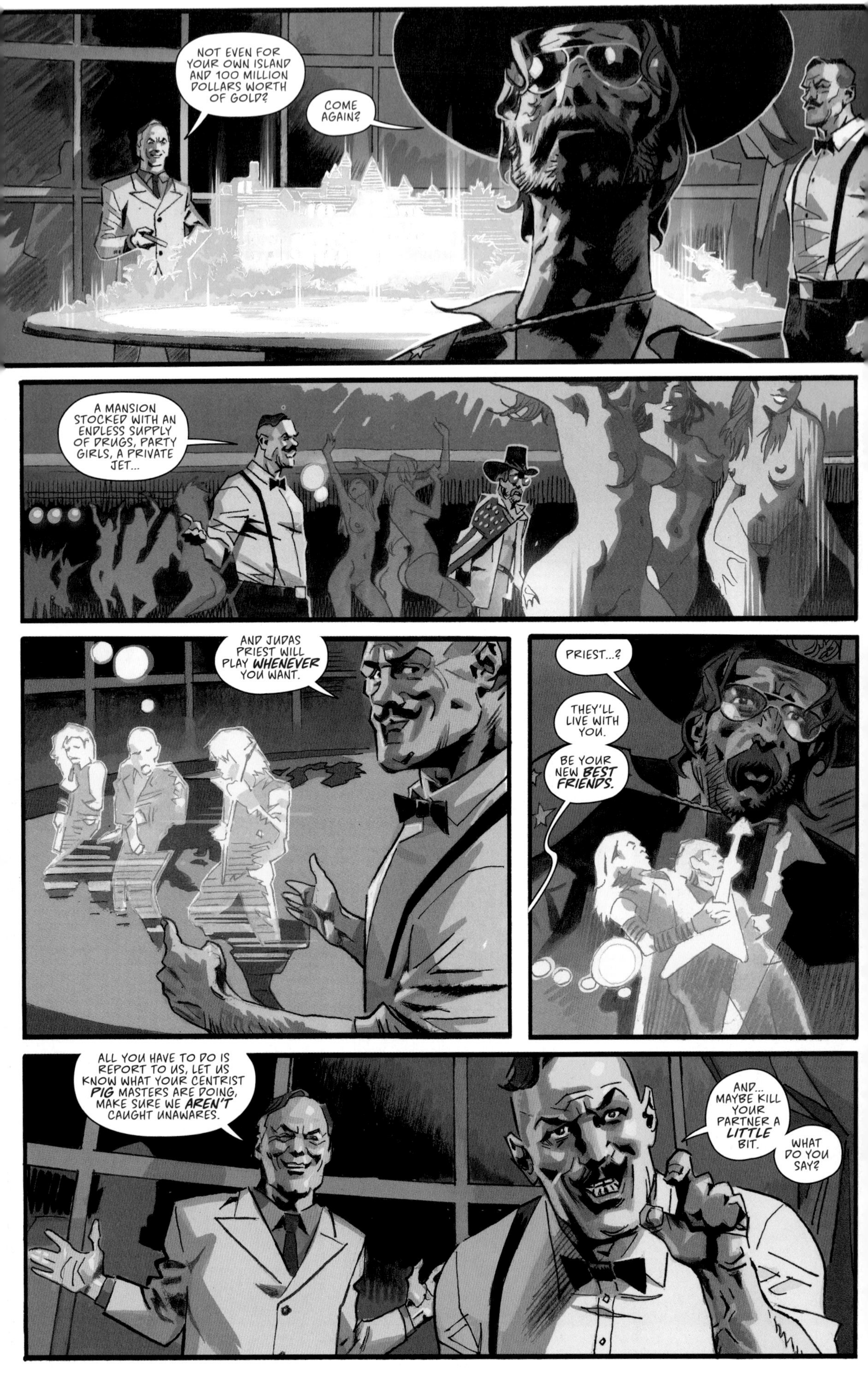
NOT EVEN FOR YOUR OWN ISLAND AND 100 MILLION DOLLARS WORTH OF GOLD?
COME AGAIN?
A MANSION STOCKED WITH AN ENDLESS SUPPLY OF DRUGS, PARTY GIRLS, A PRIVATE JET...
AND JUDAS PRIEST WILL PLAY WHENEVER YOU WANT.
PRIEST...?
THEY'LL LIVE WITH YOU.
BE YOUR NEW BEST FRIENDS.
ALL YOU HAVE TO DO IS REPORT TO US, LET US KNOW WHAT YOUR CENTRIST PIG MASTERS ARE DOING, MAKE SURE WE AREN'T CAUGHT UNAWARES.
AND... MAYBE KILL YOUR PARTNER A LITTLE BIT.
WHAT DO YOU SAY?

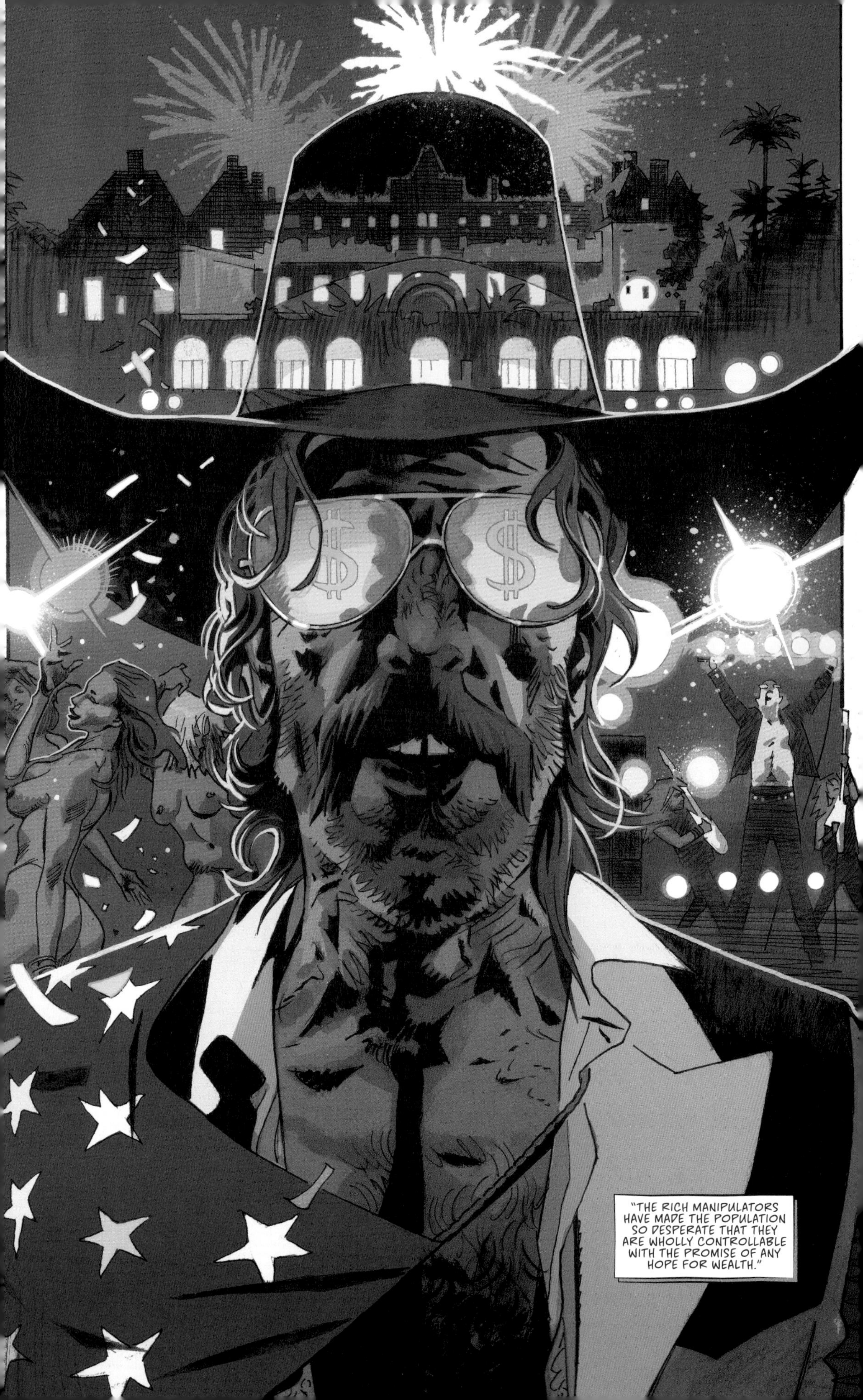
"THE RICH MANIPULATORS HAVE MADE THE POPULATION SO DESPERATE THAT THEY ARE WHOLLY CONTROLLABLE WITH THE PROMISE OF ANY HOPE FOR WEALTH."

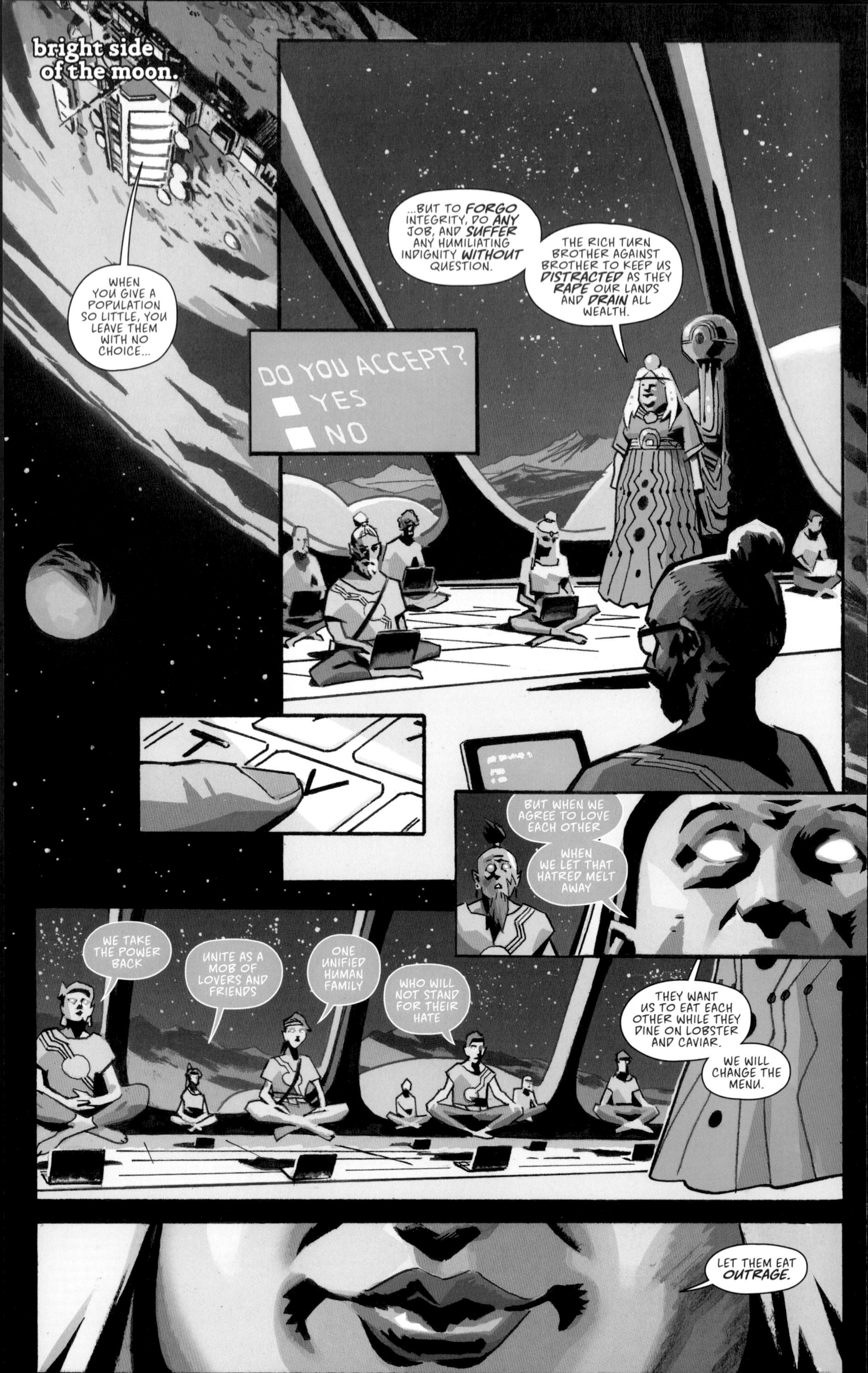
bright side of the moon.
WHEN YOU GIVE A POPULATION SO LITTLE, YOU LEAVE THEM WITH NO CHOICE...
...BUT TO FORGO INTEGRITY, DO ANY JOB, AND SUFFER ANY HUMILIATING INDIGNITY WITHOUT QUESTION.
THE RICH TURN BROTHER AGAINST BROTHER TO KEEP US DISTRACTED AS THEY RAPE OUR LANDS AND DRAIN ALL WEALTH.
DO YOU ACCEPT?
YES
NO
BUT WHEN WE AGREE TO LOVE EACH OTHER
WHEN WE LET THAT HATRED MELT AWAY
WE TAKE THE POWER BACK
UNITE AS A MOB OF LOVERS AND FRIENDS
ONE UNIFIED HUMAN FAMILY
WHO WILL NOT STAND FOR THEIR HATE
THEY WANT US TO EAT EACH OTHER WHILE THEY DINE ON LOBSTER AND CAVIAR.
WE WILL CHANGE THE MENU.
LET THEM EAT OUTRAGE.

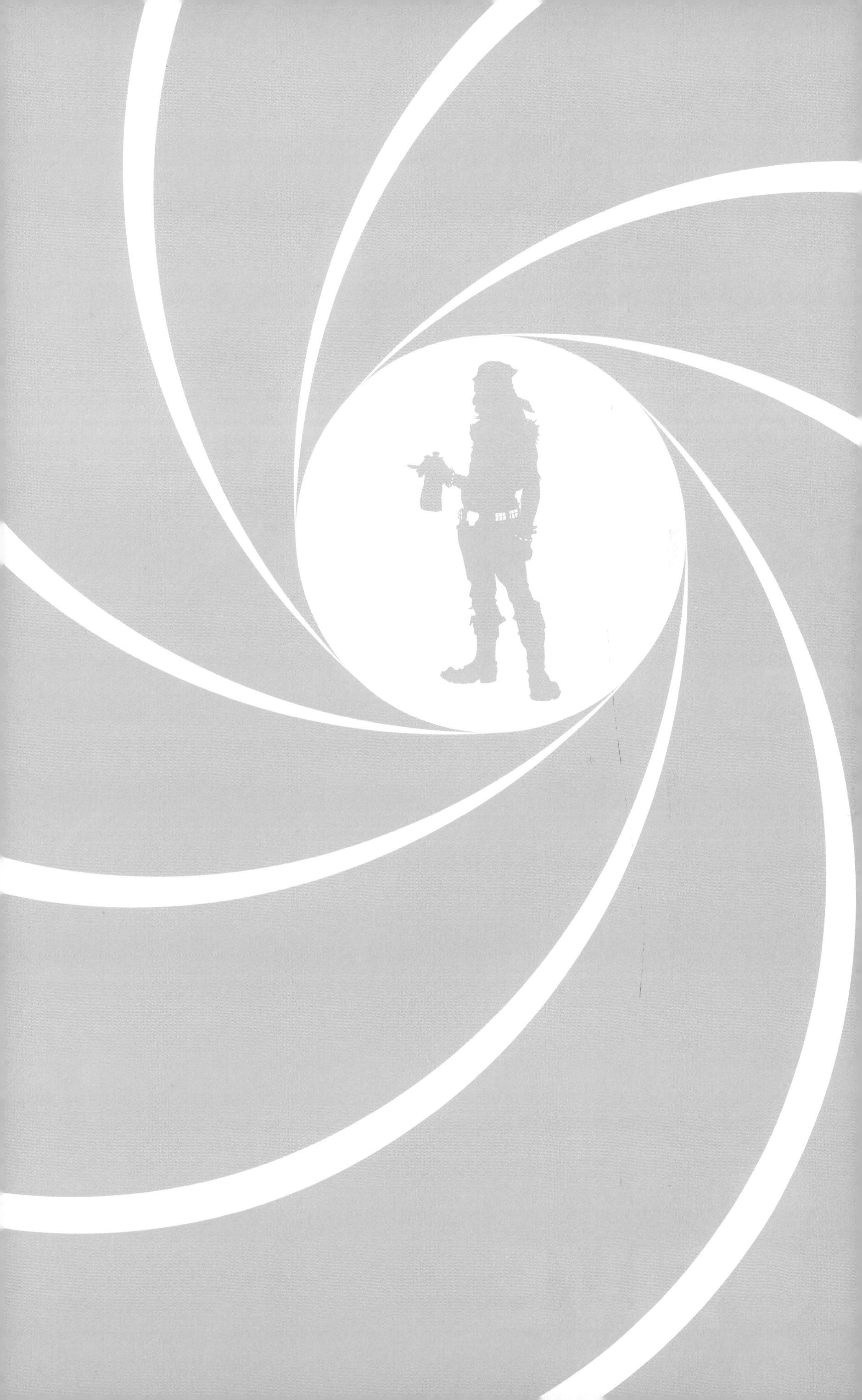

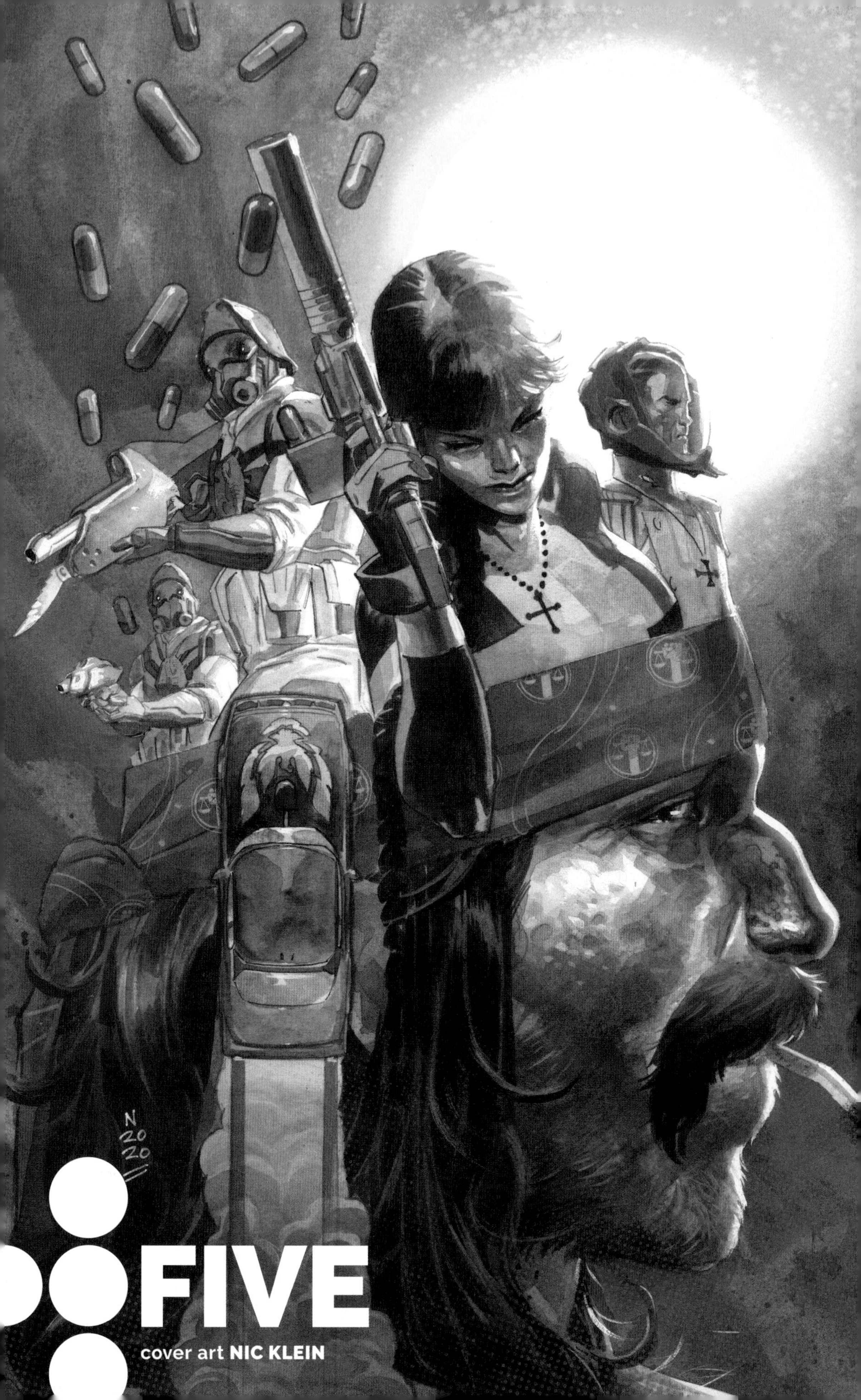

FIVE

cover art NIC KLEIN

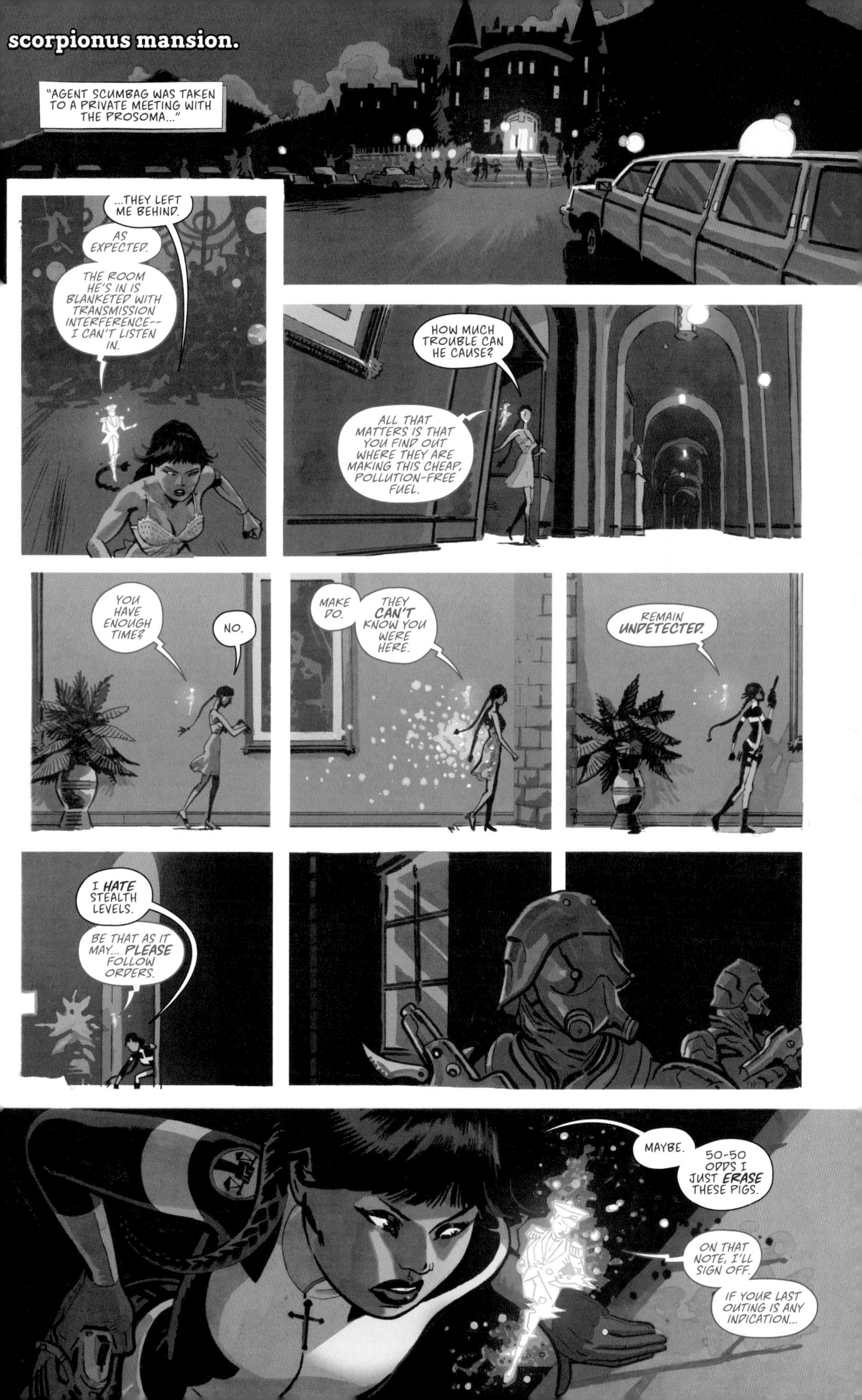
scorpionus mansion.
"AGENT SCUMBAG WAS TAKEN TO A PRIVATE MEETING WITH THE PROSOMA..."
...THEY LEFT ME BEHIND.
AS EXPECTED.
THE ROOM HE'S IN IS BLANKETED WITH TRANSMISSION INTERFERENCE-- I CAN'T LISTEN IN.
HOW MUCH TROUBLE CAN HE CAUSE?
ALL THAT MATTERS IS THAT YOU FIND OUT WHERE THEY ARE MAKING THIS CHEAP, POLLUTION-FREE FUEL.
YOU HAVE ENOUGH TIME?
NO.
MAKE DO.
THEY CAN'T KNOW YOU WERE HERE.
REMAIN UNDETECTED.
I HATE STEALTH LEVELS.
BE THAT AS IT MAY... PLEASE FOLLOW ORDERS.
MAYBE.
50-50 ODDS I JUST ERASE THESE PIGS.
ON THAT NOTE, I'LL SIGN OFF.
IF YOUR LAST OUTING IS ANY INDICATION...

"...I MAY NEED PLAUSIBLE DENIABILITY."

PT

FFTSH

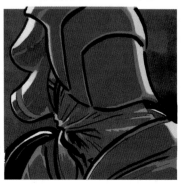

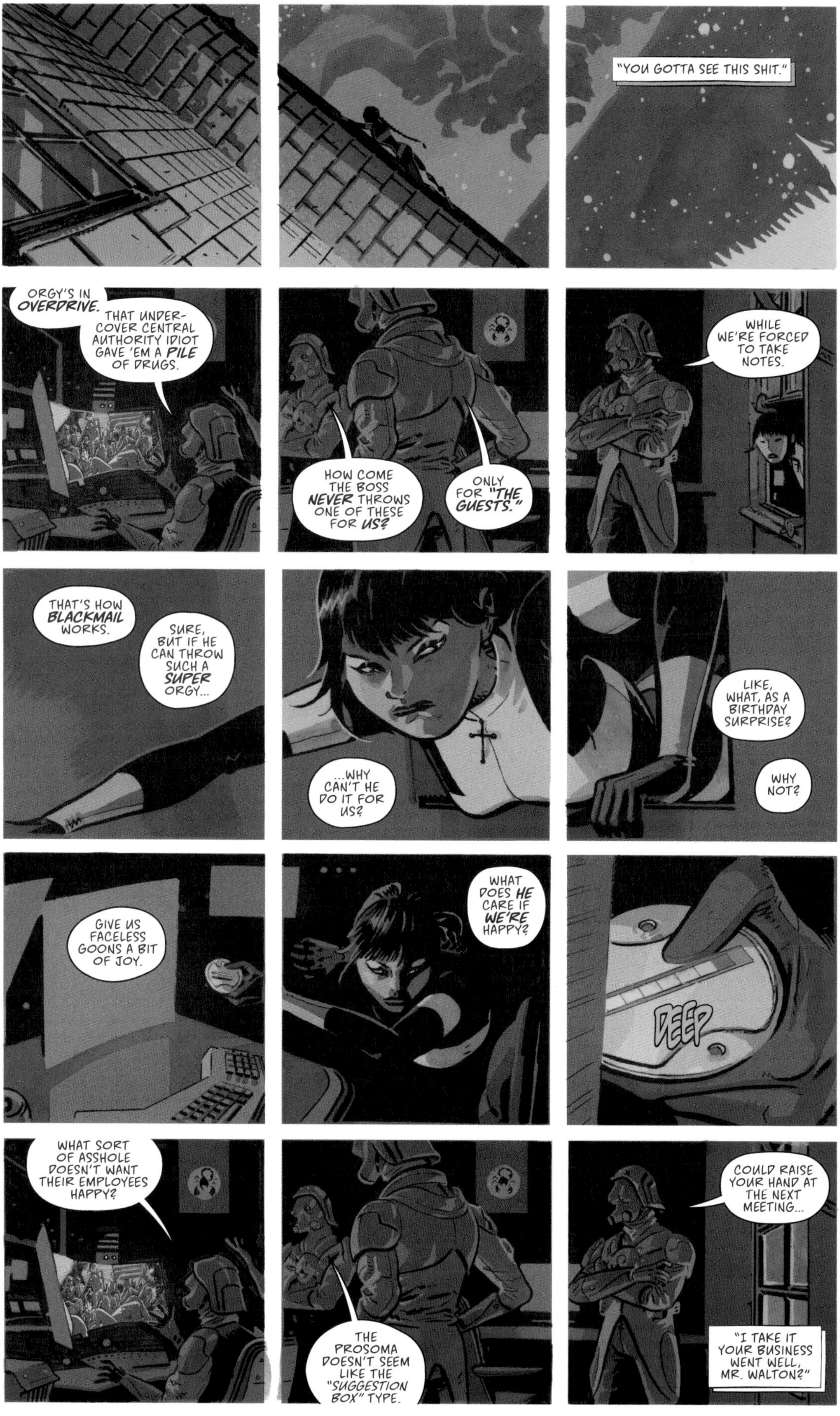
"YOU GOTTA SEE THIS SHIT."
ORGY'S IN OVERDRIVE.
THAT UNDER-COVER CENTRAL AUTHORITY IDIOT GAVE 'EM A PILE OF DRUGS.
HOW COME THE BOSS NEVER THROWS ONE OF THESE FOR US?
ONLY FOR "THE GUESTS."
WHILE WE'RE FORCED TO TAKE NOTES.
THAT'S HOW BLACKMAIL WORKS.
SURE, BUT IF HE CAN THROW SUCH A SUPER ORGY...
...WHY CAN'T HE DO IT FOR US?
LIKE, WHAT, AS A BIRTHDAY SURPRISE?
WHY NOT?
GIVE US FACELESS GOONS A BIT OF JOY.
WHAT DOES HE CARE IF WE'RE HAPPY?
DEEP
WHAT SORT OF ASSHOLE DOESN'T WANT THEIR EMPLOYEES HAPPY?
THE PROSOMA DOESN'T SEEM LIKE THE "SUGGESTION BOX" TYPE.
COULD RAISE YOUR HAND AT THE NEXT MEETING...
"I TAKE IT YOUR BUSINESS WENT WELL, MR. WALTON?"

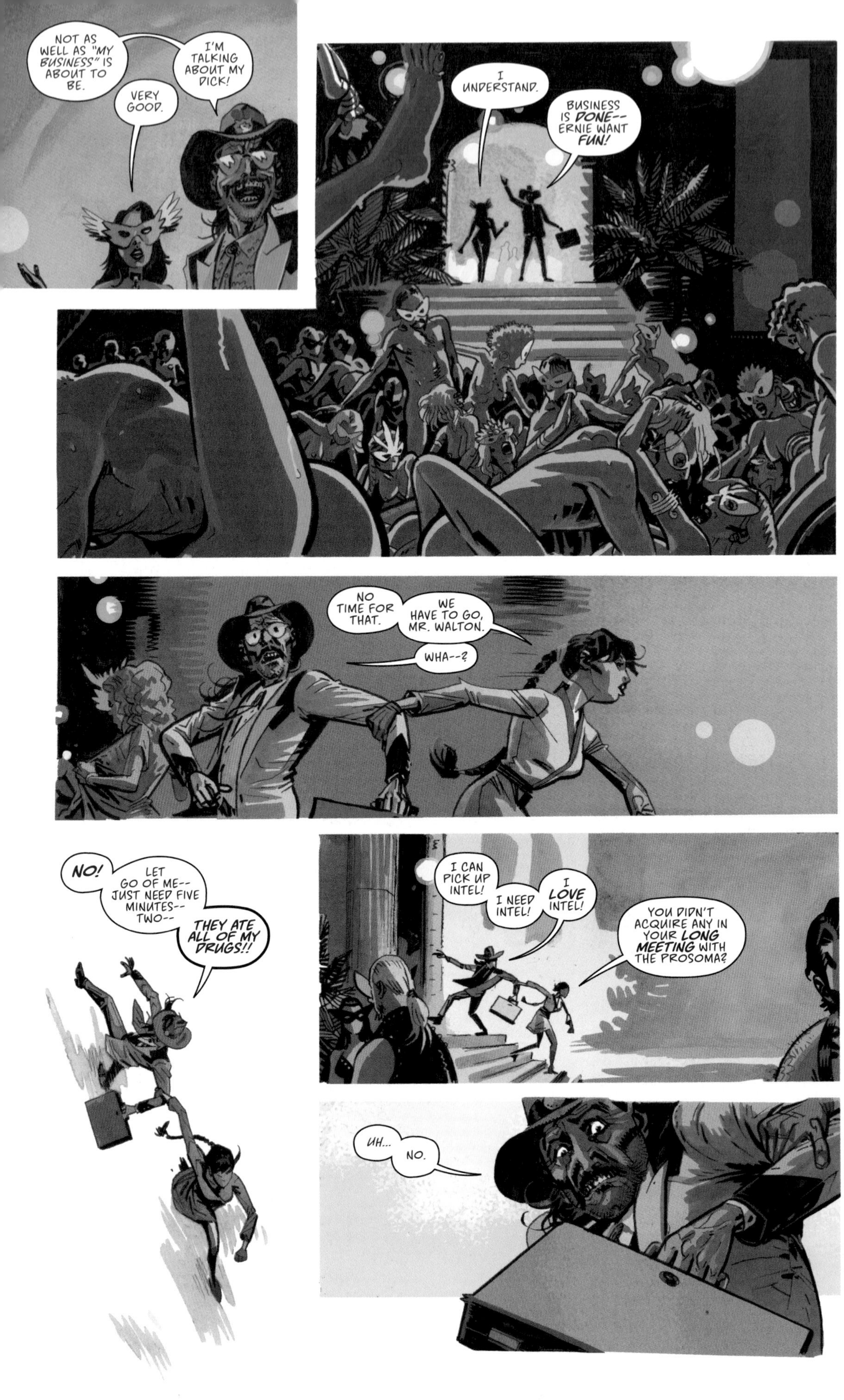
NOT AS WELL AS "MY BUSINESS" IS ABOUT TO BE.
I'M TALKING ABOUT MY DICK!
VERY GOOD.
I UNDERSTAND.
BUSINESS IS DONE-- ERNIE WANT FUN!
NO TIME FOR THAT.
WE HAVE TO GO, MR. WALTON.
WHA--?
NO!
LET GO OF ME-- JUST NEED FIVE MINUTES-- TWO--
THEY ATE ALL OF MY DRUGS!!
I CAN PICK UP INTEL!
I NEED INTEL!
I LOVE INTEL!
YOU DIDN'T ACQUIRE ANY IN YOUR LONG MEETING WITH THE PROSOMA?
UH... NO.

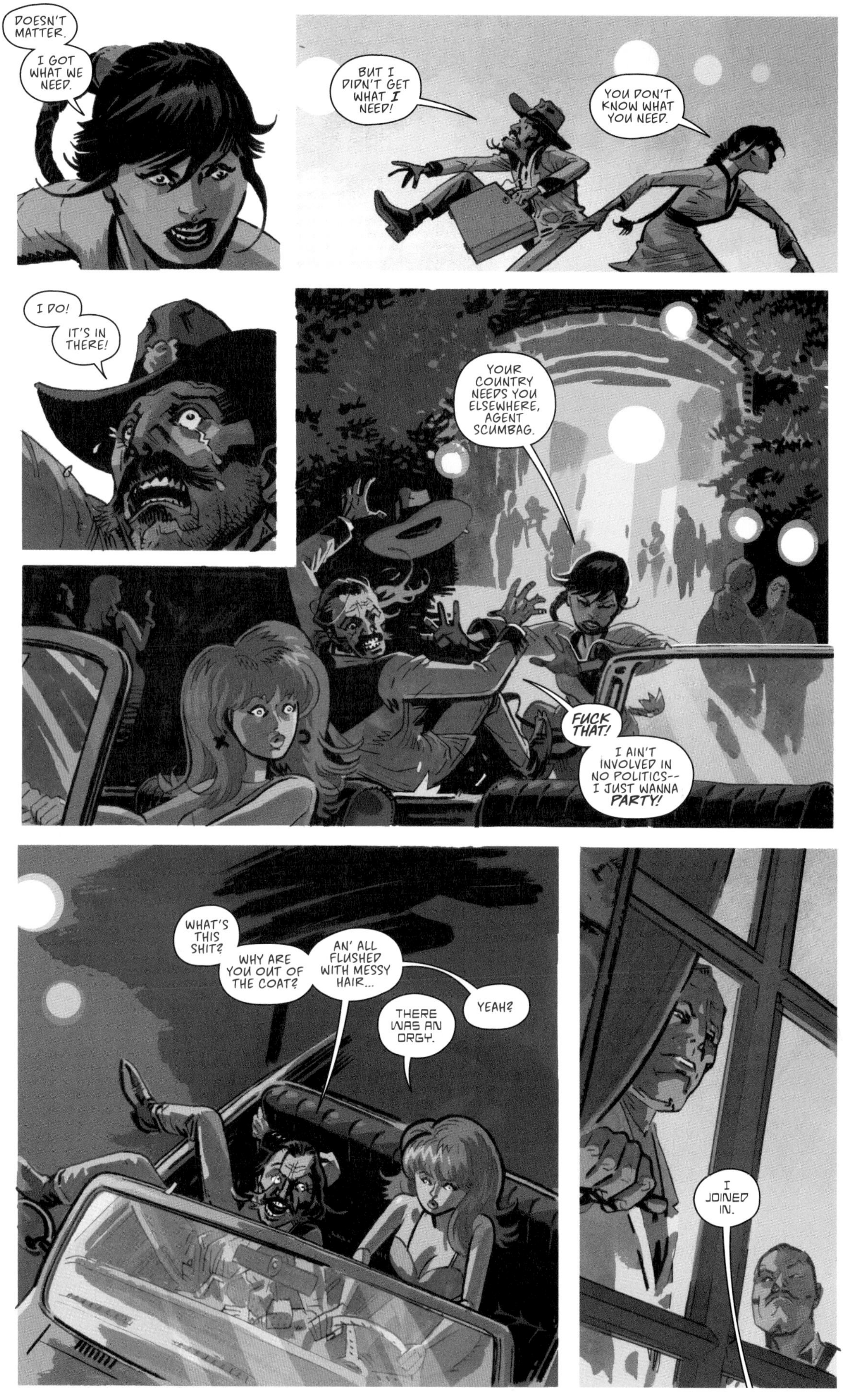
DOESN'T MATTER.
I GOT WHAT WE NEED.
BUT I DIDN'T GET WHAT I NEED!
YOU DON'T KNOW WHAT YOU NEED.
I DO!
IT'S IN THERE!
YOUR COUNTRY NEEDS YOU ELSEWHERE, AGENT SCUMBAG.
FUCK THAT!
I AIN'T INVOLVED IN NO POLITICS-- I JUST WANNA PARTY!
WHAT'S THIS SHIT?
WHY ARE YOU OUT OF THE COAT?
AN' ALL FLUSHED WITH MESSY HAIR...
YEAH?
THERE WAS AN ORGY.
I JOINED IN.

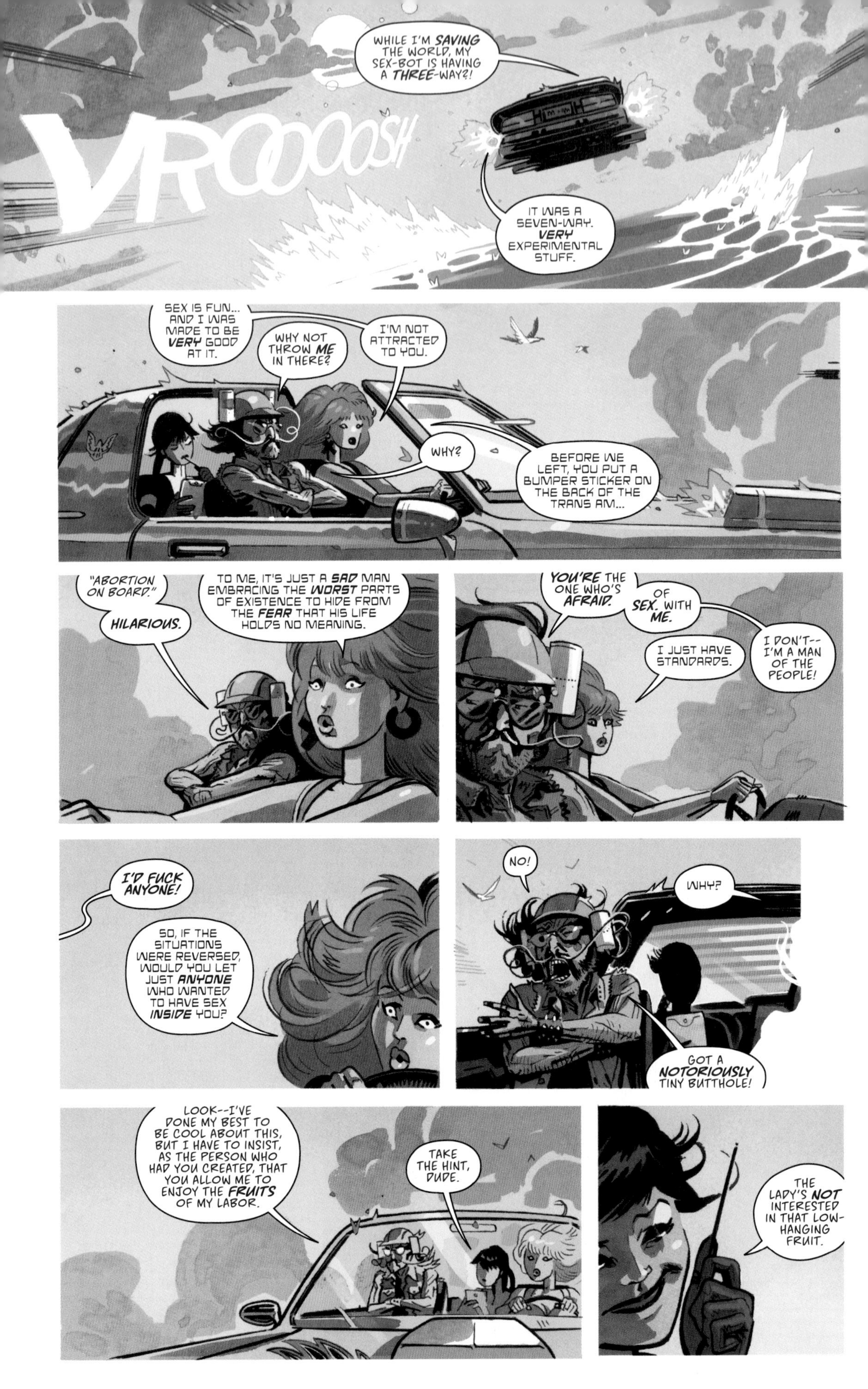
WHILE I'M SAVING THE WORLD, MY SEX-BOT IS HAVING A THREE-WAY?!
VRROOOOSH
IT WAS A SEVEN-WAY. VERY EXPERIMENTAL STUFF.
SEX IS FUN... AND I WAS MADE TO BE VERY GOOD AT IT.
WHY NOT THROW ME IN THERE?
I'M NOT ATTRACTED TO YOU.
WHY?
BEFORE WE LEFT, YOU PUT A BUMPER STICKER ON THE BACK OF THE TRANS AM...
"ABORTION ON BOARD."
HILARIOUS.
TO ME, IT'S JUST A SAD MAN EMBRACING THE WORST PARTS OF EXISTENCE TO HIDE FROM THE FEAR THAT HIS LIFE HOLDS NO MEANING.
YOU'RE THE ONE WHO'S AFRAID.
OF SEX. WITH ME.
I JUST HAVE STANDARDS.
I DON'T-- I'M A MAN OF THE PEOPLE!
I'D FUCK ANYONE!
SO, IF THE SITUATIONS WERE REVERSED, WOULD YOU LET JUST ANYONE WHO WANTED TO HAVE SEX INSIDE YOU?
NO!
WHY?
GOT A NOTORIOUSLY TINY BUTTHOLE!
LOOK--I'VE DONE MY BEST TO BE COOL ABOUT THIS, BUT I HAVE TO INSIST, AS THE PERSON WHO HAD YOU CREATED, THAT YOU ALLOW ME TO ENJOY THE FRUITS OF MY LABOR.
TAKE THE HINT, DUDE.
THE LADY'S NOT INTERESTED IN THAT LOW-HANGING FRUIT.

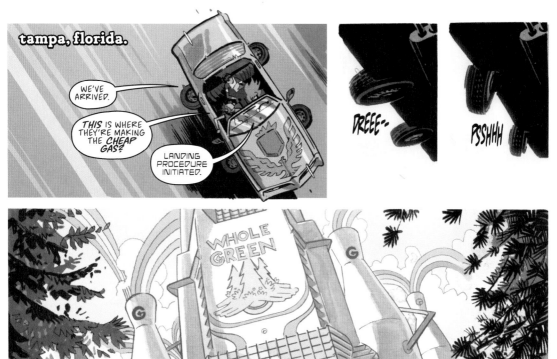

tampa, florida.

WE'VE ARRIVED.

THIS IS WHERE THEY'RE MAKING THE *CHEAP GAS?*

LANDING PROCEDURE INITIATED.

DREEE--

PSSHHH

WE DON'T KNOW WHAT TO EXPECT INSIDE, BUT EXPECT SECURITY TO BE VERY TIGHT.

TIME IS SHORT.

WHY THE BRIEFCASE? YOU GAVE ALL YOUR DRUGS AWAY.

MAKES ME LOOK BUSINESS-LIKE.

WHATEVER.

FIND OUT A WAY TO GET INSIDE.

WHAT'S WITH THE LINE OUT HERE?

THEY'RE HIRING, PAYING 20 DOLLARS AN HOUR WITH FULL HEALTH BENEFITS.

C'MON. GONNA WALK YOU RIGHT IN.

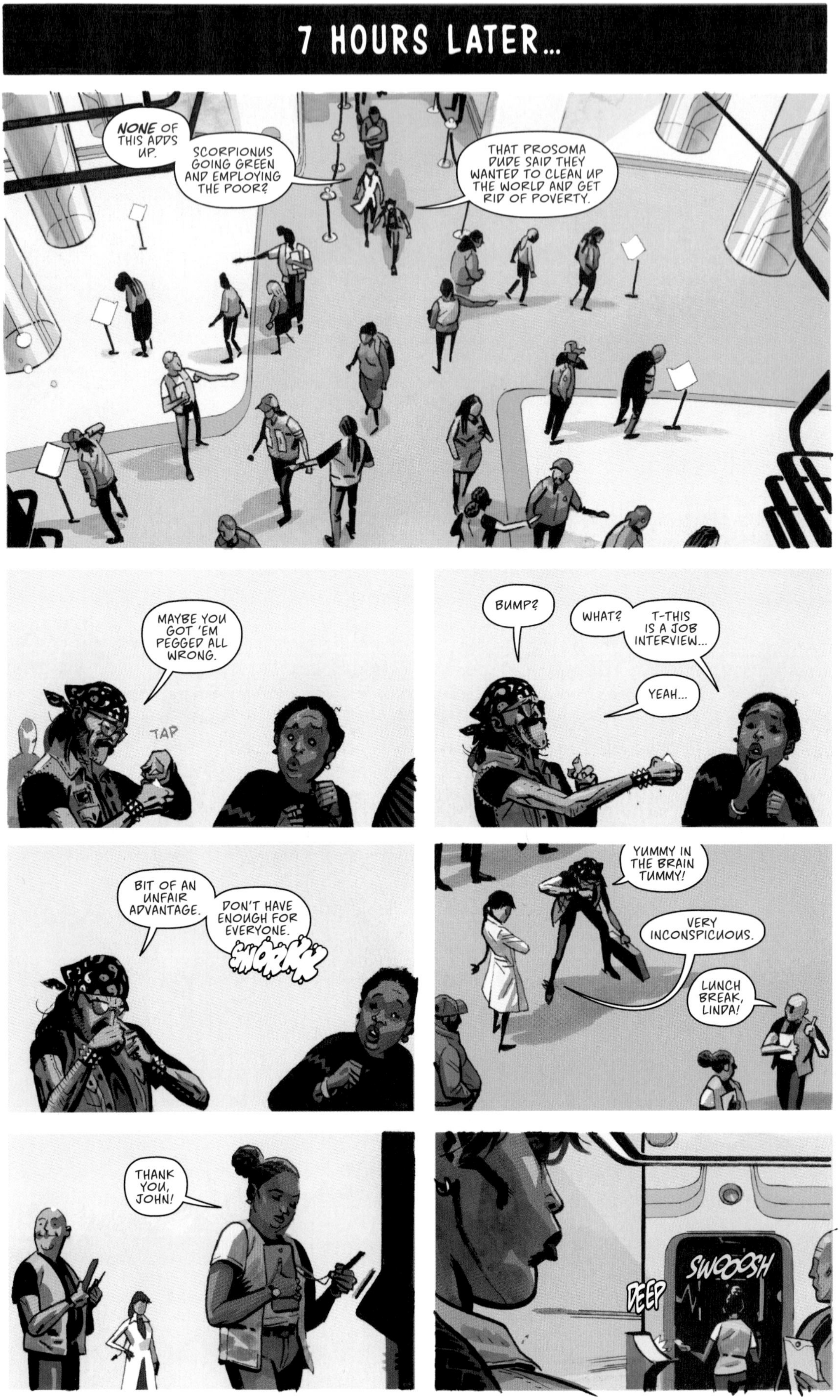
7 HOURS LATER...
NONE OF THIS ADDS UP.
SCORPIONUS GOING GREEN AND EMPLOYING THE POOR?
THAT PROSOMA DUDE SAID THEY WANTED TO CLEAN UP THE WORLD AND GET RID OF POVERTY.
MAYBE YOU GOT 'EM PEGGED ALL WRONG.
TAP
BUMP?
WHAT?
T-THIS IS A JOB INTERVIEW...
YEAH...
BIT OF AN UNFAIR ADVANTAGE.
DON'T HAVE ENOUGH FOR EVERYONE.
SNORK
YUMMY IN THE BRAIN TUMMY!
VERY INCONSPICUOUS.
LUNCH BREAK, LINDA!
THANK YOU, JOHN!
SWOOOSH
BEEP

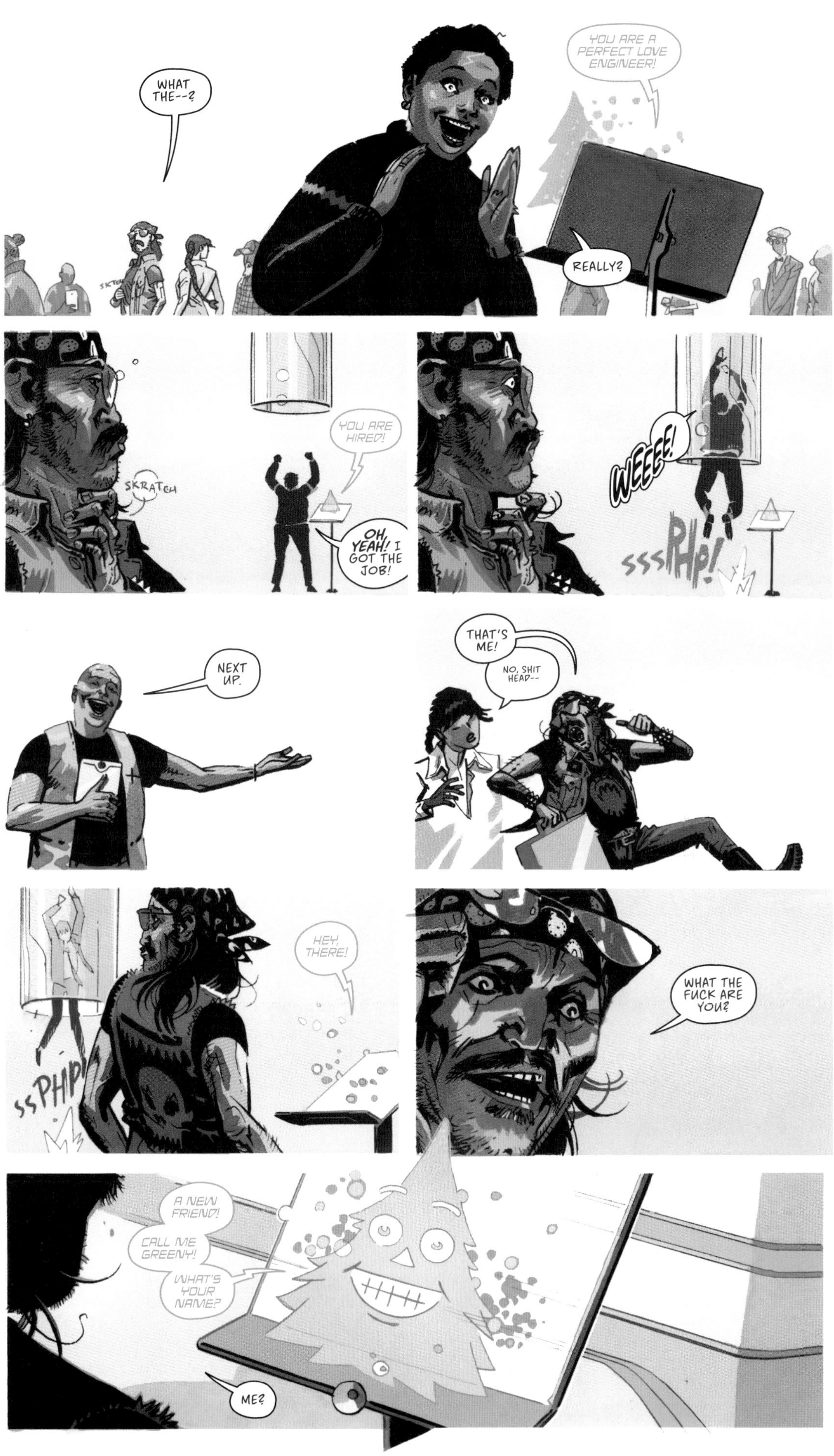
WHAT THE--?
YOU ARE A PERFECT LOVE ENGINEER!
SKTCH
REALLY?
SKRATCH
YOU ARE HIRED!
OH, YEAH! I GOT THE JOB!
WEEEE!
SSSRHP!
NEXT UP.
THAT'S ME!
NO, SHIT HEAD--
HEY, THERE!
SSPHP!
WHAT THE FUCK ARE YOU?
A NEW FRIEND!
CALL ME GREENY!
WHAT'S YOUR NAME?
ME?

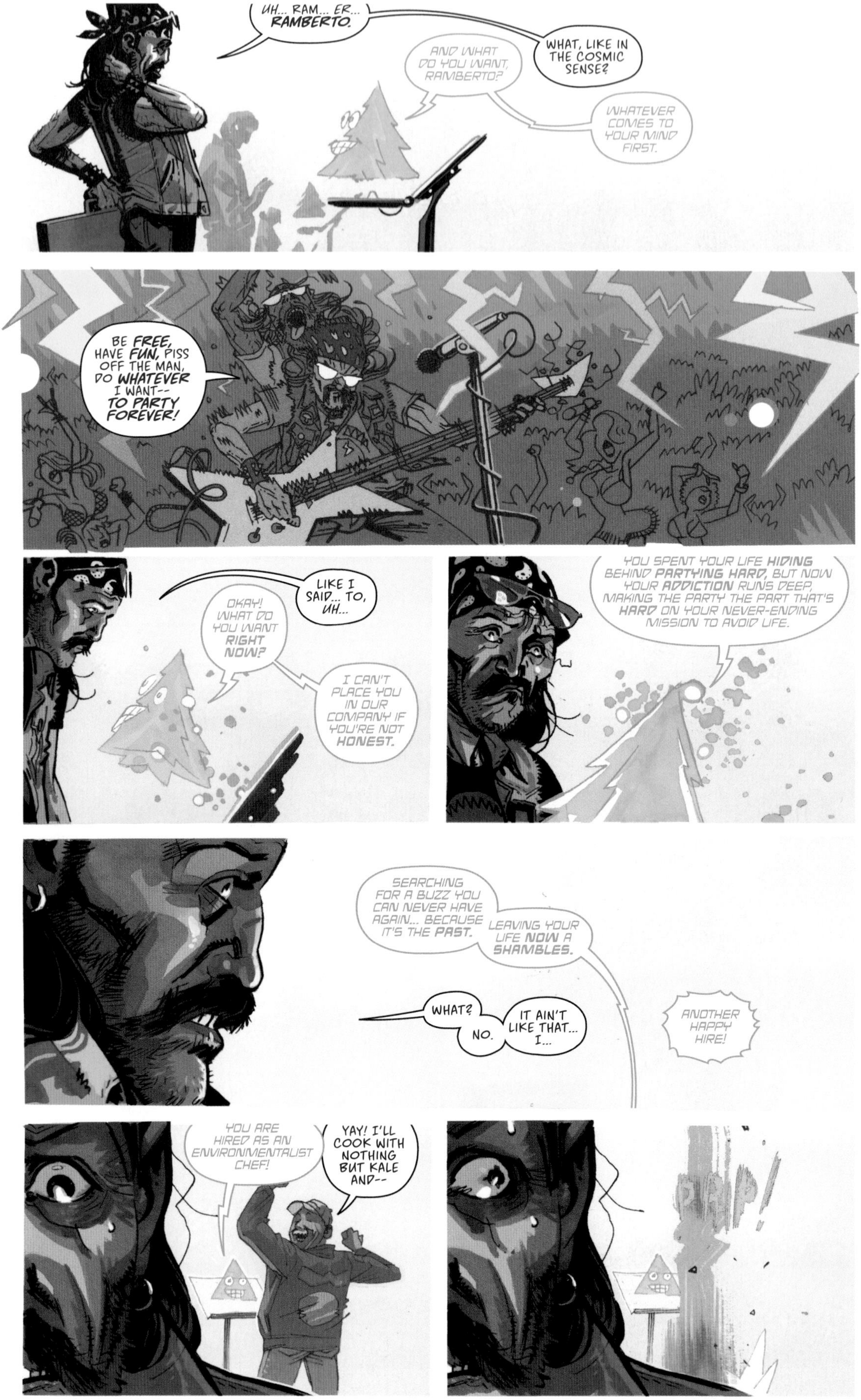
UH... RAM... ER... RAMBERTO.
AND WHAT DO YOU WANT, RAMBERTO?
WHAT, LIKE IN THE COSMIC SENSE?
WHATEVER COMES TO YOUR MIND FIRST.
BE FREE, HAVE FUN, PISS OFF THE MAN, DO WHATEVER I WANT-- TO PARTY FOREVER!
OKAY! WHAT DO YOU WANT RIGHT NOW?
LIKE I SAID... TO, UH...
I CAN'T PLACE YOU IN OUR COMPANY IF YOU'RE NOT HONEST.
YOU SPENT YOUR LIFE HIDING BEHIND PARTYING HARD, BUT NOW YOUR ADDICTION RUNS DEEP, MAKING THE PARTY THE PART THAT'S HARD ON YOUR NEVER-ENDING MISSION TO AVOID LIFE.
SEARCHING FOR A BUZZ YOU CAN NEVER HAVE AGAIN... BECAUSE IT'S THE PAST.
LEAVING YOUR LIFE NOW A SHAMBLES.
WHAT?
NO.
IT AIN'T LIKE THAT... I...
ANOTHER HAPPY HIRE!
YOU ARE HIRED AS AN ENVIRONMENTALIST CHEF!
YAY! I'LL COOK WITH NOTHING BUT KALE AND--

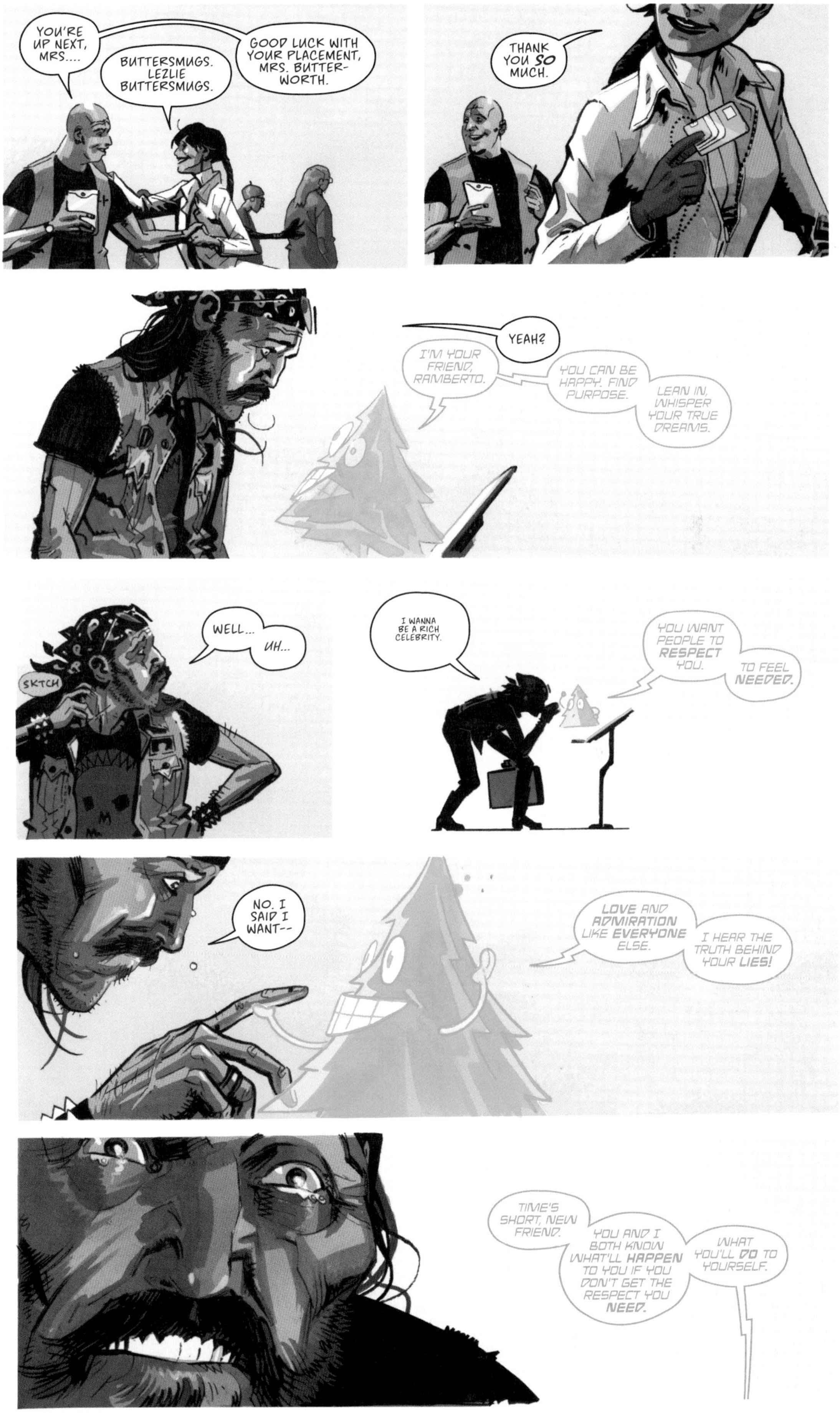
YOU'RE UP NEXT, MRS....
BUTTERSMUGS. LEZLIE BUTTERSMUGS.
GOOD LUCK WITH YOUR PLACEMENT, MRS. BUTTER-WORTH.
THANK YOU SO MUCH.
YEAH?
I'M YOUR FRIEND, RAMBERTO.
YOU CAN BE HAPPY. FIND PURPOSE.
LEAN IN, WHISPER YOUR TRUE DREAMS.
WELL...
UH...
SKTCH
I WANNA BE A RICH CELEBRITY.
YOU WANT PEOPLE TO RESPECT YOU.
TO FEEL NEEDED.
NO. I SAID I WANT--
LOVE AND ADMIRATION LIKE EVERYONE ELSE.
I HEAR THE TRUTH BEHIND YOUR LIES!
TIME'S SHORT, NEW FRIEND.
YOU AND I BOTH KNOW WHAT'LL HAPPEN TO YOU IF YOU DON'T GET THE RESPECT YOU NEED.
WHAT YOU'LL DO TO YOURSELF.

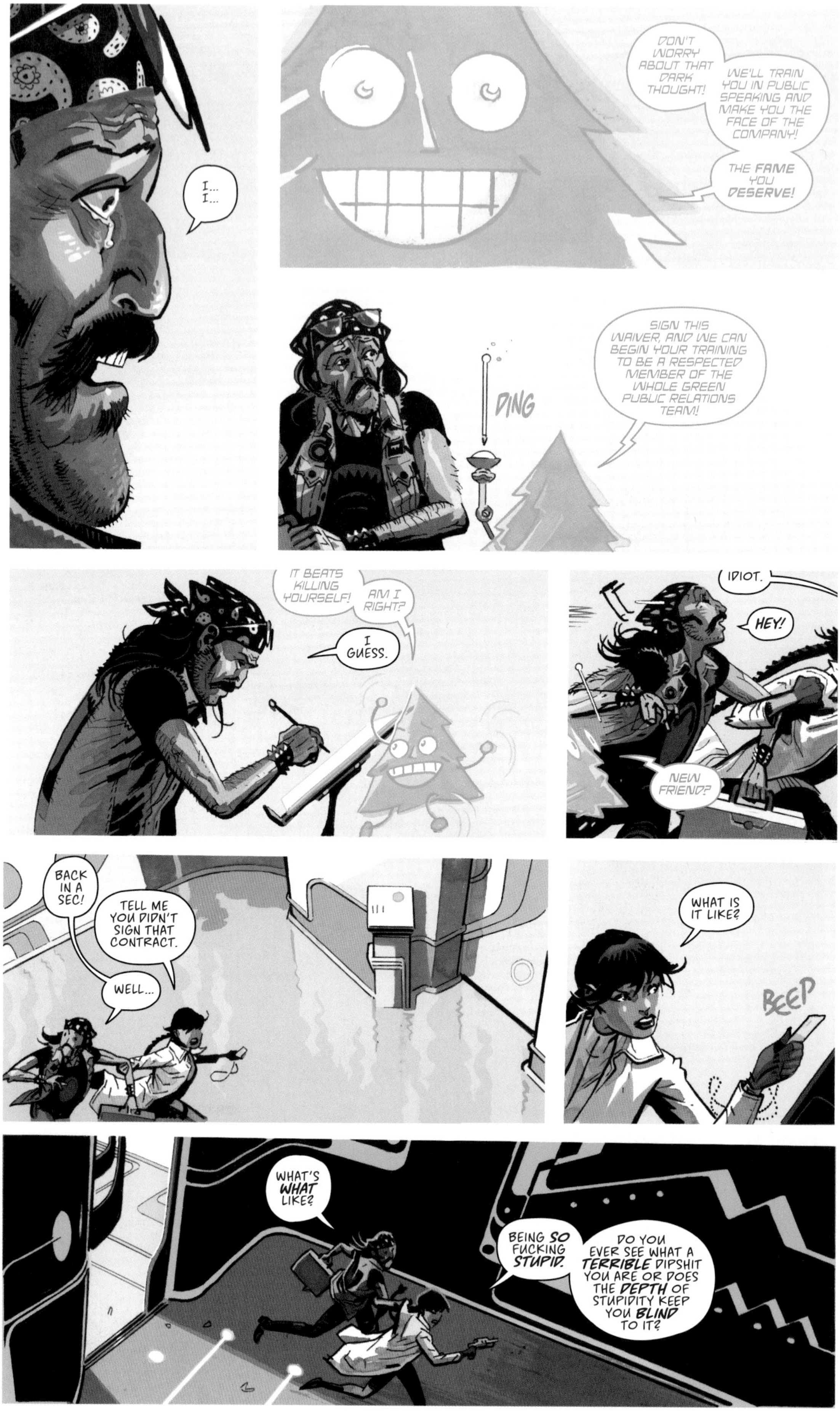
I... I...
DON'T WORRY ABOUT THAT DARK THOUGHT!
WE'LL TRAIN YOU IN PUBLIC SPEAKING AND MAKE YOU THE FACE OF THE COMPANY!
THE FAME YOU DESERVE!
SIGN THIS WAIVER, AND WE CAN BEGIN YOUR TRAINING TO BE A RESPECTED MEMBER OF THE WHOLE GREEN PUBLIC RELATIONS TEAM!
DING
IT BEATS KILLING YOURSELF!
AM I RIGHT?
I GUESS.
IDIOT.
HEY!
NEW FRIEND?
BACK IN A SEC!
TELL ME YOU DIDN'T SIGN THAT CONTRACT.
WELL...
WHAT IS IT LIKE?
BEEP
WHAT'S WHAT LIKE?
BEING SO FUCKING STUPID.
DO YOU EVER SEE WHAT A TERRIBLE DIPSHIT YOU ARE OR DOES THE DEPTH OF STUPIDITY KEEP YOU BLIND TO IT?

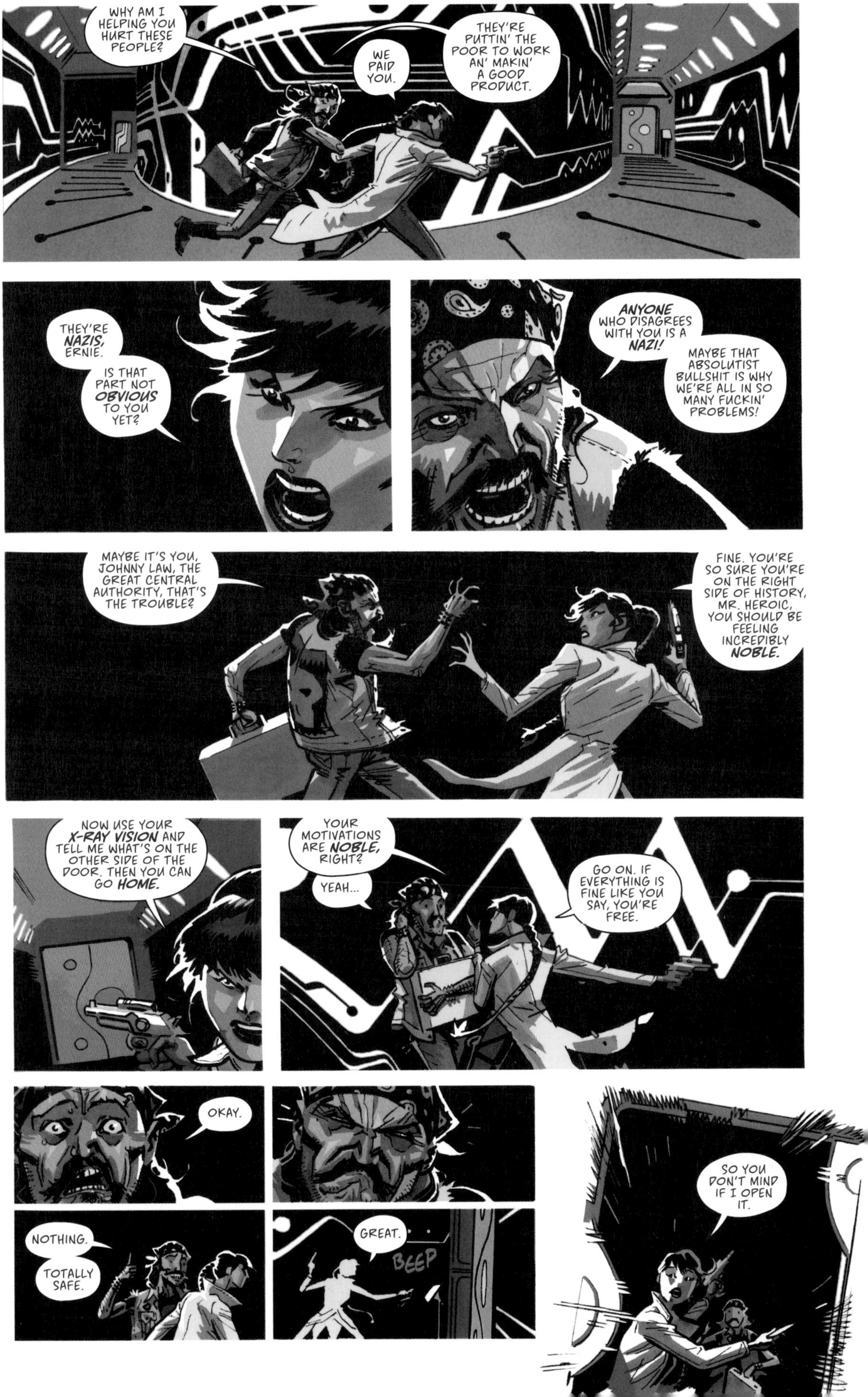
WHY AM I HELPING YOU HURT THESE PEOPLE?
WE PAID YOU.
THEY'RE PUTTIN' THE POOR TO WORK AN' MAKIN' A GOOD PRODUCT.
THEY'RE NAZIS, ERNIE.
IS THAT PART NOT OBVIOUS TO YOU YET?
ANYONE WHO DISAGREES WITH YOU IS A NAZI!
MAYBE THAT ABSOLUTIST BULLSHIT IS WHY WE'RE ALL IN SO MANY FUCKIN' PROBLEMS!
MAYBE IT'S YOU, JOHNNY LAW, THE GREAT CENTRAL AUTHORITY, THAT'S THE TROUBLE?
FINE. YOU'RE SO SURE YOU'RE ON THE RIGHT SIDE OF HISTORY, MR. HEROIC, YOU SHOULD BE FEELING INCREDIBLY NOBLE.
NOW USE YOUR X-RAY VISION AND TELL ME WHAT'S ON THE OTHER SIDE OF THE DOOR. THEN YOU CAN GO HOME.
YOUR MOTIVATIONS ARE NOBLE, RIGHT?
YEAH...
GO ON. IF EVERYTHING IS FINE LIKE YOU SAY, YOU'RE FREE.
OKAY.
NOTHING.
TOTALLY SAFE.
GREAT.
BEEP
SO YOU DON'T MIND IF I OPEN IT.

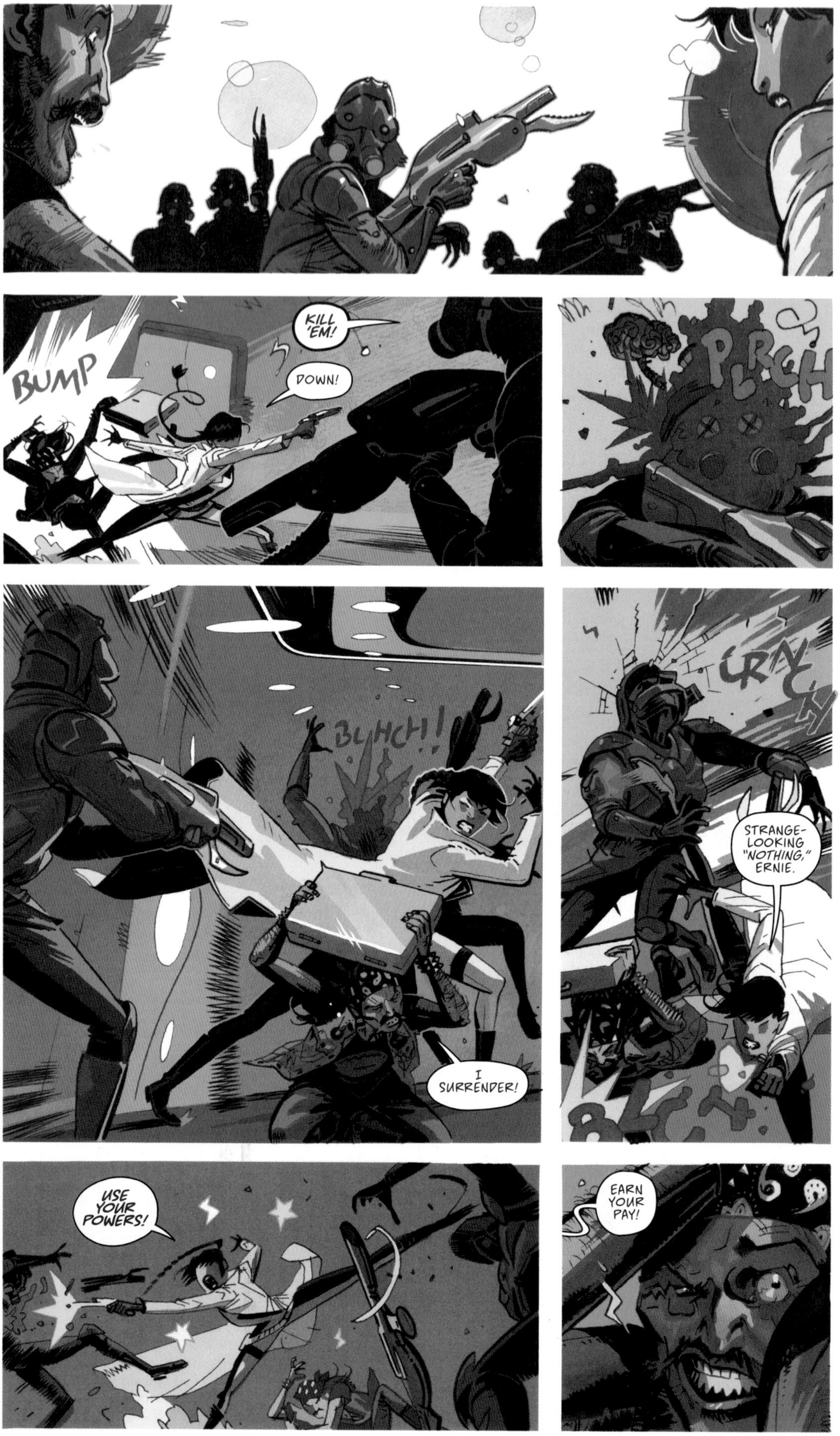
BUMP
KILL 'EM!
DOWN!
PLRCH
BLHCH!!
I SURRENDER!
CRACH
STRANGE-LOOKING "NOTHING," ERNIE.
USE YOUR POWERS!
EARN YOUR PAY!

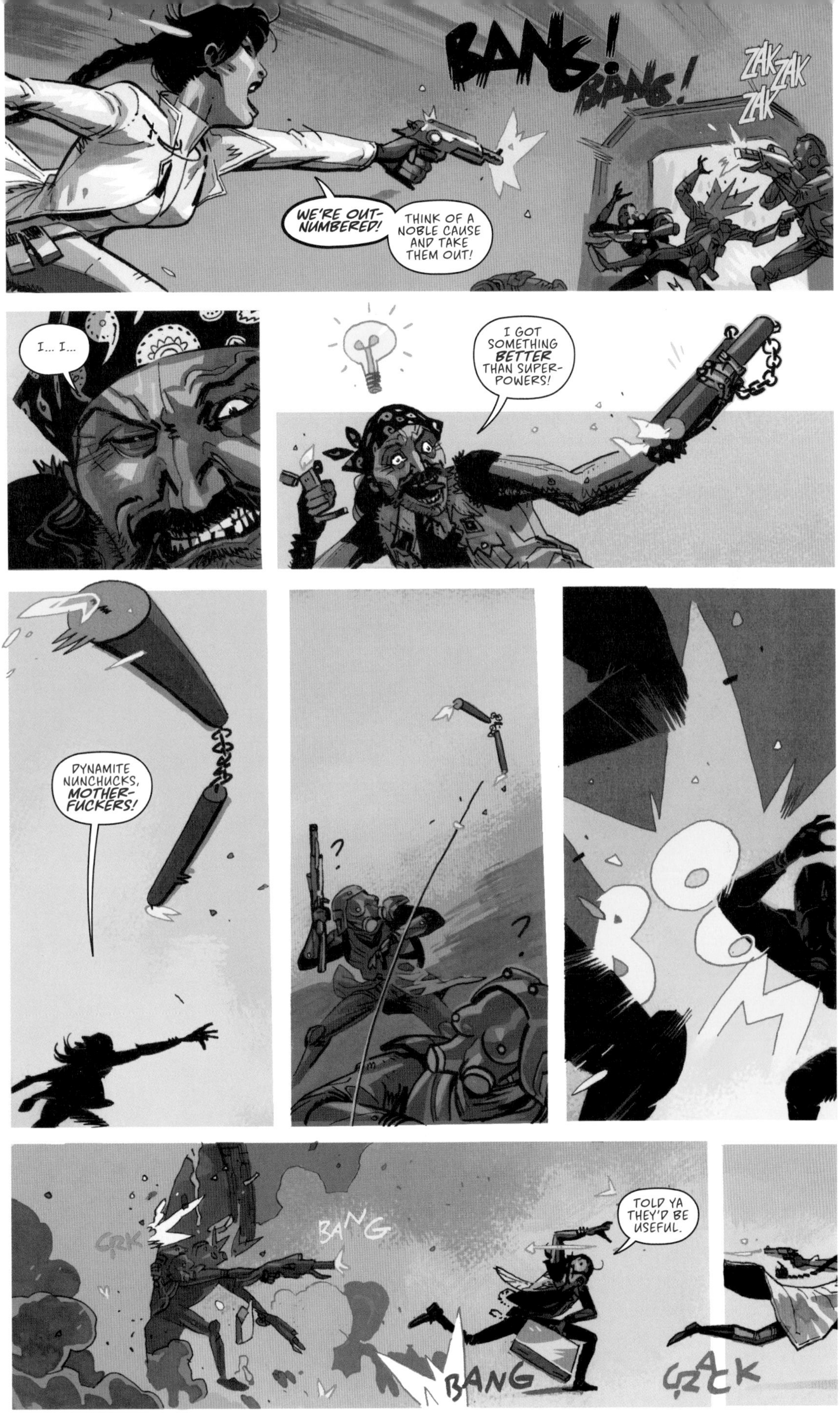
BANG!
BANG!
ZAK ZAK ZAK
WE'RE OUT-NUMBERED!
THINK OF A NOBLE CAUSE AND TAKE THEM OUT!
I... I...
I GOT SOMETHING BETTER THAN SUPER-POWERS!
DYNAMITE NUNCHUCKS, MOTHER-FUCKERS!
?
?
BOOM
CRK
BANG
TOLD YA THEY'D BE USEFUL.
BANG
CRACK

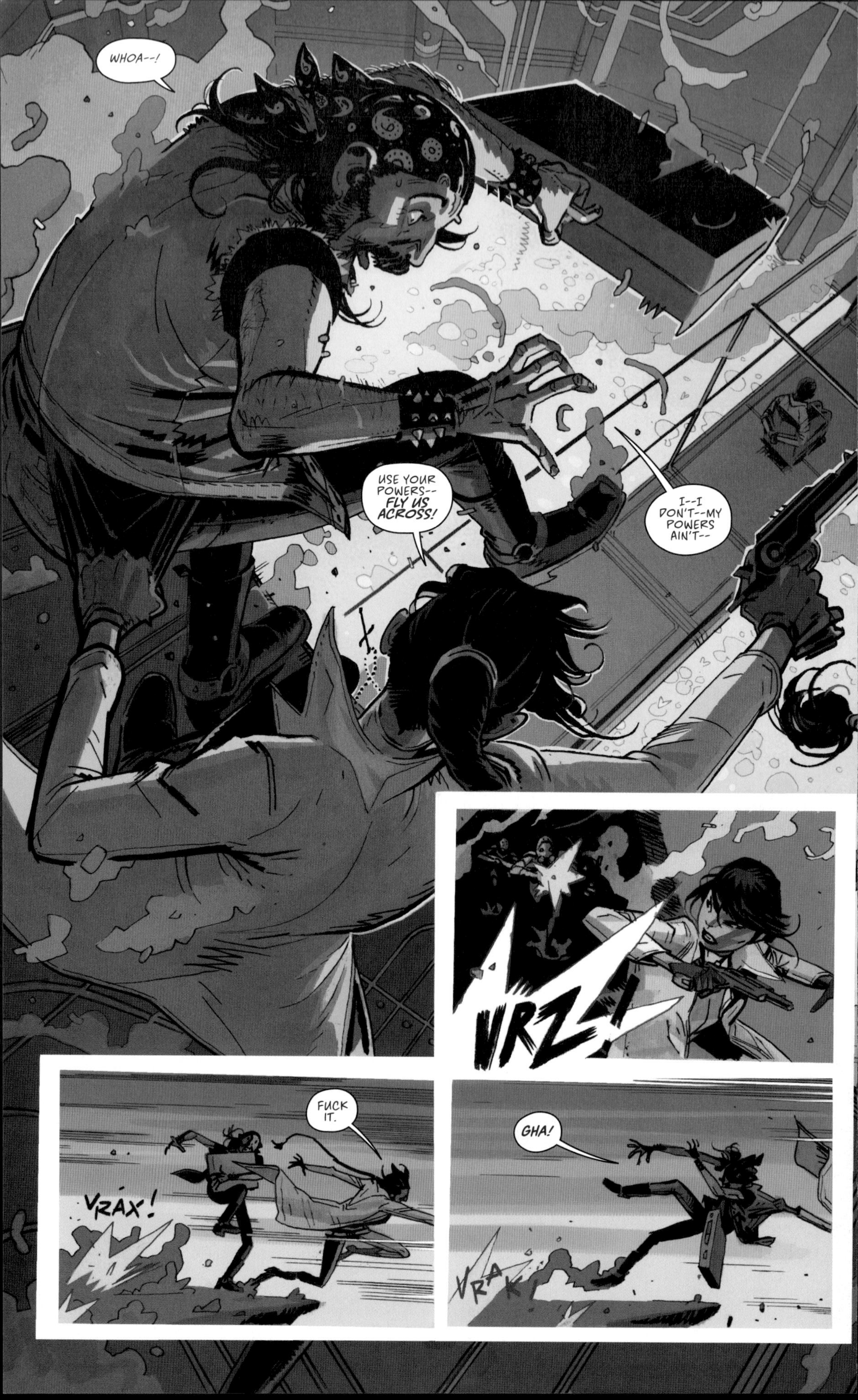
WHOA--!
USE YOUR POWERS--FLY US ACROSS!
I--I DON'T--MY POWERS AIN'T--
VRZZ!
FUCK IT.
VRAX!
GHA!
VRAK!

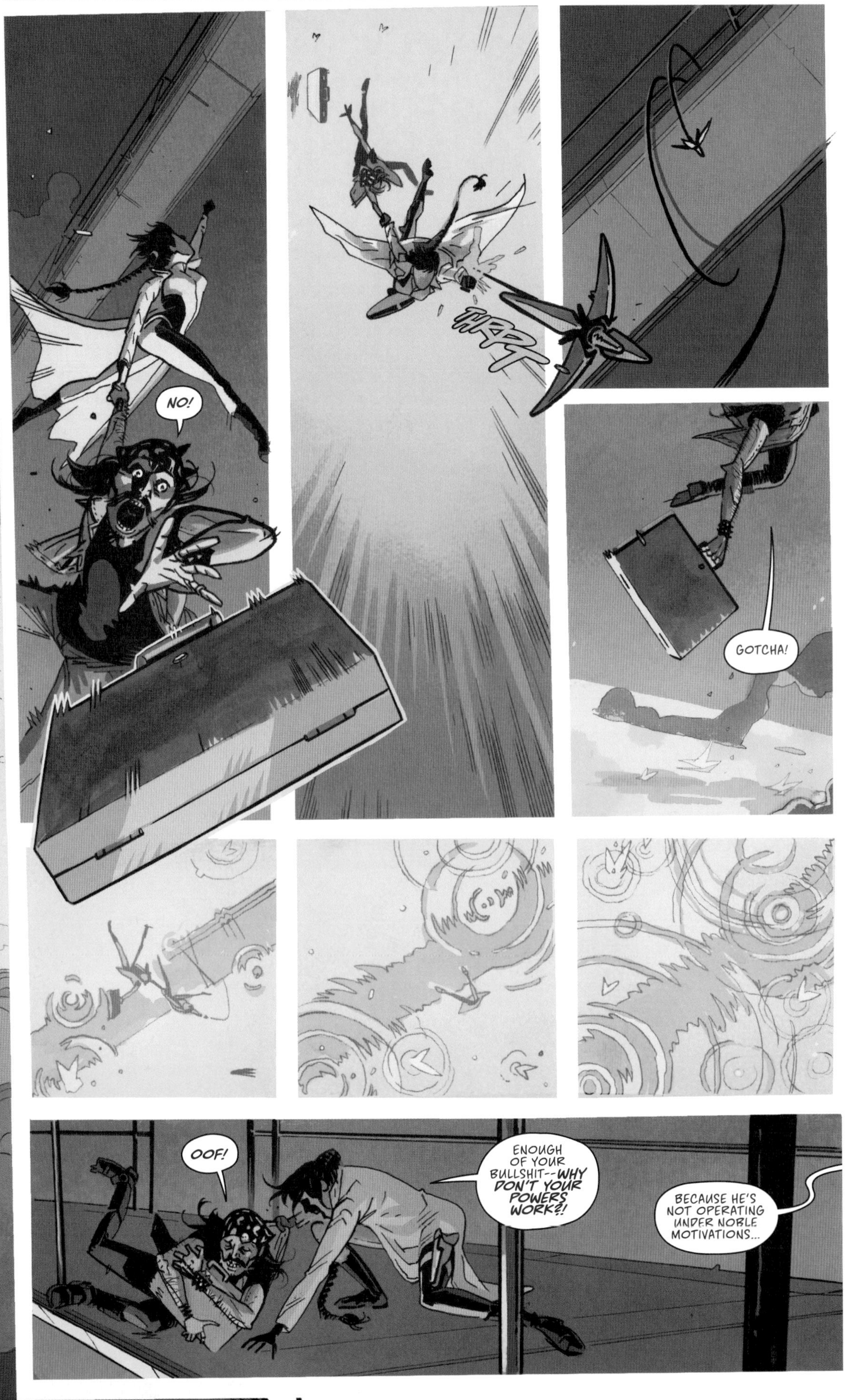
NO!
THPPT
GOTCHA!
OOF!
ENOUGH OF YOUR BULLSHIT--WHY DON'T YOUR POWERS WORK?!
BECAUSE HE'S NOT OPERATING UNDER NOBLE MOTIVATIONS...

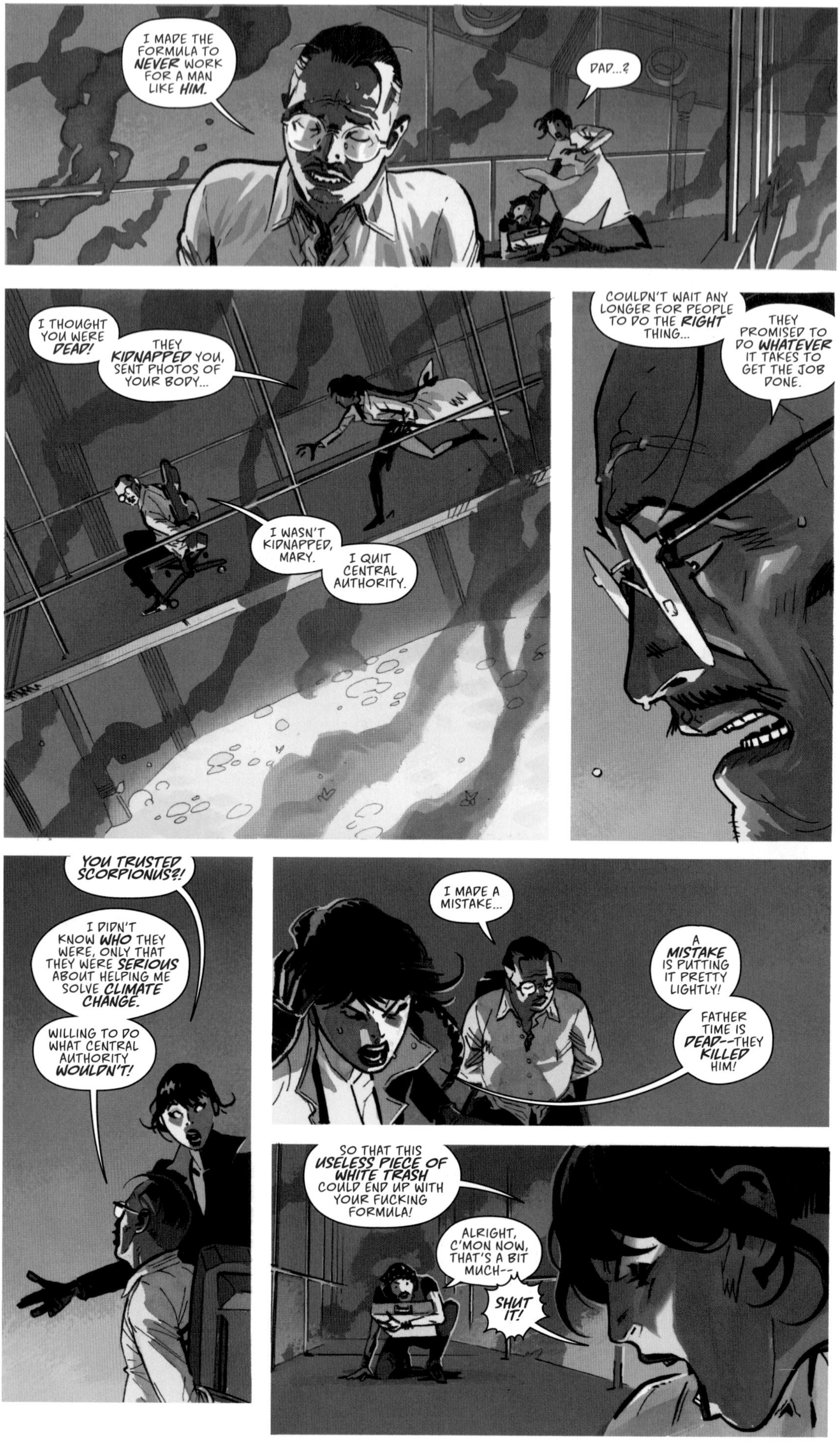
I MADE THE FORMULA TO NEVER WORK FOR A MAN LIKE HIM.
DAD...?
I THOUGHT YOU WERE DEAD!
THEY KIDNAPPED YOU, SENT PHOTOS OF YOUR BODY...
I WASN'T KIDNAPPED, MARY.
I QUIT CENTRAL AUTHORITY.
COULDN'T WAIT ANY LONGER FOR PEOPLE TO DO THE RIGHT THING...
THEY PROMISED TO DO WHATEVER IT TAKES TO GET THE JOB DONE.
YOU TRUSTED SCORPIONUS?!
I DIDN'T KNOW WHO THEY WERE, ONLY THAT THEY WERE SERIOUS ABOUT HELPING ME SOLVE CLIMATE CHANGE.
WILLING TO DO WHAT CENTRAL AUTHORITY WOULDN'T!
I MADE A MISTAKE...
A MISTAKE IS PUTTING IT PRETTY LIGHTLY!
FATHER TIME IS DEAD--THEY KILLED HIM!
SO THAT THIS USELESS PIECE OF WHITE TRASH COULD END UP WITH YOUR FUCKING FORMULA!
ALRIGHT, C'MON NOW, THAT'S A BIT MUCH--
SHUT IT!

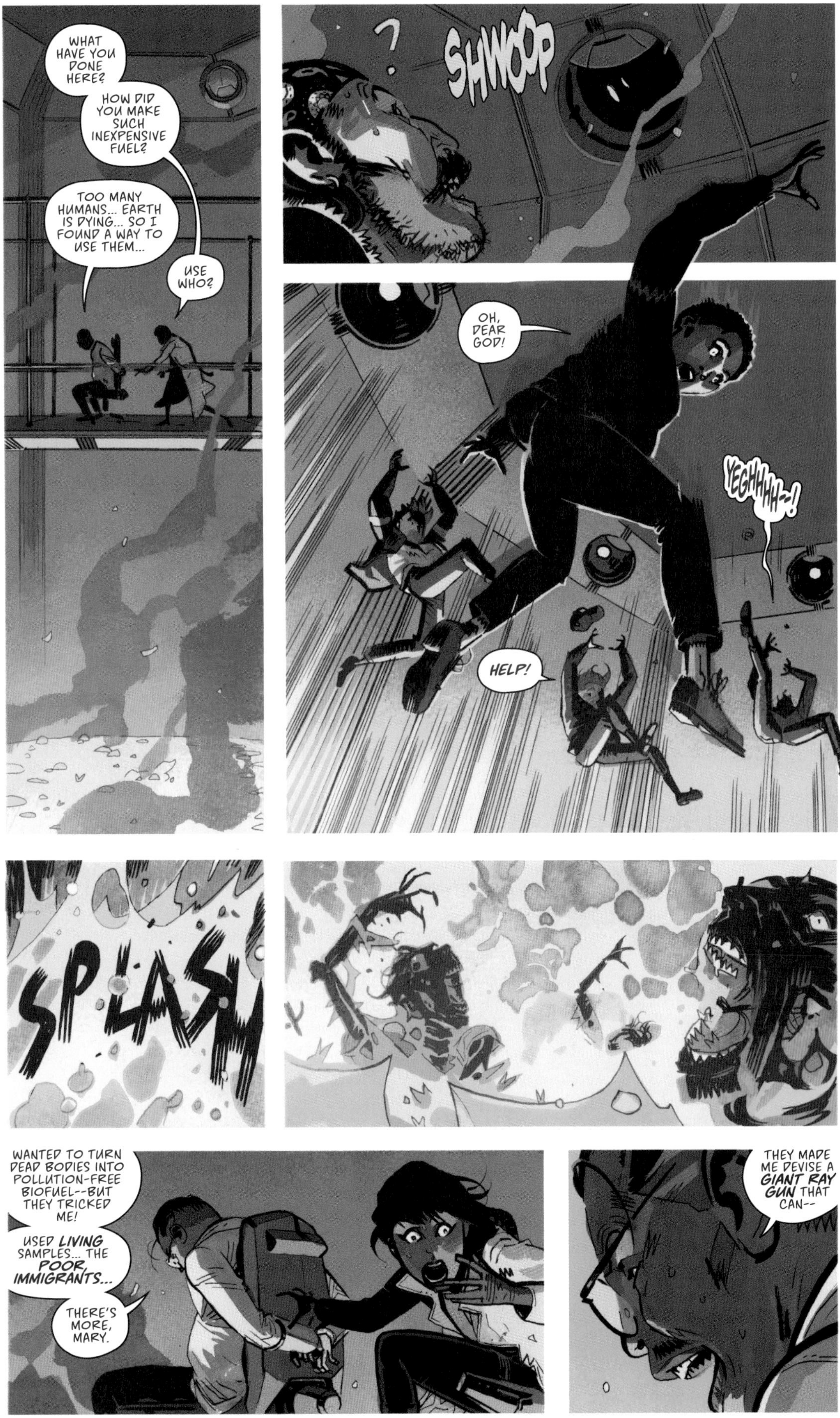
WHAT HAVE YOU DONE HERE?
HOW DID YOU MAKE SUCH INEXPENSIVE FUEL?
TOO MANY HUMANS... EARTH IS DYING... SO I FOUND A WAY TO USE THEM...
USE WHO?
?
SHWOOP
OH, DEAR GOD!
YEGHHHH--!
HELP!
SPLASH
WANTED TO TURN DEAD BODIES INTO POLLUTION-FREE BIOFUEL--BUT THEY TRICKED ME!
USED LIVING SAMPLES... THE POOR, IMMIGRANTS...
THERE'S MORE, MARY.
THEY MADE ME DEVISE A GIANT RAY GUN THAT CAN--

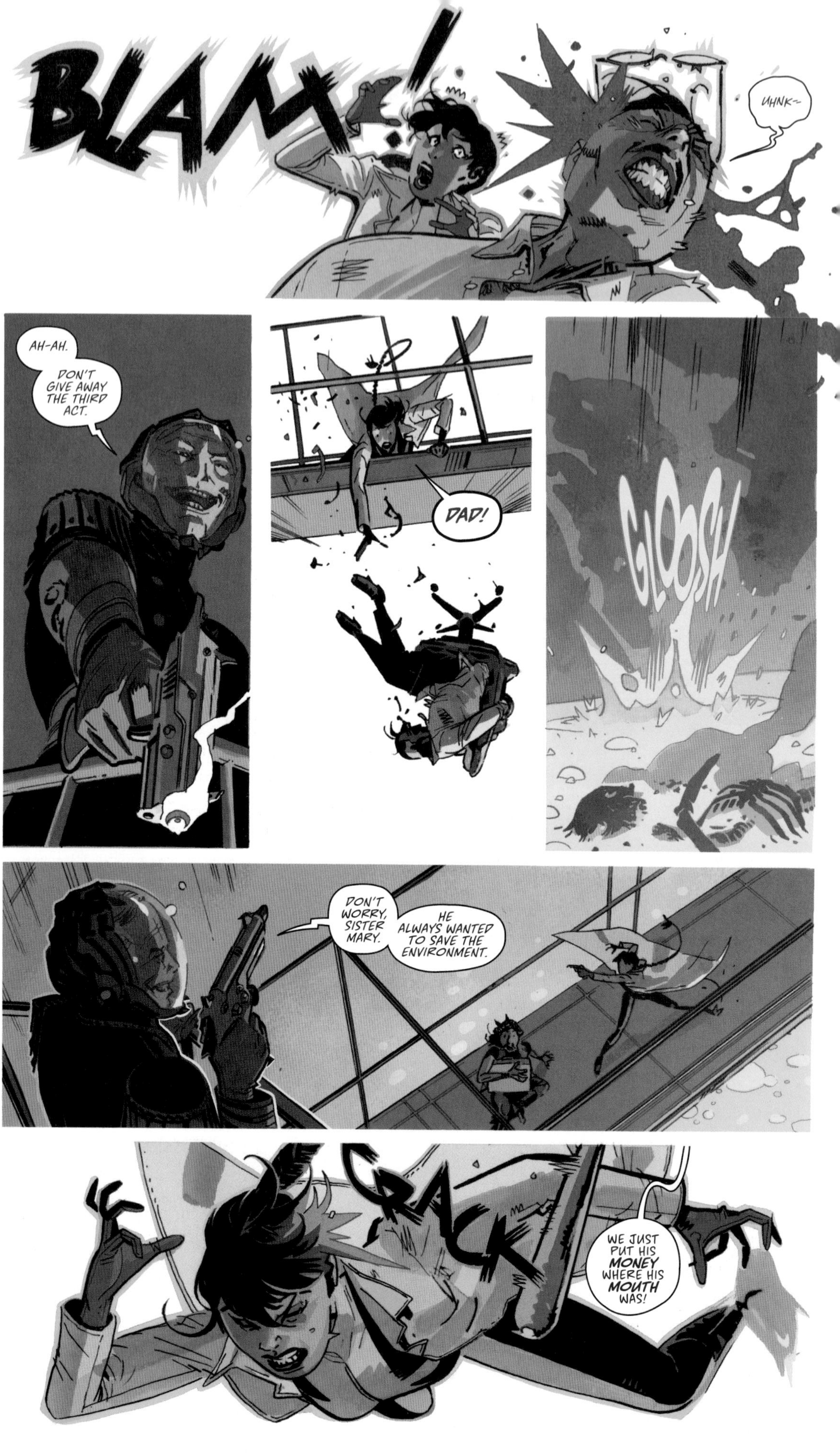
BLAM!
UHNK--
AH-AH.
DON'T GIVE AWAY THE THIRD ACT.
DAD!
GLOOSH
DON'T WORRY, SISTER MARY.
HE ALWAYS WANTED TO SAVE THE ENVIRONMENT.
CRACK
WE JUST PUT HIS MONEY WHERE HIS MOUTH WAS!

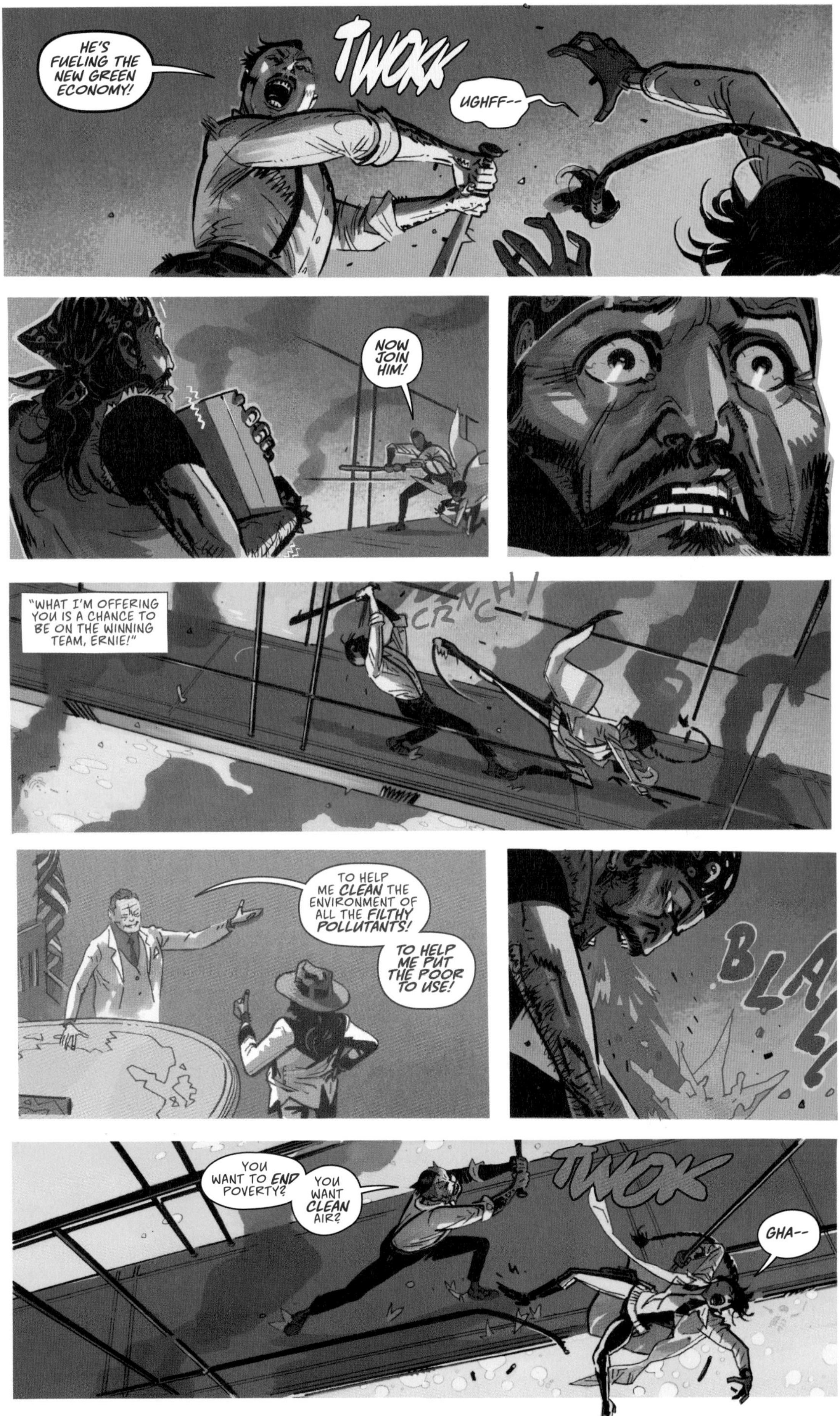

HE'S FUELING THE NEW GREEN ECONOMY!
TWOKK
UGHFF--
NOW JOIN HIM!
"WHAT I'M OFFERING YOU IS A CHANCE TO BE ON THE WINNING TEAM, ERNIE!"
CRNCH!
TO HELP ME CLEAN THE ENVIRONMENT OF ALL THE FILTHY POLLUTANTS!
TO HELP ME PUT THE POOR TO USE!
BLA
YOU WANT TO END POVERTY?
YOU WANT CLEAN AIR?
TWOK
GHA--

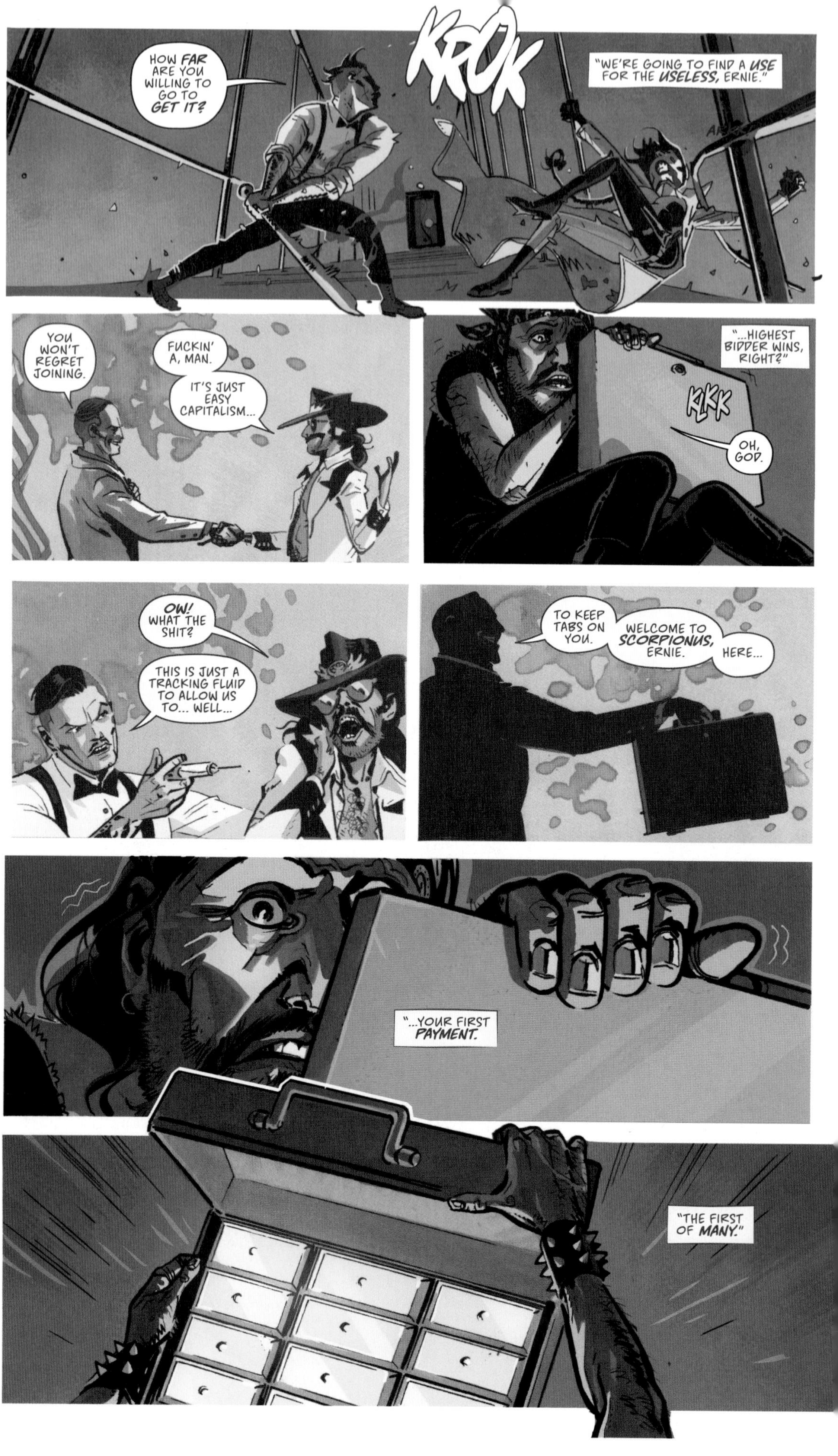
HOW FAR ARE YOU WILLING TO GO TO GET IT?
KROK
"WE'RE GOING TO FIND A USE FOR THE USELESS, ERNIE."
YOU WON'T REGRET JOINING.
FUCKIN' A, MAN.
IT'S JUST EASY CAPITALISM...
"...HIGHEST BIDDER WINS, RIGHT?"
KLIKK
OH, GOD.
OW! WHAT THE SHIT?
THIS IS JUST A TRACKING FLUID TO ALLOW US TO... WELL...
TO KEEP TABS ON YOU.
WELCOME TO SCORPIONUS, ERNIE.
HERE...
"...YOUR FIRST PAYMENT.
"THE FIRST OF MANY."

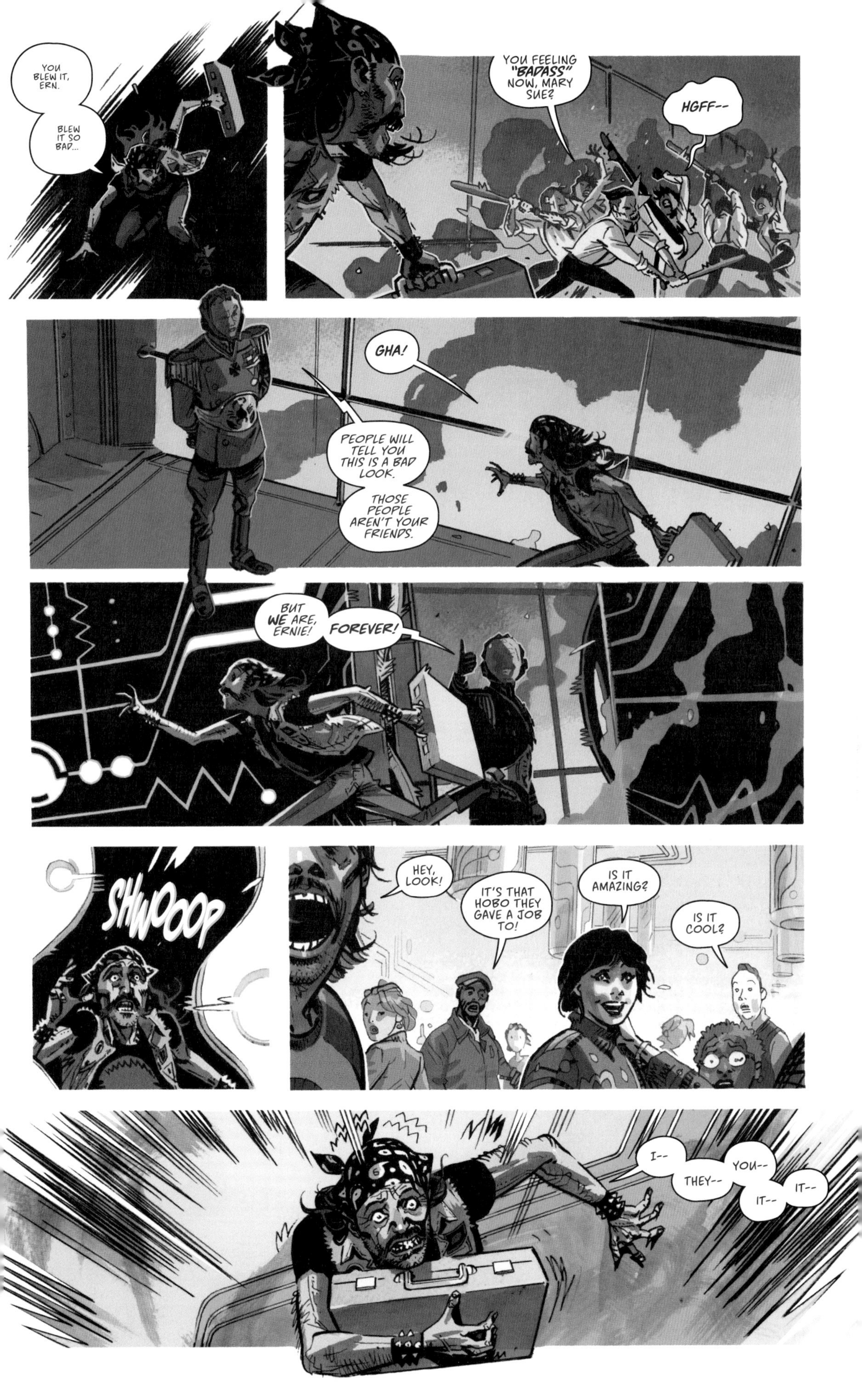
YOU BLEW IT, ERN.
BLEW IT SO BAD...
YOU FEELING "BADASS" NOW, MARY SUE?
HGFF--
GHA!
PEOPLE WILL TELL YOU THIS IS A BAD LOOK.
THOSE PEOPLE AREN'T YOUR FRIENDS.
BUT WE ARE, ERNIE!
FOREVER!
SHWOOOP
HEY, LOOK!
IT'S THAT HOBO THEY GAVE A JOB TO!
IS IT AMAZING?
IS IT COOL?
I--
THEY--
YOU--
IT--
IT--

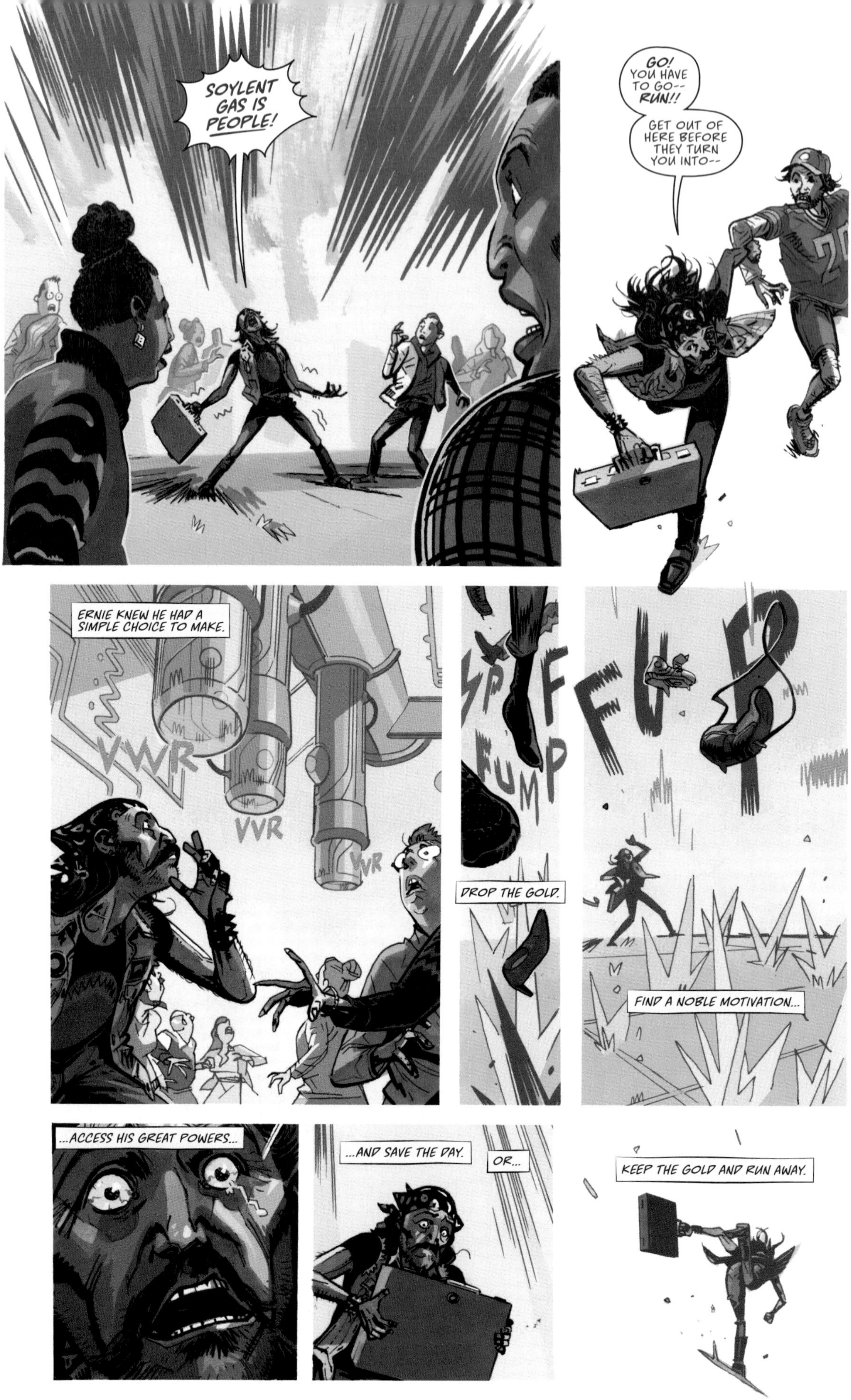
SOYLENT GAS IS PEOPLE!
GO! YOU HAVE TO GO-- RUN!!
GET OUT OF HERE BEFORE THEY TURN YOU INTO--
ERNIE KNEW HE HAD A SIMPLE CHOICE TO MAKE.
VWR
VVR
VVR
SPFF
FUMP
FFUP
DROP THE GOLD.
FIND A NOBLE MOTIVATION...
...ACCESS HIS GREAT POWERS...
...AND SAVE THE DAY.
OR...
KEEP THE GOLD AND RUN AWAY.

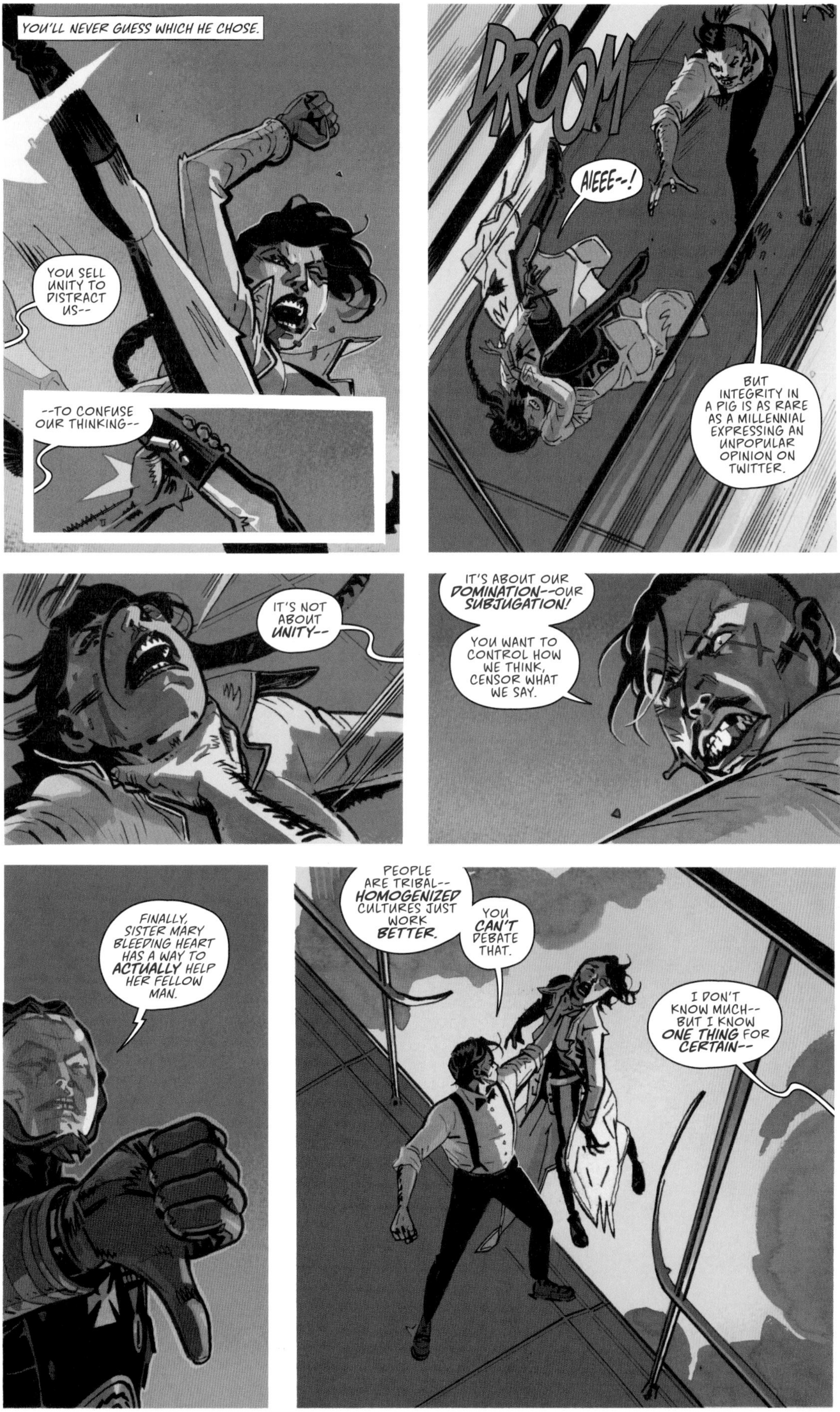
YOU'LL NEVER GUESS WHICH HE CHOSE.
YOU SELL UNITY TO DISTRACT US--
--TO CONFUSE OUR THINKING--
DROOM
AIEEE--!
BUT INTEGRITY IN A PIG IS AS RARE AS A MILLENNIAL EXPRESSING AN UNPOPULAR OPINION ON TWITTER.
IT'S NOT ABOUT UNITY--
IT'S ABOUT OUR DOMINATION--OUR SUBJUGATION!
YOU WANT TO CONTROL HOW WE THINK, CENSOR WHAT WE SAY.
FINALLY, SISTER MARY BLEEDING HEART HAS A WAY TO ACTUALLY HELP HER FELLOW MAN.
PEOPLE ARE TRIBAL--HOMOGENIZED CULTURES JUST WORK BETTER.
YOU CAN'T DEBATE THAT.
I DON'T KNOW MUCH--BUT I KNOW ONE THING FOR CERTAIN--

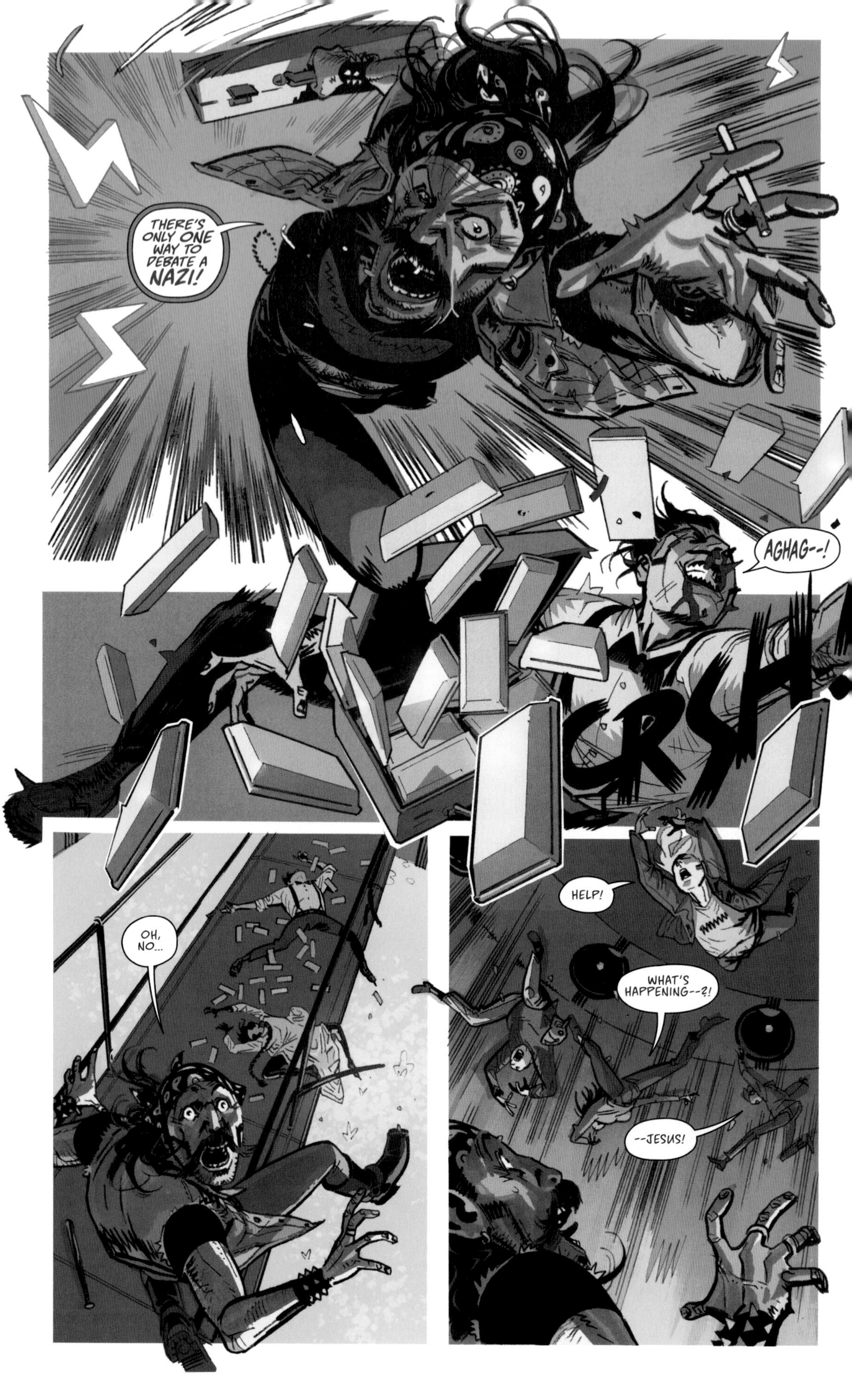
THERE'S ONLY ONE WAY TO DEBATE A NAZI!
AGHAG--!
CRSH
OH, NO...
HELP!
WHAT'S HAPPENING--?!
--JESUS!

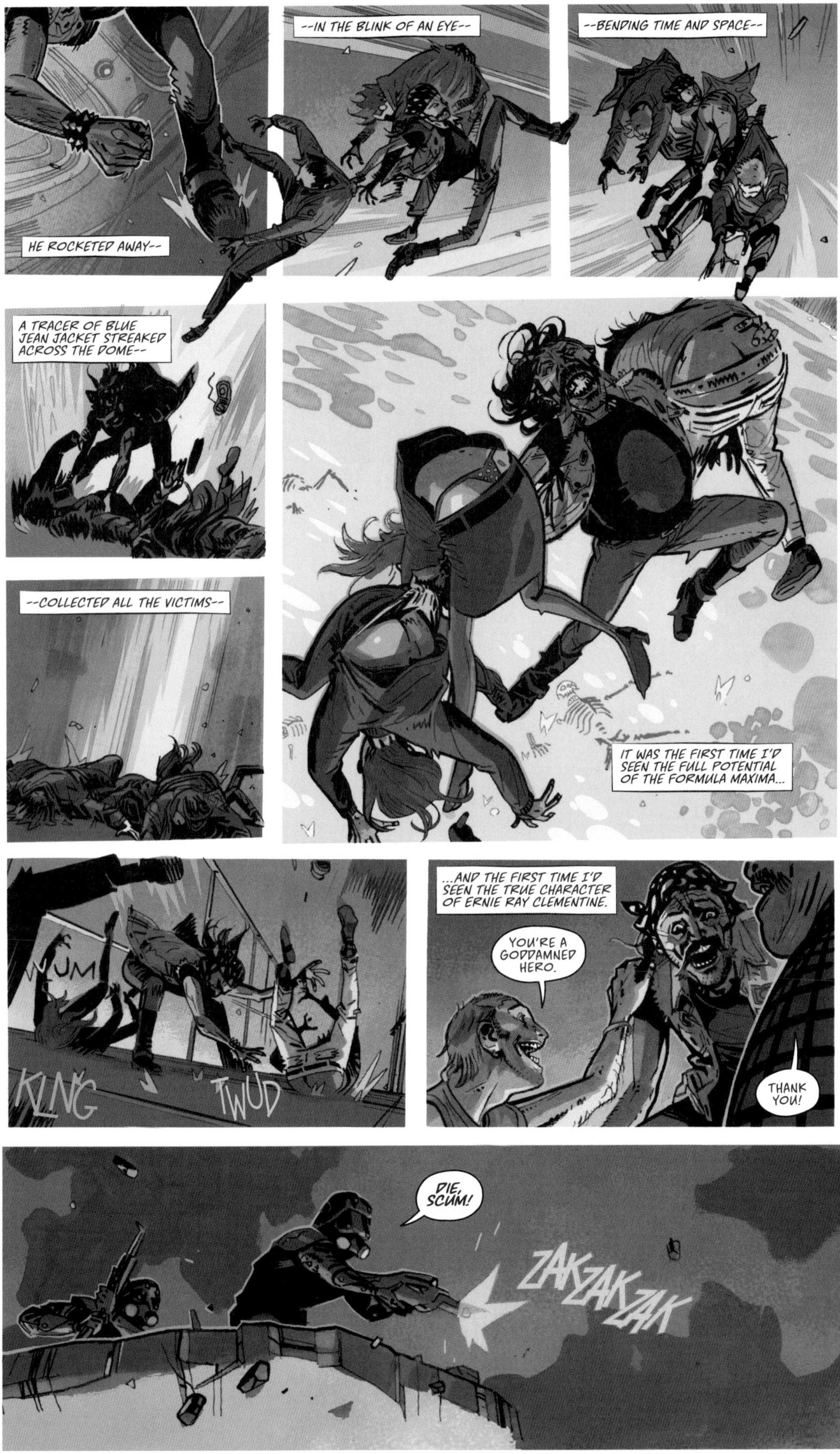
HE ROCKETED AWAY--
--IN THE BLINK OF AN EYE--
--BENDING TIME AND SPACE--
A TRACER OF BLUE JEAN JACKET STREAKED ACROSS THE DOME--
--COLLECTED ALL THE VICTIMS--
IT WAS THE FIRST TIME I'D SEEN THE FULL POTENTIAL OF THE FORMULA MAXIMA...
KLNG
TWUD
...AND THE FIRST TIME I'D SEEN THE TRUE CHARACTER OF ERNIE RAY CLEMENTINE.
YOU'RE A GODDAMNED HERO.
THANK YOU!
DIE, SCUM!
ZAKZAKZAK

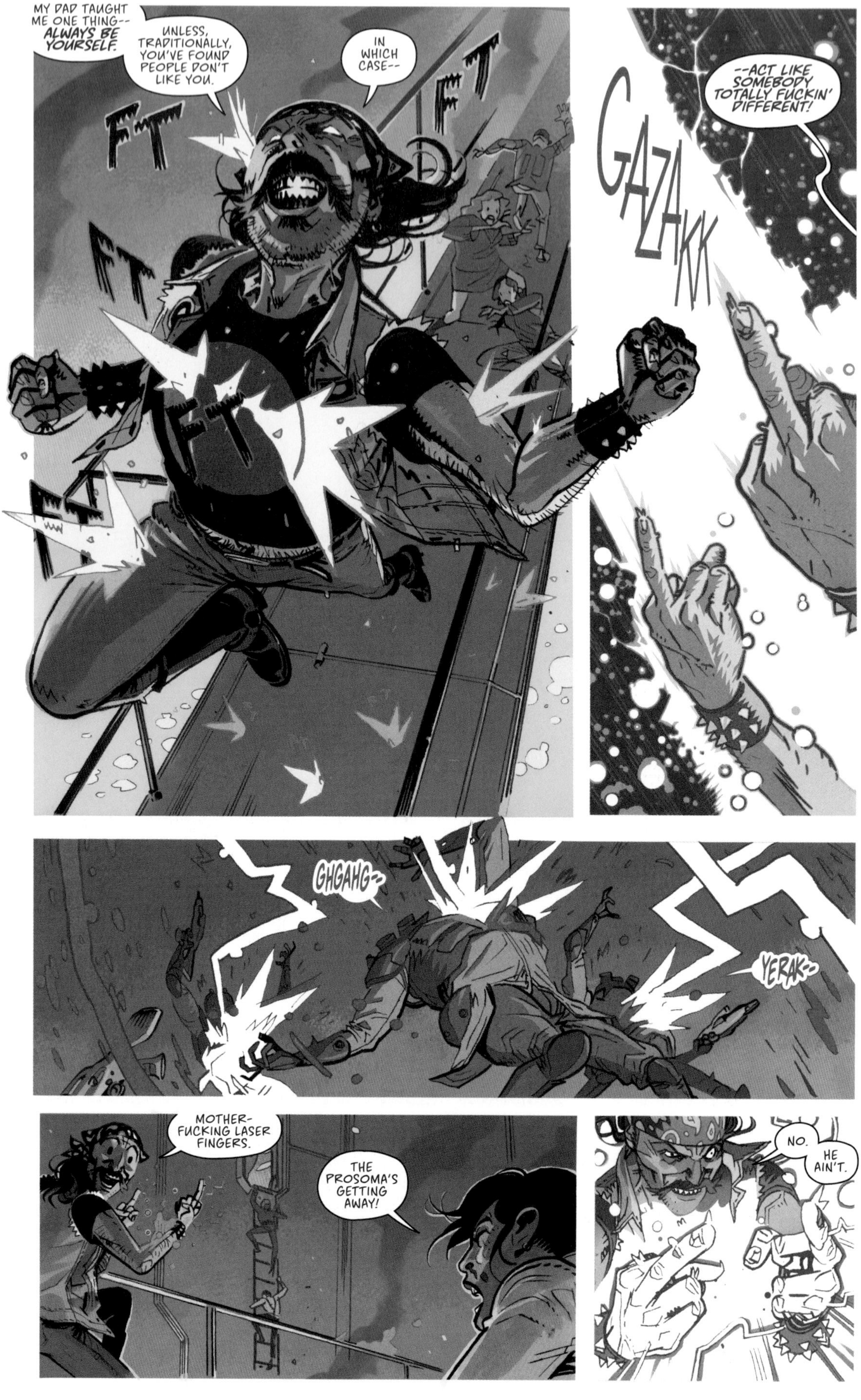
MY DAD TAUGHT ME ONE THING-- ALWAYS BE YOURSELF.
UNLESS, TRADITIONALLY, YOU'VE FOUND PEOPLE DON'T LIKE YOU.
IN WHICH CASE--
FT
FT
FT
FT
FT
--ACT LIKE SOMEBODY TOTALLY FUCKIN' DIFFERENT!
GAZAKK
GHGAHG
YERAK
MOTHER-FUCKING LASER FINGERS.
THE PROSOMA'S GETTING AWAY!
NO.
HE AIN'T.

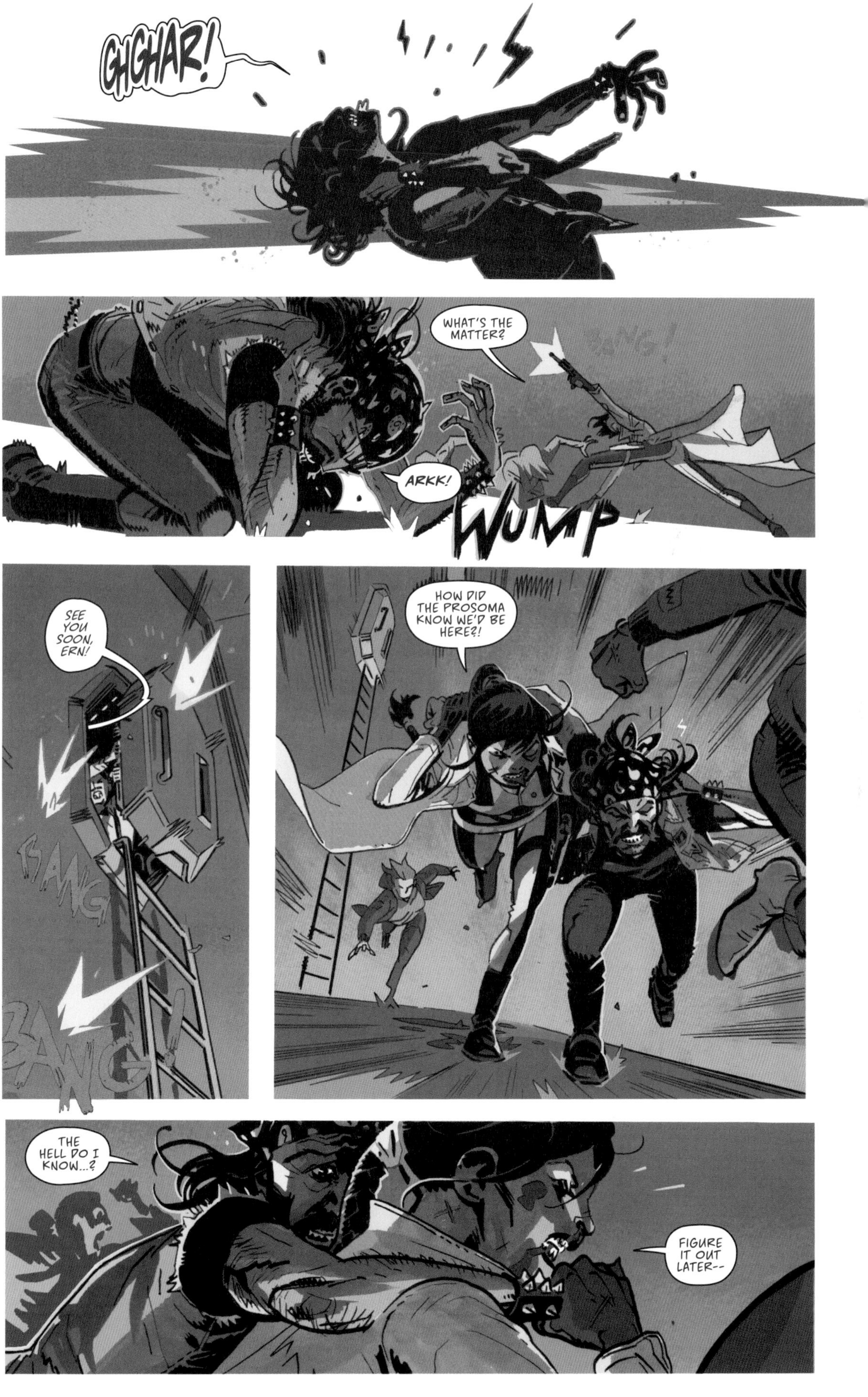
GHGHAR!
WHAT'S THE MATTER?
BANG!
ARKK!
WUMP
SEE YOU SOON, ERN!
BANG
BANG!
HOW DID THE PROSOMA KNOW WE'D BE HERE?!
THE HELL DO I KNOW...?
FIGURE IT OUT LATER--

"RIGHT NOW WE HAVE TO EVACUATE THIS BUILDING!"

IS EVERYONE OUT?

YES.

THAT'S THE LAST OF THEM.

BEEP

GOOD.

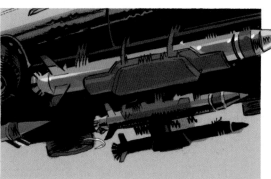

FWOOOOSH

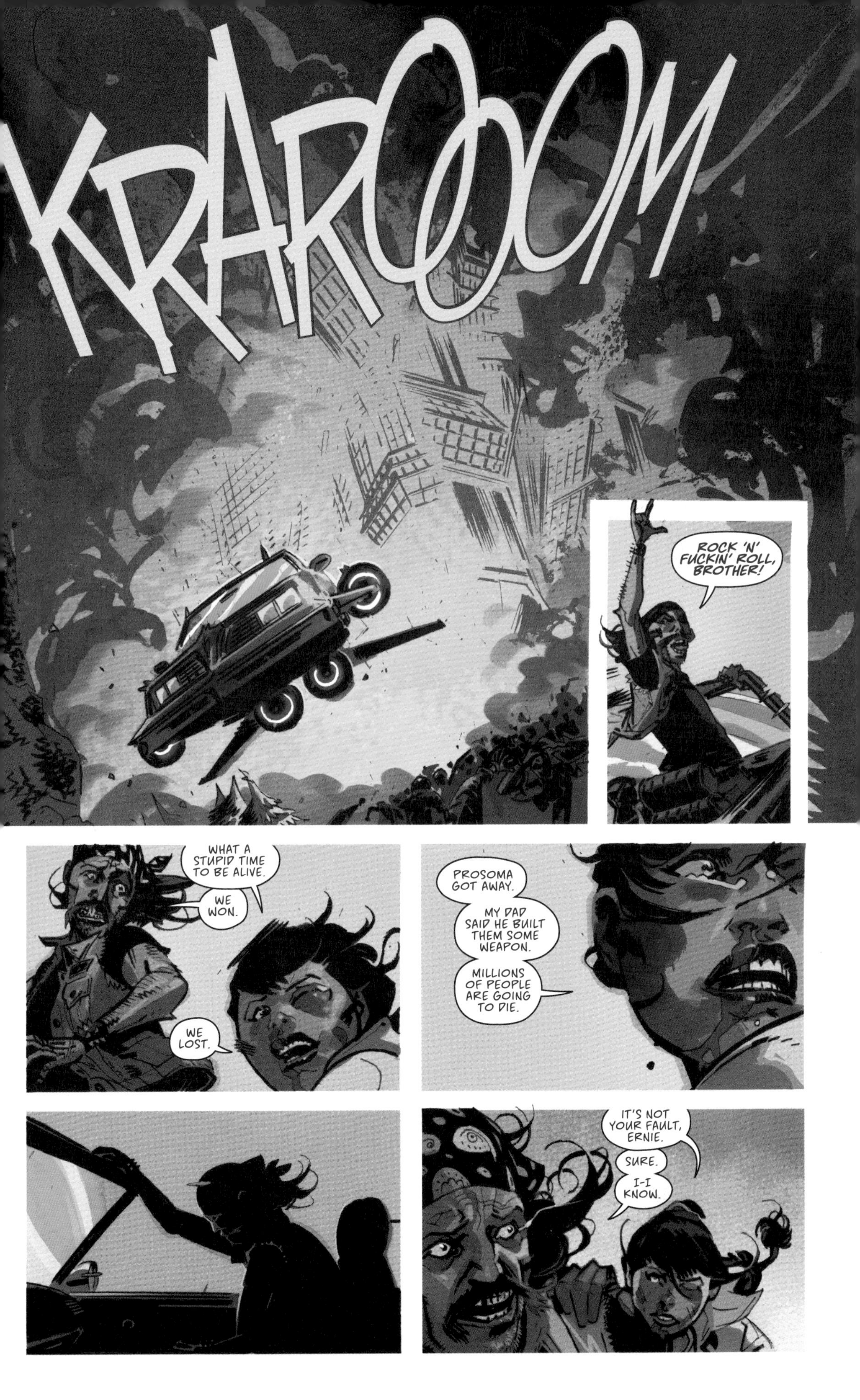
KRAROOOM
ROCK 'N' FUCKIN' ROLL, BROTHER!
WHAT A STUPID TIME TO BE ALIVE.
WE WON.
WE LOST.
PROSOMA GOT AWAY.
MY DAD SAID HE BUILT THEM SOME WEAPON.
MILLIONS OF PEOPLE ARE GOING TO DIE.
IT'S NOT YOUR FAULT, ERNIE.
SURE.
I-I KNOW.

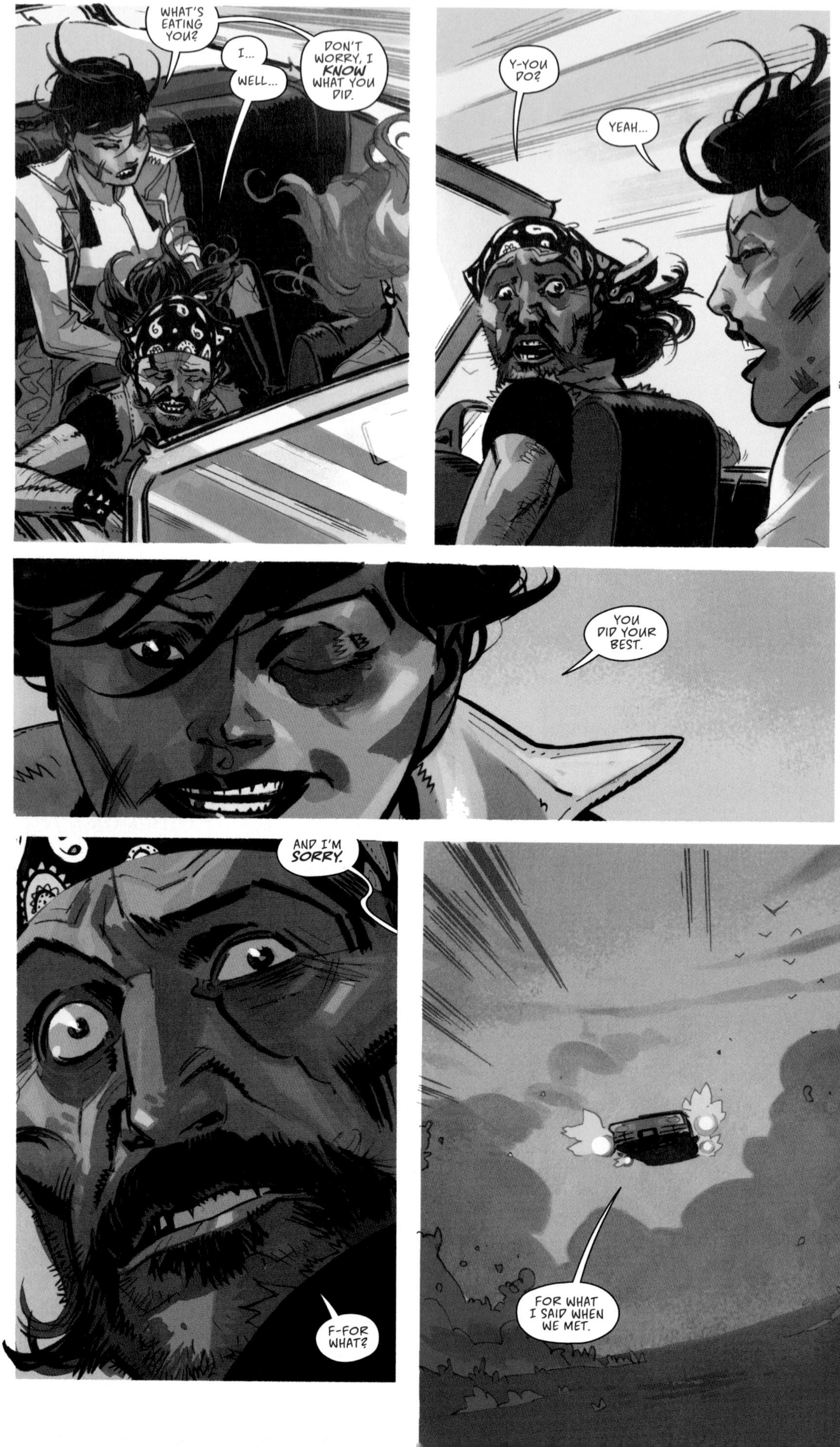
WHAT'S EATING YOU?
I... WELL...
DON'T WORRY, I KNOW WHAT YOU DID.
Y-YOU DO?
YEAH...
YOU DID YOUR BEST.
AND I'M SORRY.
F-FOR WHAT?
FOR WHAT I SAID WHEN WE MET.

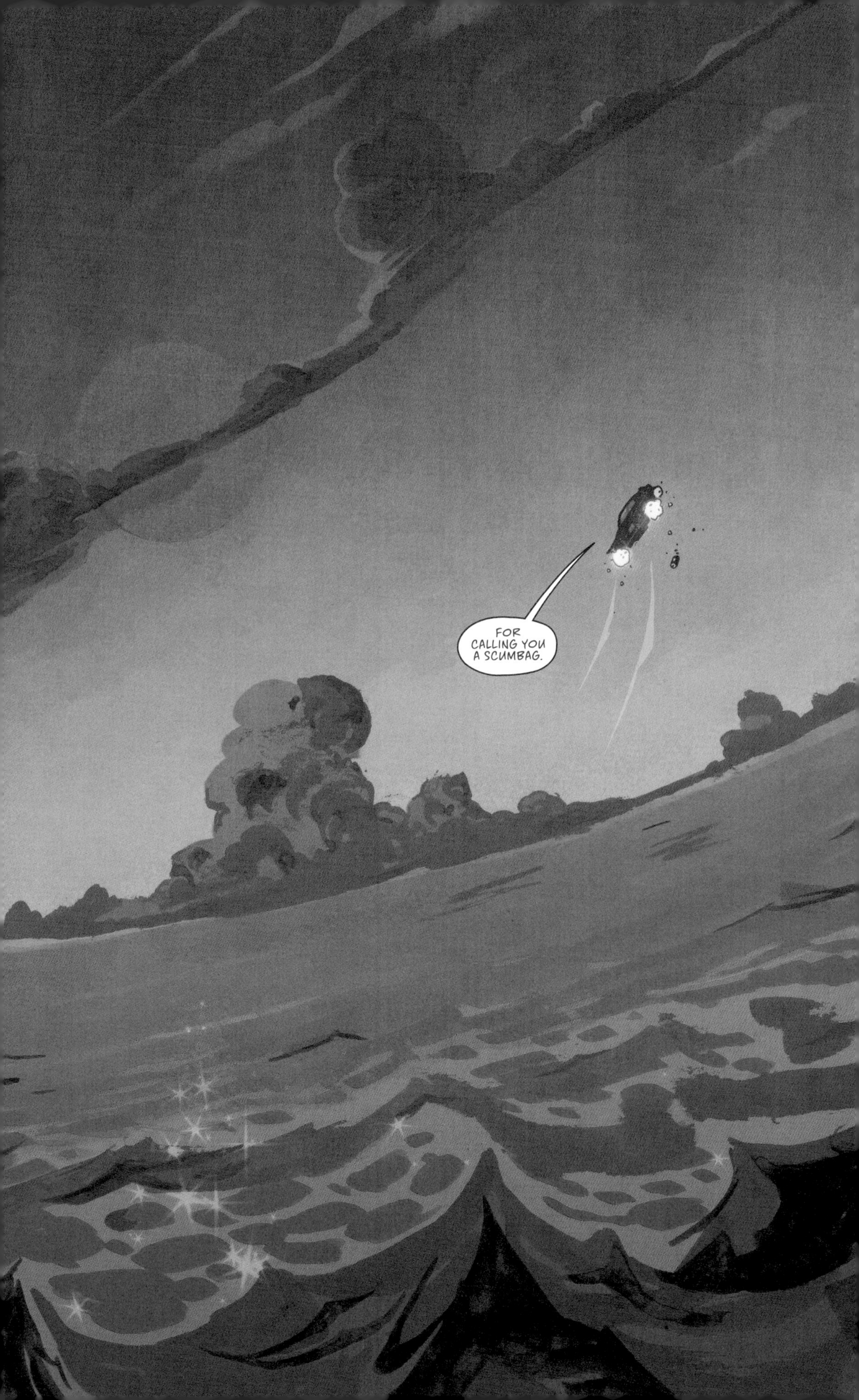
FOR CALLING YOU A SCUMBAG.

COVER
GALLERY

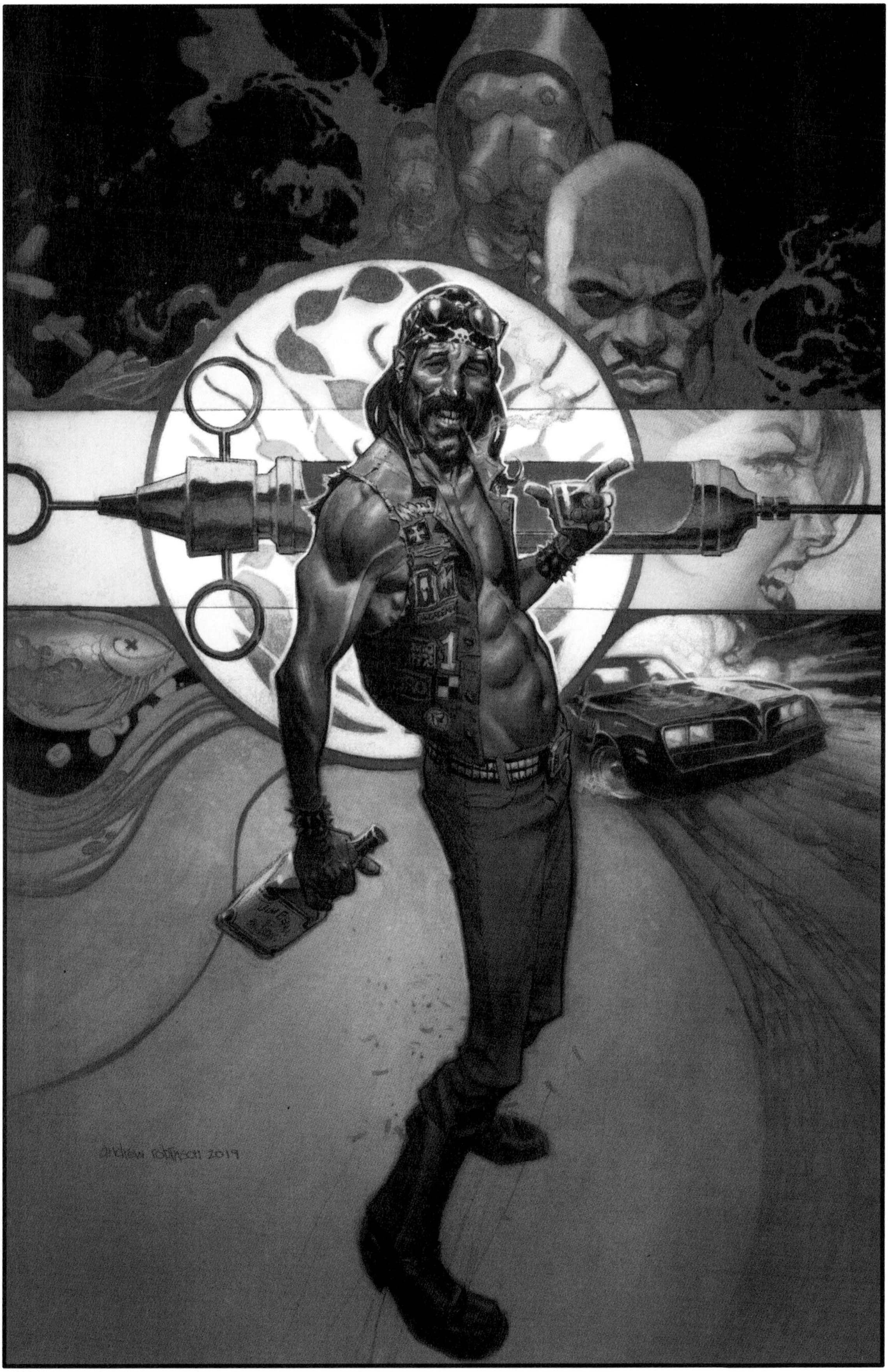

// ISSUE ONE VARIANT // ANDREW ROBINSON //

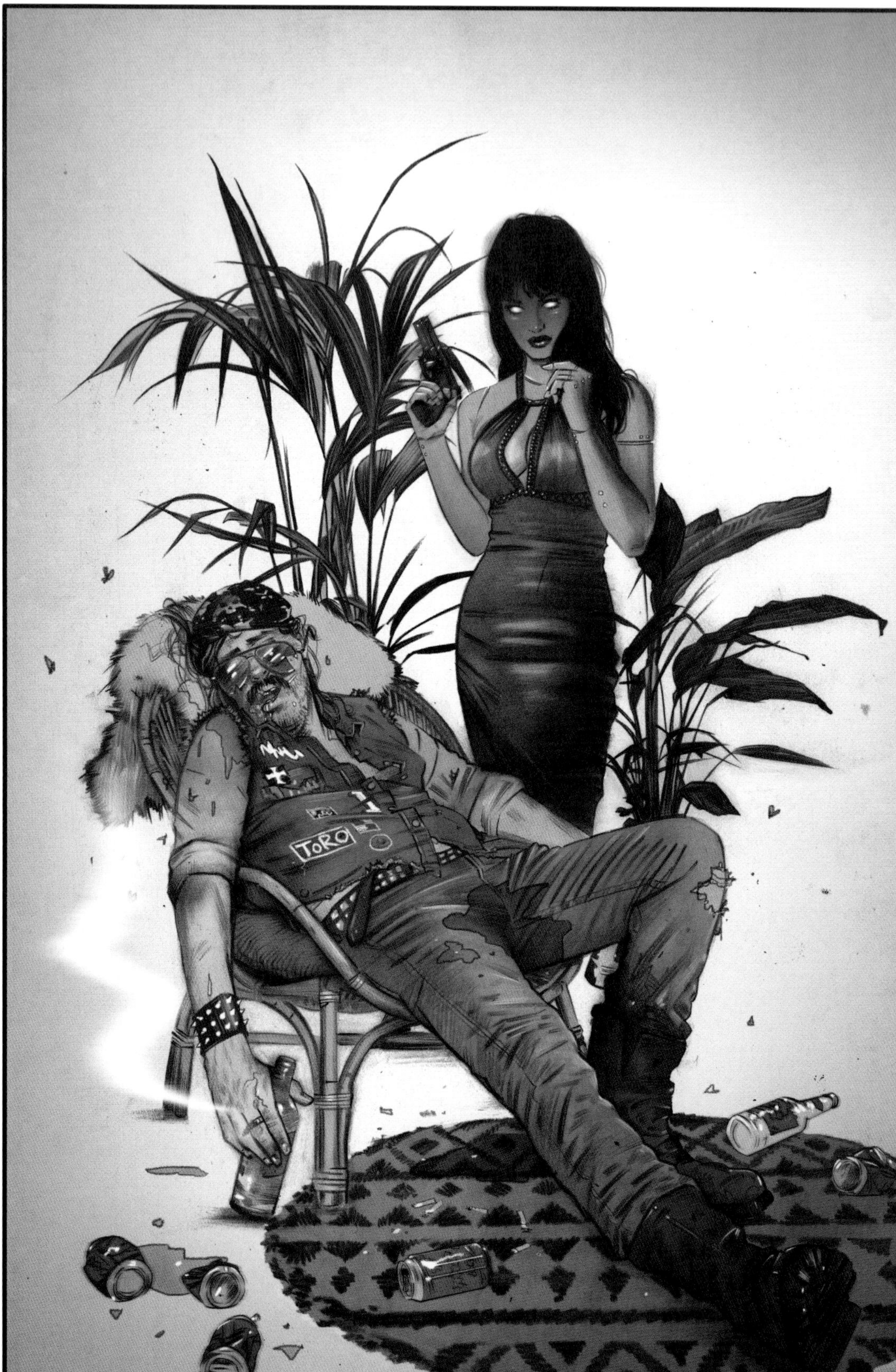
TORO

// ISSUE ONE VARIANT // TULA LOTAY //

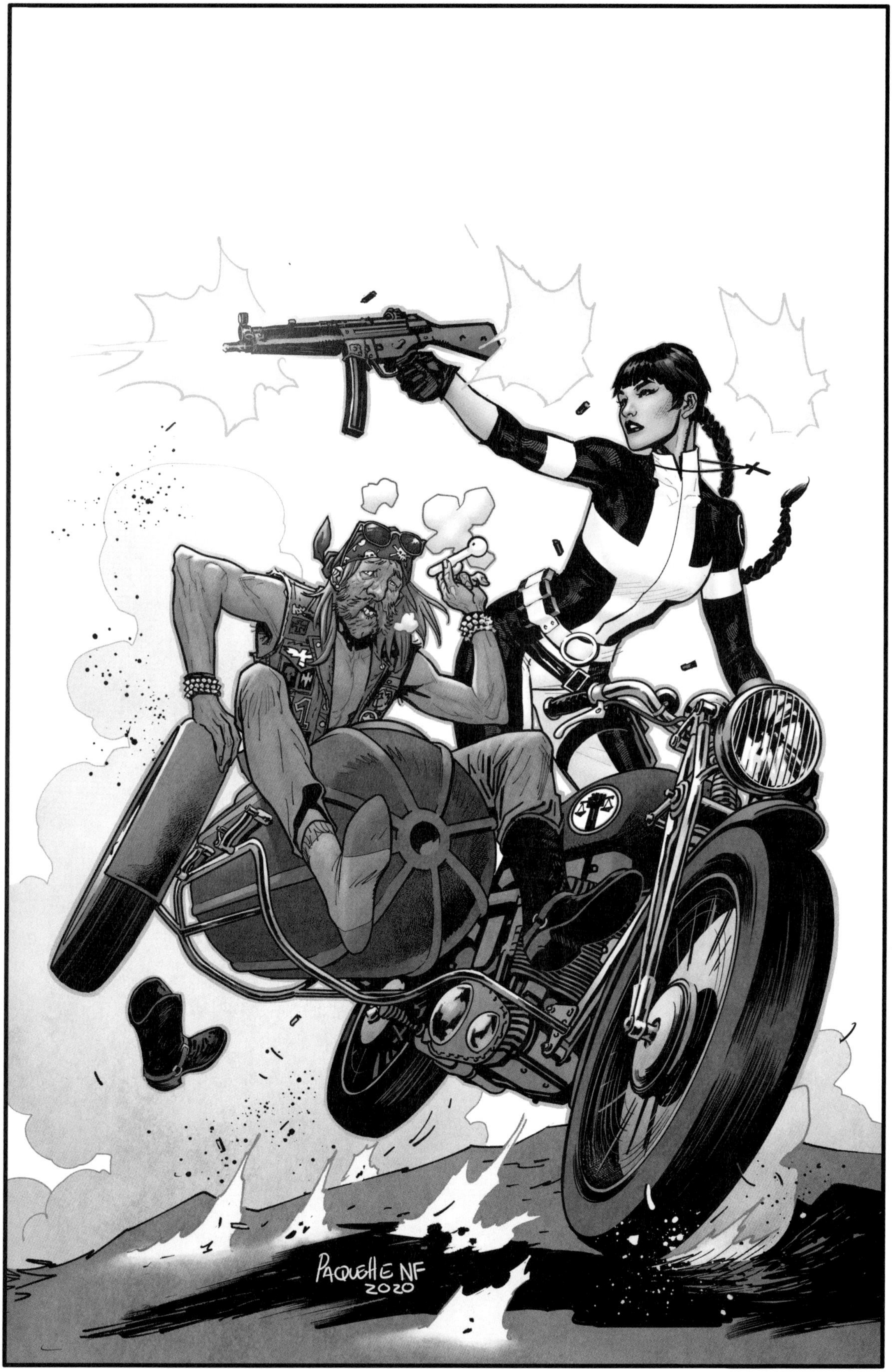

// ISSUE ONE VARIANT // YANICK PAQUETTE & NATHAN FAIRBAIRN //

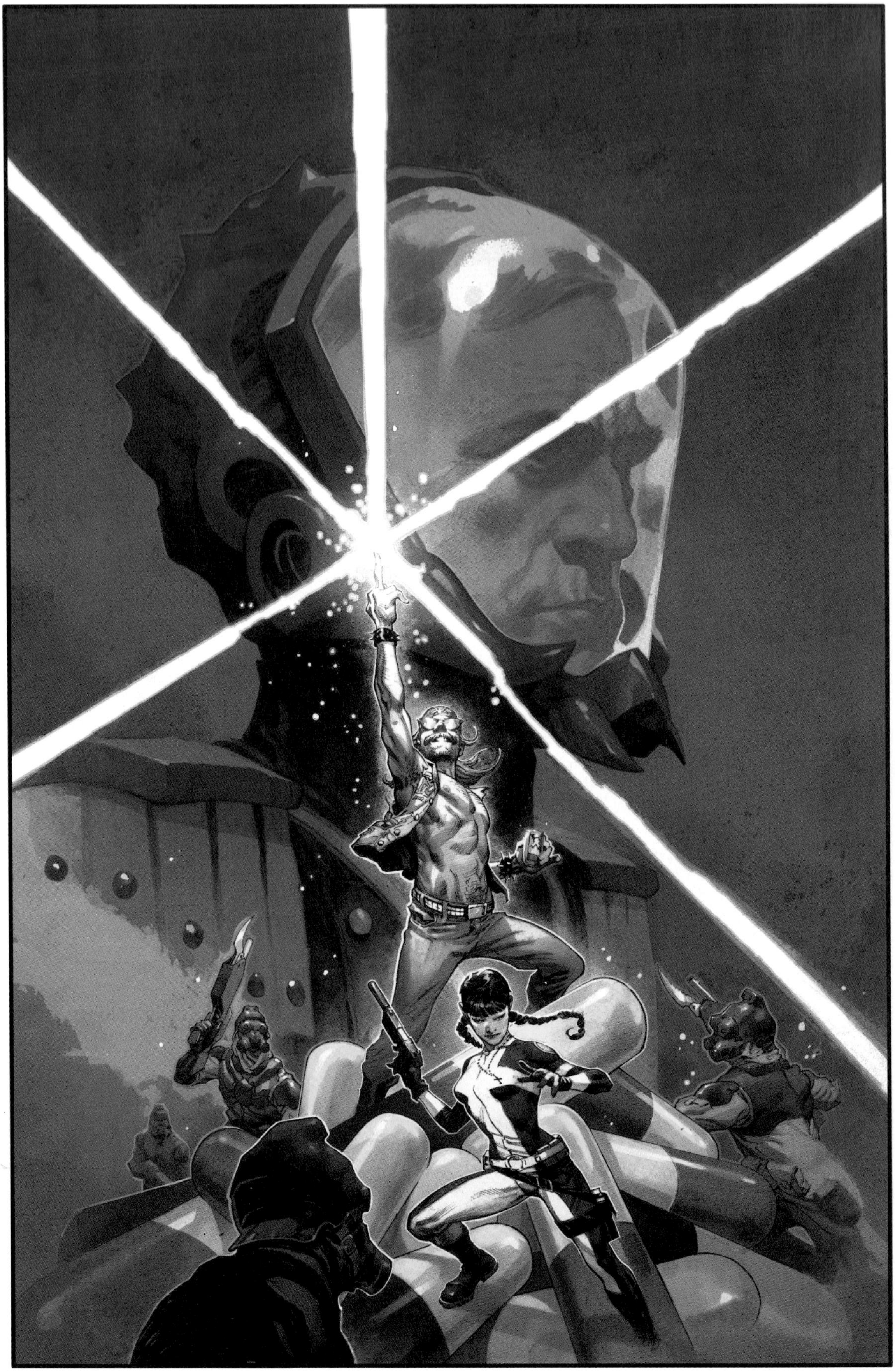

// ISSUE ONE VARIANT // JEROME OPEÑA & MORENO DINISIO //

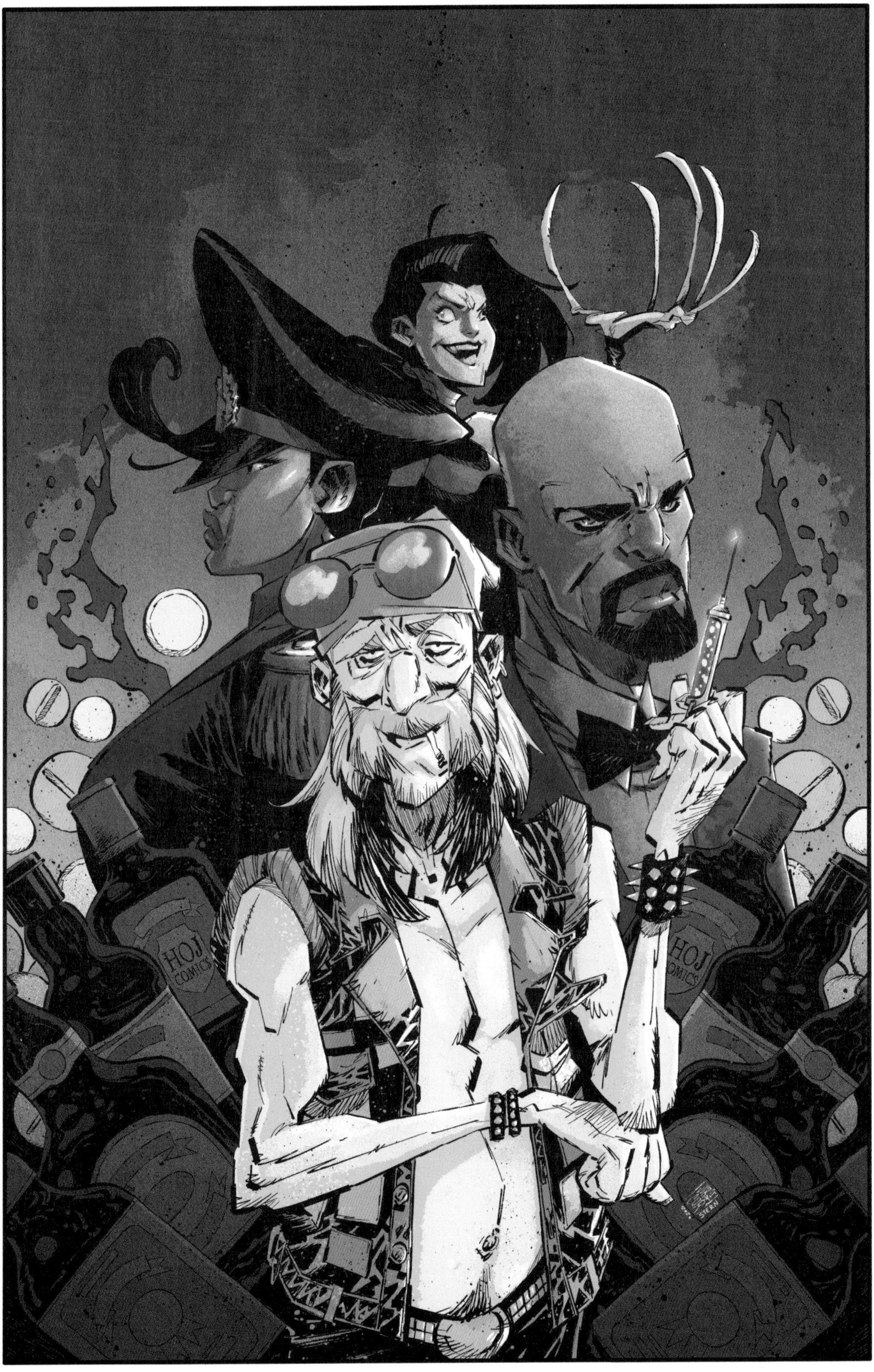
HOJ
COMICS
HOJ
COMICS

// ISSUE ONE VARIANT // JORGE CORONA & SARAH STERN //

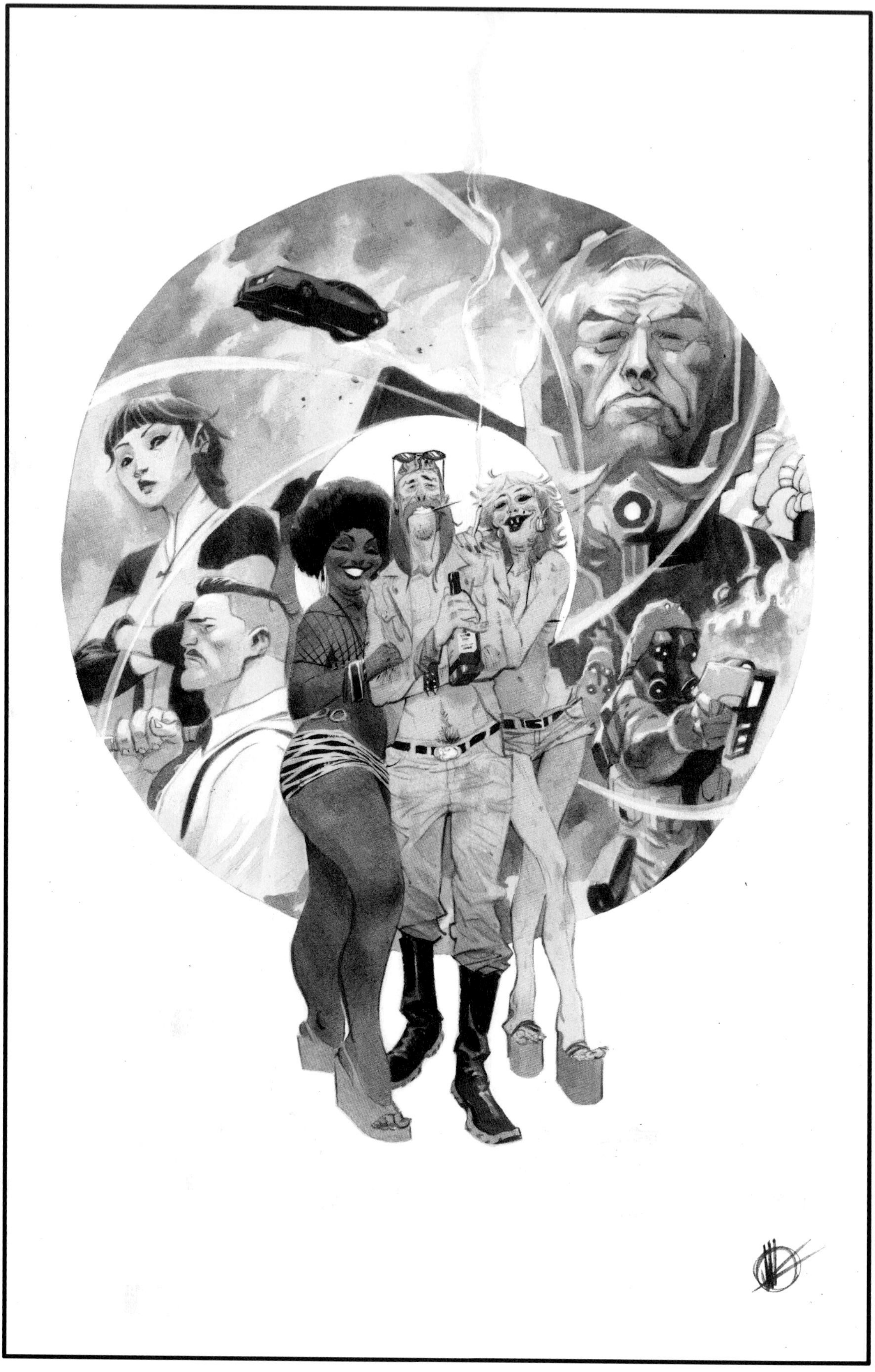

// ISSUE TWO VARIANT // MATTEO SCALERA //

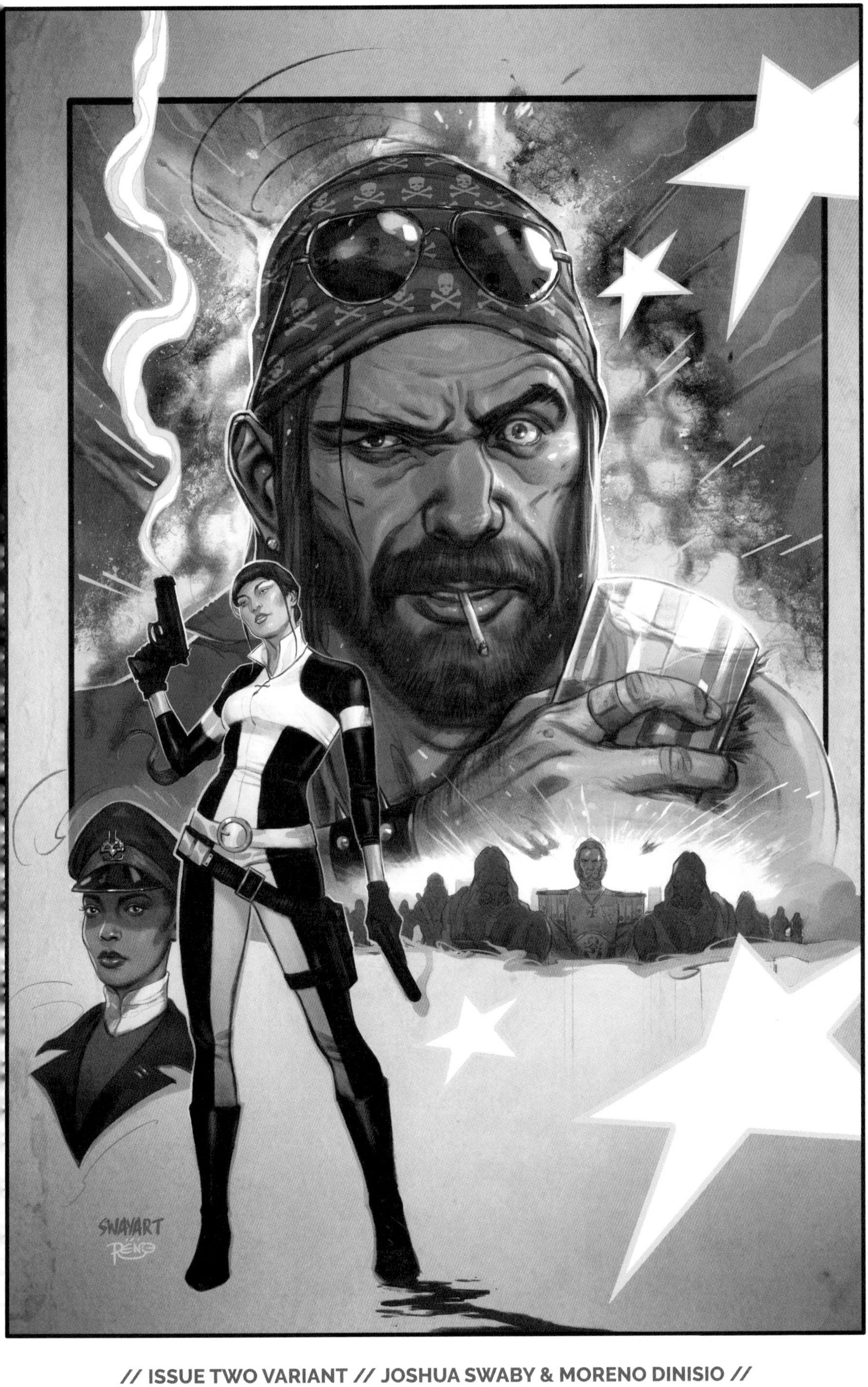
SWAYART
RENO

// ISSUE TWO VARIANT // JOSHUA SWABY & MORENO DINISIO //

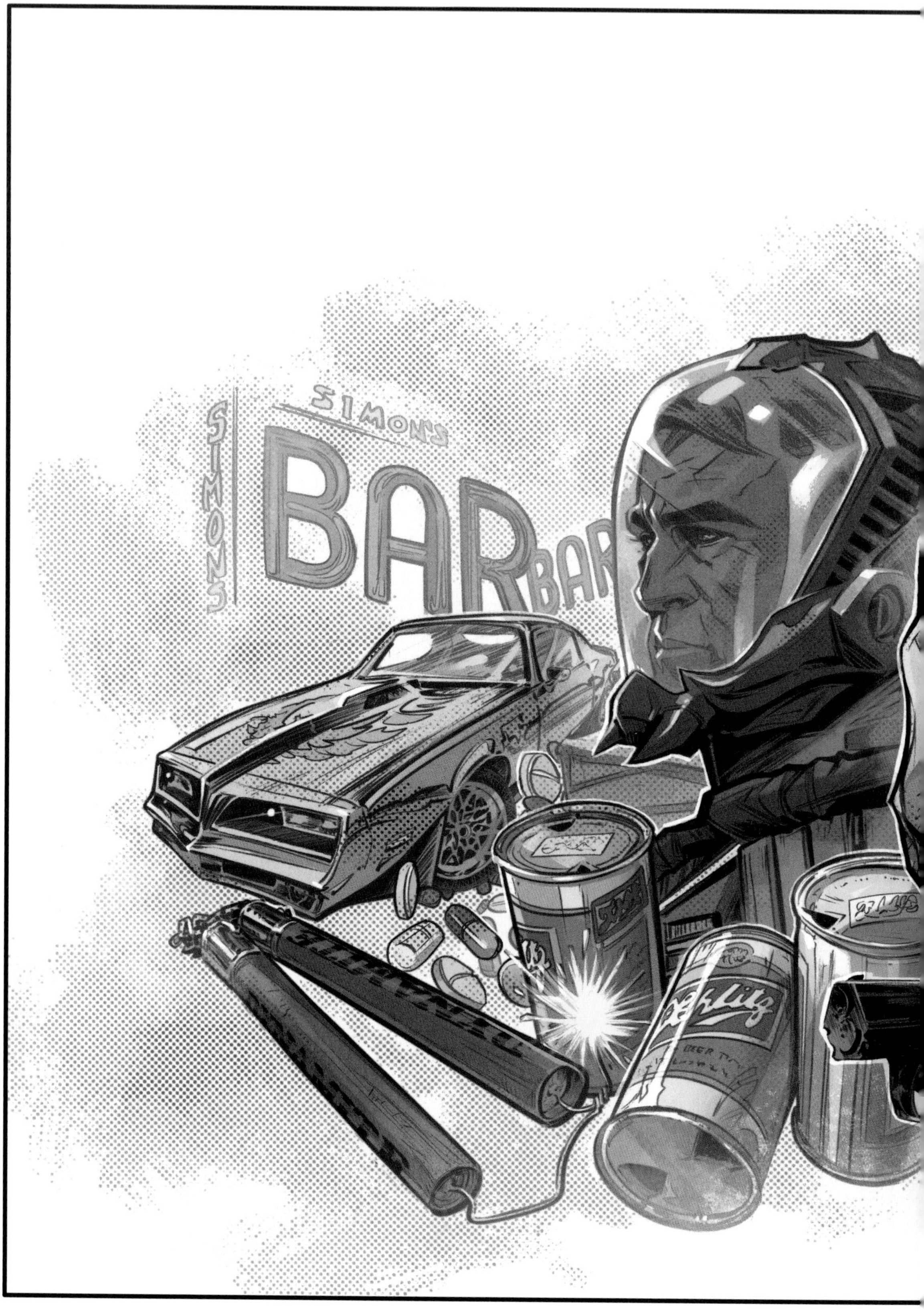
SIMON'S
SIMONS
BAR
BAR

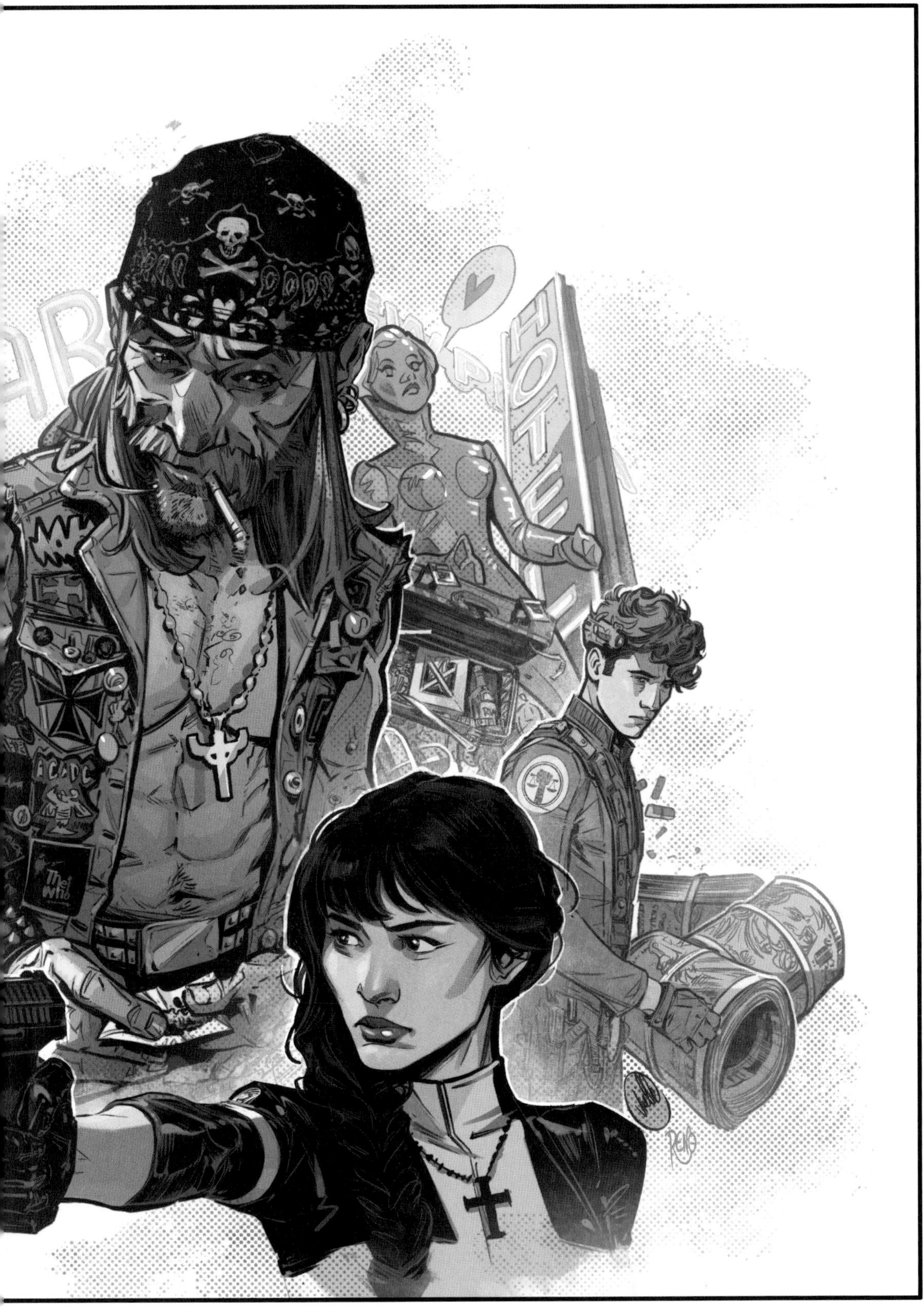

// ISSUE THREE // JOËLLE JONES & MORENO DINISIO //

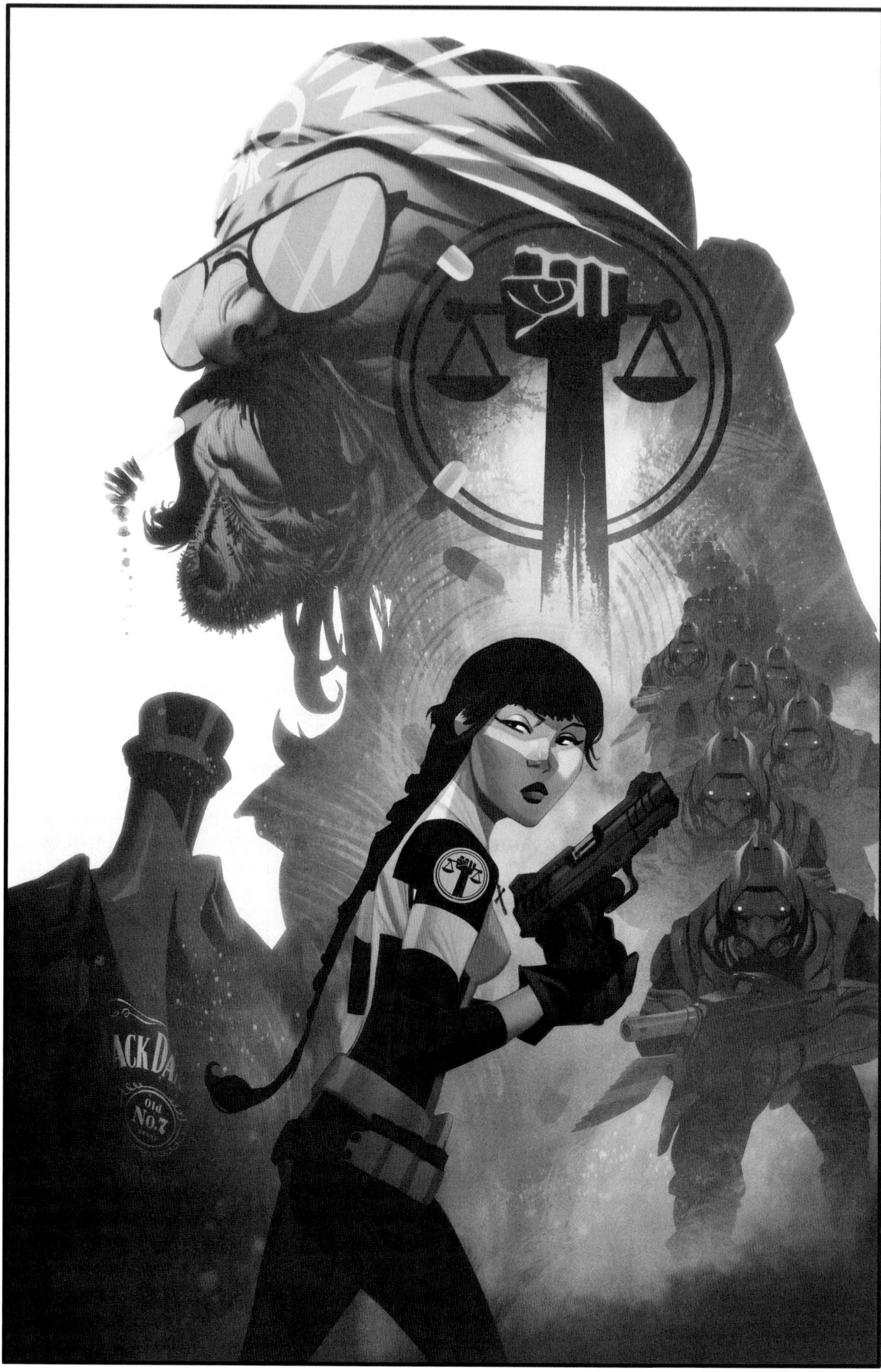
Old
No.7

// ISSUE THREE VARIANT // DAVE GUERTIN //

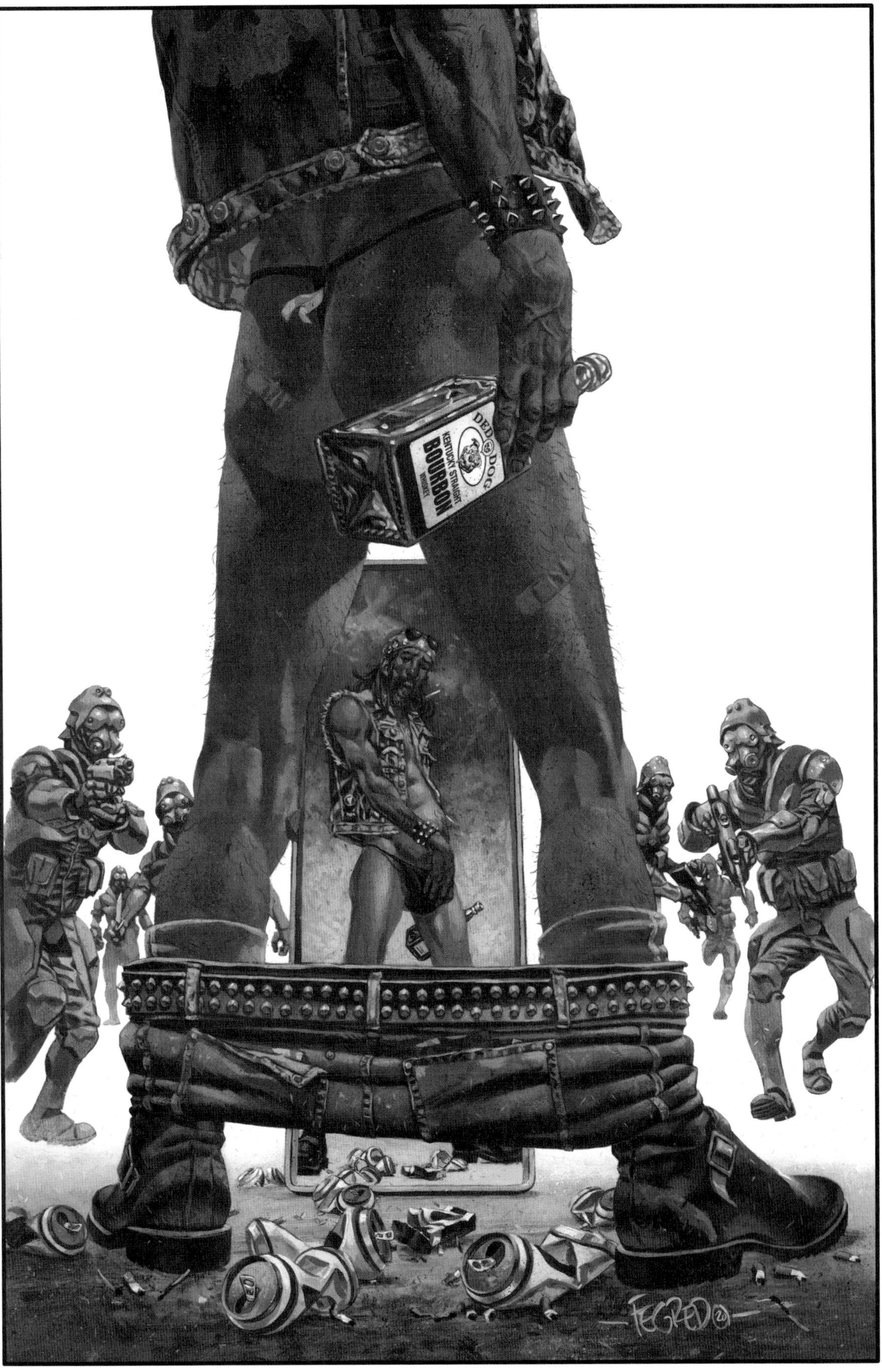
DED DOG
KENTUCKY STRAIGHT
BOURBON
FEGREDO

// ISSUE FOUR VARIANT // DUNCAN FEGREDO //

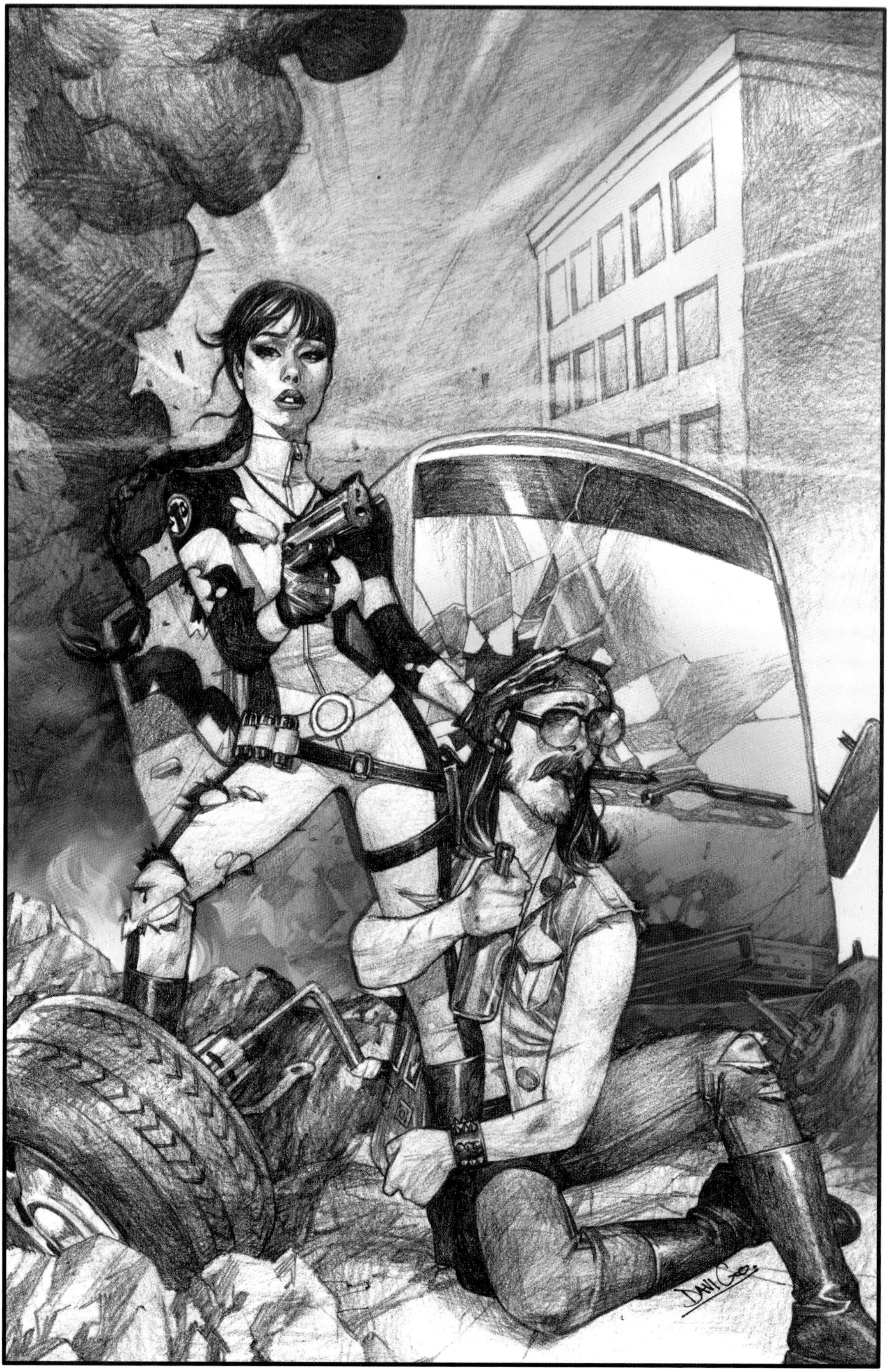

// ISSUE FIVE VARIANT // DAVI GO //